Rochelle
Premium Pt.
PINE ISL.
Pelham M
WESTCH
NASS
MW00583177
Williamsbridge
Dyre
Bay Chester
Gun Hill Rd
O N X
City Isl.
Pelham Pk
Bay Chester
PELHAM BAY
Westchester
Morris Pk
EASTERN
E. TREMONT
E. 177th
CITY ISLAND
HART ISL.
Sands Pt.
Prospect Pt.
Sands Point
HEMPSTEAD
MANHASSETT NECK
Barker Pt.
Kings Pt.
BRONX CO.
NASSAU CO.
New Rochelle
Plum Pt.
Mott Pt.
HARBOR
Beacon Hill
Port Washington
Locust Pt.
Old Ferry Pt.
MANHASSET BAY
Kings Point
GREAT NECK
FORT SCHUYLER
Whitestone Pt.
Whitestone Landing
QUEENS CO.
Willetts Pt.
FT. TOTTEN
BAR BEACH
Malba
Beechhurst
U.S. GOV. RES.
Plandome
College Point
Whitestone
Great Neck
LITTLE NECK BAY
NORTH
Airport Inc.
Bridge St
Saddle Rock
Great Neck Est
Kensington
Manhasset
Flushing
Great Neck Sta
Manhasset
Roslyn
Murray Hill
Broadway
Auburndale
Douglaston
HEMPSTEAD
Little Neck
Bayside
Lakeville
KISSENA PARK
Success
Toll Gate
ALLEY POND PARK
Albertson
Williston Pk
E. Williston
QUEENS
L. I. MOTOR
Creedmoor
HILLSIDE PARK
Mineola
Union
Hall St
Hillside
Bellaire
Queens Village
Merillon
Floral Park
New Hyde Park
Hollis
Bellerose
Belmont Park Race Track
Nassau Blvd
Jamaica
Stewart Manor
Garden City
Belmont Pk Sta.
Elmont
Cedar Manor
St. Albans
Franklin Square
Co. Life Press
Hem
Munson
Pioneer Field
Springfield
Locust Av
Jamaica Race Track
BAISLEYS POND
W. Hempstead
Jamaica South
Higbie
Hempstead Gardens
Laurelton
Lakeview
VALLEY STREAM PARK
Rosedale
Valley
Malverne

AN UNYEARED PLANNER

×

THE PERPETUALLY LATE SHOW

×

IF FOUND:

. . . .

. . . .

. . . .

IS REALLY SAD.

PROUDLY DESIGNED ON THE UPPER WEST SIDE
(OF KANSAS CITY).

THIS PLANNER IS DEDICATED TO ALL OF THE OTHER THINGS THAT WE PROBABLY COULD HAVE ACCOMPLISHED IN THE TIME THAT WE SPENT ON IT.

× × ×

WE'LL LEARN HOW TO PLAY THAT SAXOPHONE SOMEDAY.

DISCLAIMER

× × ×

LOOK, WE TRIED OUR BEST.

WE FILLED THIS PLANNER WITH ALL OF THE EXTRA LITTLE DETAILS THAT WE COULD, JUST BECAUSE WE LOVE THAT KIND OF THING...AND WE HOPE THAT YOU DO TOO.

THAT SAID, WE PROBABLY MADE A FEW MISTAKES...EVEN THOUGH WE TRIED REALLY HARD TO AVOID THEM. WE'RE JUST A COUPLE OF DESIGNERS THAT LOVE TO BITE OFF MORE THAN THEY CAN CHEW...AND HONESTLY, THIS PLANNER REQUIRED THE HEIMLICH MORE THAN A FEW TIMES.

SO, IF IT TURNS OUT THAT 'NATIONAL TOASTER APPRECIATION DAY' ISN'T OFFICIALLY RECOGNIZED IN TENNESSEE, WELL WE'RE REALLY SORRY FOR THE PAIN THAT IT MAY HAVE CAUSED YOU. SEND US AN EMAIL ABOUT IT IF IT HELPS YOU SLEEP AT NIGHT.

15

YOUR WEEK AT A GLANCE

MONDAY	TUESDAY	WEDNESDAY	THURSDAY	FRIDAY	SATURDAY ☐
		15th			
TODAY ☐	TODAY ☐	TODAY ☒	TODAY ☐	TODAY ☐	☐ SUNDAY

IT'S NATIONAL BAGEL DAY

BAGELS WENT TO SPACE IN 2008. THE CREAM CHEESE DIDN'T MAKE IT.

MARTIN LUTHER KING JR. WAS BORN IN 1929 — PITBULL WAS BORN IN 1981

9 AM — 9:15AM - WEEKLY touchbase
10 AM
11 AM — ↳ MEETING ID# 21 047 873 P.C. 5532
NOON
1 PM — 1 PM - Lunch w/ AMY & CANDICE @ THE Iron District
2 PM
3 PM
4 PM
5 PM — MEETING w/ PHOTOGRAPHERS - Go over SHOT LIST
6 PM

ON THIS DAY IN 2009: SULLY SULLENBERGER LANDED A PLANE ON THE HUDSON.

NOTES AND/OR DOODLES

×THE IRON× DISTRICT

A+

THE Burger

16

YOUR WEEK AT A GLANCE

MONDAY	TUESDAY	WEDNESDAY	THURSDAY	FRIDAY	SATURDAY ☐
			16th		
TODAY ☐	TODAY ☐	TODAY ☐	TODAY ☒	TODAY ☐	☐ SUNDAY

IT'S NATIONAL FIG NEWTON DAY

OVER 1 BILLION ARE EATEN EVERY YEAR, AND YET WE'VE NEVER HAD ONE.

KATE MOSS WAS BORN IN 1974 — AALIYAH WAS BORN IN 1979

9 AM
10 AM — 10AM CHECK IN w/ Sales Team - Q2 PLAN
11 AM — ↳ MEETING ID# 737 251 443 P.C. 239
NOON
1 PM
2 PM
3 PM — * * DESIGN FILES DUE EOD * *
4 PM
5 PM
6 PM — 7PM - DINNER w/ THE Neighbors - GET DESSERT

ON THIS DAY IN 1939: THE SUPERMAN DAILY COMIC STRIP DEBUTED.

NOTES AND/OR DOODLES

* DON'T * forget to pickup DOG FOOD

HOW TO USE A DAILY PLANNER

THIS ONE – SPECIFICALLY

IT'S ACTUALLY UNYEARED. NOT UNDATED.

THIS ISN'T YOUR TYPICAL UNDATED PLANNER. INSTEAD OF A BUNCH OF BLANK BOXES, WE'VE ALREADY DONE THE HARD WORK FOR YOU. WE PUT IN THE DATES, THE FIXED HOLIDAYS, AND A BUNCH OF EXTRA STUFF (LIKE TRIVIA, CELEBRITY BIRTHDAYS, & OTHER USEFULLY-USELESS STUFF).

NOW ALL YOU HAVE TO DO IS FILL IN THE YEAR, AND WHAT DAY OF THE WEEK EACH DAY FALLS ON. IT'S AS SIMPLE AS THAT. SO IF YOU WANT, YOU CAN BUY THIS PLANNER IN 2023 AND PROCRASTINATE ACTUALLY USING IT UNTIL 2054.

YOU'RE WELCOME.

VISUAL LEARNER? LOOK LEFT.

WE FILLED OUT A SAMPLE PAGE OVER THERE FOR YOU TO SEE.

IS JANUARY 19TH ON A TUESDAY THIS YEAR? MARK IT ON THE WEEK AT A GLANCE ROW, AND THEN JUST FOLLOW SUIT FOR THE REST OF THE PLANNER.

CAN'T WAIT AND DECIDE TO START USING THIS PLANNER IN AUGUST? JUST USE THE BOOKMARK (PSST...IT'S THAT RIBBON ATTACHED TO THE SPINE) AND START THERE. WHEN YOU GET BACK AROUND TO JANUARY, MOVE ON TO THE NEXT YEAR.

AND NOW YOU KNOW.

THAT WAS A LOT OF INFORMATION, SO HERE'S AN INTERMISSION. AKA: CHUG AN OVERPRICED DRINK IN 5 MINUTES.

A FEW THINGS TO KEEP IN MIND

ALSO KNOWN AS: CALENDARS ARE WEIRD

MOST HOLIDAYS FLOAT. FEW ARE FIXED.

WE AREN'T TALKING ABOUT 'TAKE YOUR IGUANA TO WORK DAY.' WE CHOSE THE RANDOM HOLIDAYS THAT FALL ON SPECIFIC DATES FOR THAT VERY REASON.

WE MEAN THE BIG ONES, YOU KNOW, LIKE THANKSGIVING. SURE, IT ALWAYS FALLS ON THE 4TH THURSDAY OF NOVEMBER. THE PROBLEM IS, THAT'S A DIFFERENT DAY EVERY YEAR. SO, WE EXPLAIN THE RULES OF THESE HOLIDAYS ON THE MONTH AT A GLANCE PAGE PRECEDING EACH MONTH. JUST REMEMBER THEY'RE NOT INCLUDED IN THE DAILY CALENDAR PORTION. YOUR MOM WILL BE MAD IF YOU FORGET TO CALL.

NO, IT'S NOT A CONSPIRACY. WE DON'T HAVE SOME AGENDA AGAINST PRESIDENTS' DAY. WE JUST DON'T KNOW WHEN IT WILL FALL...SO WE NEED YOUR HELP.

THANKS AGAIN.

DON'T FORGET LEAP DAY. OR ACTUALLY, DO.

ONCE EVERY FOUR YEARS (WELL, MOST OF THE TIME ANYWAY...MORE ON THAT LATER) WE HAVE A LEAP YEAR, ADDING FEBRUARY 29TH TO THE CALENDAR.

SO...OUR PLANNER HAS TO HAVE IT TOO, REGARDLESS OF WHETHER YOU NEED IT THAT YEAR OR NOT. YOUR JOB IS JUST TO IGNORE IT...UNLESS, WELL, IT'S LEAP YEAR.

WHEN ARE LEAP YEARS? HERE ARE THE RULES (WE'LL ALSO REMIND YOU LATER):

LEAP YEARS ARE EVENLY DIVISIBLE BY 4.

HOWEVER: IF THE YEAR IS ALSO EVENLY DIVISIBLE BY 100, IT'S NOT A LEAP YEAR.

UNLESS: IT'S ALSO EVENLY DIVISIBLE BY 400...THEN IT ACTUALLY IS A LEAP YEAR.

BLAME JULIUS CAESAR.

ON AVERAGE THE COLDEST MONTH OF THE YEAR (NORTHERN HEMISPHERE).

WELCOME TO

× JANUARY ×

OF WHATEVER YEAR
YOU SAY IT IS.

LET'S GO WITH:

☐☐☐☐

. . . .

. . . .

. . . .

NAMED AFTER THE ROMAN GOD JANUS. HE WAS TWO-FACED. LITERALLY.

JANUARY AT A GLANCE :YEAR

YOU MADE IT
TO JANUARY

×

CELEBRATE, IT'S:

NATIONAL BLOOD DONOR MONTH

NATIONAL BRAILLE LITERACY MONTH

NATIONAL HOBBY MONTH

NATIONAL SOUP MONTH

NATIONAL STAYING HEALTHY MONTH

×

OFFICIAL SYMBOLS:

BIRTHSTONE: GARNET

FLOWERS: CARNATION & SNOWDROP

TREES: FIR, ELM, & CYPRESS

CAPRICORN (DEC 22 / JAN 19)

AQUARIUS (JAN 20 / FEB 18)

DATES TO KNOW*
LIKE, IMPORTANT ONES

×

NEW YEAR'S DAY
JANUARY 1ST

WORLD BRAILLE DAY
JANUARY 4TH

CHRISTMAS
(EASTERN ORTHODOX)
JANUARY 7TH

MAHAYANA NEW YEAR
FIRST FULL MOON OF THE YEAR

WORLD RELIGION DAY
THIRD SUNDAY IN JANUARY

MARTIN LUTHER KING JR. DAY
THIRD MONDAY IN JANUARY

CHINESE NEW YEAR
SECOND NEW MOON AFTER THE WINTER SOLSTICE (MAY BE IN FEB.)

REPUBLIC DAY
(OF INDIA)
JANUARY 26TH

INTL. HOLOCAUST REMEMBRANCE DAY
JANUARY 27TH

THINGS TO ACCOMPLISH THIS MONTH
FOR EXAMPLE: FILL OUT A TO-DO LIST

1
2
3
4
5
6
7
8
9
10
11
12
13
14
15

THINGS THAT ARE NEVER GOING TO HAPPEN
THERE'S ALWAYS FEBRUARY (OR MARCH)

1
2
3
4
5
6
7
8
9
10
11
12
13
14
15

*A DISCLAIMER OF SORTS

HEY THERE. WE HERE AT BRASS MONKEY LIKE TO JOKE AROUND.. BUT WE ALSO WANT TO TAKE A MINUTE TO RECOGNIZE JUST A FEW OF THE MANY HOLIDAYS & EVENTS THAT ARE IMPORTANT TO OUR FRIENDS AROUND THE GLOBE (AND AT HOME). YOU MAY BE DIFFERENT THAN US. WE MAY HAVE NEVER MET. BUT WE LOVE YOU ALL THE SAME.

SO IF YOU HAVEN'T HEARD OF A DAY, LOOK IT UP. LEARNING ABOUT & APPRECIATING CULTURES DIFFERENT THAN YOURS IS IMPORTANT...WAY MORE THAN POSTING A FEW "STRAWBERRY JAM DAY" SELFIES.

JANUARY AT A GLANCE

YEAR:

IT'S JANUARY

START PLANNING

×

NEW YEAR'S DAY

JANUARY 1ST
(SORRY ABOUT THE HANGOVER)

MARTIN LUTHER KING JR. DAY*

OBSERVED ON
THE 3RD MONDAY
OF JANUARY

×

BIRTHDAYS

TO REMEMBER

*PSST: SINCE THIS HOLIDAY MOVES AROUND EACH YEAR (AND WE DON'T KNOW WHEN IN THE FUTURE YOU'RE USING THIS), HELP US OUT AND ADD IT TO THE CALENDAR.

ALSO, ARE THERE JET PACKS YET? OUR FINGERS ARE CROSSED.

DAY OF WEEK S M T W T F S	DAY OF WEEK S M T W T F S	DAY OF WEEK S M T W T F S	DAY OF WEEK S M T W T F S	DAY OF WEEK S M T W T F S	DAY OF WEEK S M T W T F S	DAY OF WEEK S M T W T F S
NEW YEAR'S DAY 01	02	03	04	05	06	07
08	09	10	11	12	13	14
15	16	17	18	19	20	21
22	23	24	25	26	27	28
29	30	31				

NOTES:

JANUARY, AS EXPRESSED IN A DRAWING

JANUARY PREVIEW

A JANUARY VENN DIAGRAM

WHAT DO THEY HAVE IN COMMON?

1 STOPPED BEING FUN LONG AGO
2
3
4
5
6
7
8

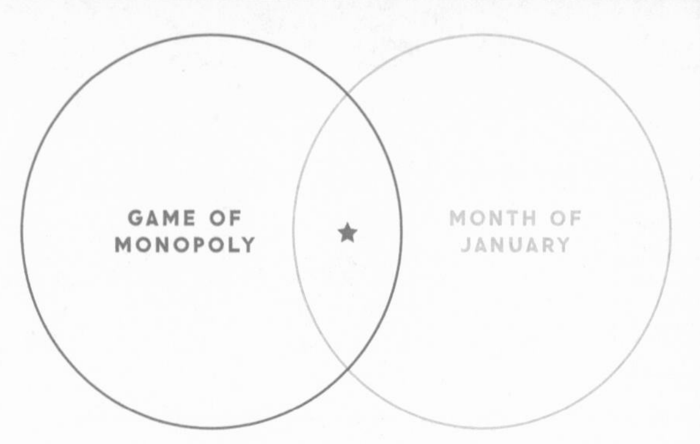

A DRAWING OF NEW YEAR'S EVE

(EXPECTATIONS VS. REALITY)

SUPPLIES NEEDED FOR THE MONTH

ALCOHOL, AND OTHER NECESSITIES

1
2
3
4
5
6
7
8
9
10
11
12
13
14
15
16
17

JANUARY ENJOYMENT INDEX

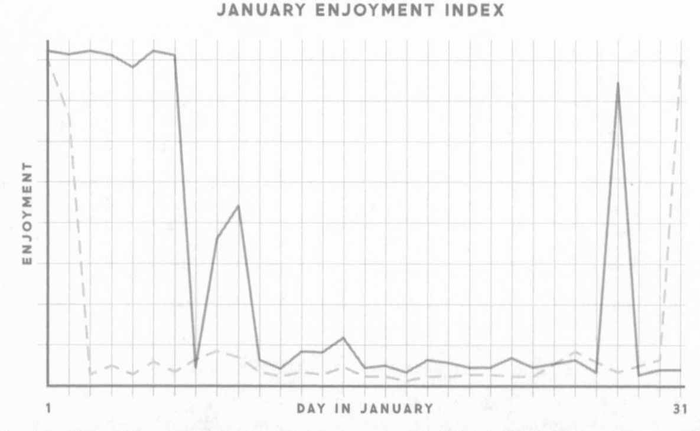

ENJOYMENT OVER TIME

CHOOSE A COLOR KEY

LINE	ITEM
——	NEW YEAR'S RESOLUTIONS
— —	DRY JANUARY
	KNOWING WHAT YEAR IT IS
	TALKING ABOUT WEATHER
	RETURNING GIFTS
	POTENTIAL SNOWSTORMS
	DISCOUNT ANYTHING
	GOING BACK TO WORK
	WEARING LAYERS
	TAKING LAYERS ON & OFF

YEAR: **JANUARY**

YOUR WEEK AT A GLANCE

MONDAY	TUESDAY	WEDNESDAY	THURSDAY	FRIDAY	SATURDAY ☐
☐ TODAY	☐ TODAY	☐ TODAY	☐ TODAY	☐ TODAY	☐ SUNDAY

01

NOTES AND/OR DOODLES

IT'S NEW YEAR'S DAY

OH, AND IT'S ALSO NATIONAL BLOODY MARY DAY.

VERNE TROYER WAS BORN IN 1969

COLIN MORGAN WAS BORN IN 1986

9 AM

10 AM

11 AM

NOON

1 PM

2 PM

3 PM

4 PM

5 PM

6 PM

ON THIS DAY IN 1984: NYC TRANSIT FARE ROSE FROM 75 CENTS TO 90 CENTS.

YOUR WEEK AT A GLANCE

MONDAY	TUESDAY	WEDNESDAY	THURSDAY	FRIDAY	SATURDAY ☐
☐ TODAY	☐ TODAY	☐ TODAY	☐ TODAY	☐ TODAY	☐ SUNDAY

02

NOTES AND/OR DOODLES

IT'S WORLD INTROVERT DAY

ONE THIRD OF ALL PEOPLE ARE INTROVERTS.

JACK HANNA WAS BORN IN 1947

TAYE DIGGS WAS BORN IN 1971

9 AM

10 AM

11 AM

NOON

1 PM

2 PM

3 PM

4 PM

5 PM

6 PM

ON THIS DAY IN 1973: THE 55 MPH SPEED LIMIT WAS INTRODUCED.

03

YOUR WEEK AT A GLANCE

MONDAY	TUESDAY	WEDNESDAY	THURSDAY	FRIDAY	SATURDAY ☐
TODAY ☐	TODAY ☐	TODAY ☐	TODAY ☐	TODAY ☐	☐ SUNDAY

IT'S FESTIVAL OF SLEEP DAY

HUMANS ARE THE ONLY ANIMALS THAT WILLINGLY PUT OFF SLEEP.

J.R.R. TOLKIEN WAS BORN IN 1892 ELI MANNING WAS BORN IN 1981

9 AM

10 AM

11 AM

NOON

1 PM

2 PM

3 PM

4 PM

5 PM

6 PM

ON THIS DAY IN 2009: BITCOIN WAS CREATED.

NOTES AND/OR DOODLES

04

YOUR WEEK AT A GLANCE

MONDAY	TUESDAY	WEDNESDAY	THURSDAY	FRIDAY	SATURDAY ☐
TODAY ☐	TODAY ☐	TODAY ☐	TODAY ☐	TODAY ☐	☐ SUNDAY

IT'S NATIONAL TRIVIA DAY

ELMO IS THE ONLY NON-HUMAN TO TESTIFY BEFORE CONGRESS.

JUSTIN TOWNES EARLE WAS BORN IN 1982 CHARLYNE YI WAS BORN IN 1986

9 AM

10 AM

11 AM

NOON

1 PM

2 PM

3 PM

4 PM

5 PM

6 PM

ON THIS DAY IN 1980: THE U.S. BOYCOTTED THE MOSCOW OLYMPICS.

NOTES AND/OR DOODLES

YEAR: JANUARY

YOUR WEEK AT A GLANCE

MONDAY	TUESDAY	WEDNESDAY	THURSDAY	FRIDAY	SATURDAY ☐	05
☐ TODAY	☐ TODAY	☐ TODAY	☐ TODAY	☐ TODAY	☐ SUNDAY	

NOTES AND/OR DOODLES

IT'S NATIONAL WHIPPED CREAM DAY

IT WAS ORIGINALLY KNOWN AS 'MILK SNOW' UNTIL THE 17TH CENTURY.

TED LANGE WAS BORN IN 1948

DIANE KEATON WAS BORN IN 1946

9 AM

10 AM

11 AM

NOON

1 PM

2 PM

3 PM

4 PM

5 PM

6 PM

ON THIS DAY IN 1933: WORK STARTED ON THE GOLDEN GATE BRIDGE.

YOUR WEEK AT A GLANCE

MONDAY	TUESDAY	WEDNESDAY	THURSDAY	FRIDAY	SATURDAY ☐	06
☐ TODAY	☐ TODAY	☐ TODAY	☐ TODAY	☐ TODAY	☐ SUNDAY	

NOTES AND/OR DOODLES

IT'S NATIONAL TECHNOLOGY DAY

MORE THAN 570 NEW WEBSITES ARE CREATED EVERY MINUTE.

FOR EXAMPLE: BRASSMONKEYGOODS.COM

NIGELLA LAWSON WAS BORN IN 1960

EDDIE REDMAYNE WAS BORN IN 1982

9 AM

10 AM

11 AM

NOON

1 PM

2 PM

3 PM

4 PM

5 PM

6 PM

ON THIS DAY IN 1975: 'WHEEL OF FORTUNE' DEBUTED ON NBC.

07

YOUR WEEK AT A GLANCE

MONDAY	TUESDAY	WEDNESDAY	THURSDAY	FRIDAY	SATURDAY ☐
TODAY ☐	TODAY ☐	TODAY ☐	TODAY ☐	TODAY ☐	☐ SUNDAY

IT'S NATIONAL BOBBLEHEAD DAY

THE BIGGEST ONE ON RECORD IS A 15 FOOT TALL ST. BERNARD.

KATIE COURIC WAS BORN IN 1957

NICOLAS CAGE WAS BORN IN 1964

9 AM

10 AM

11 AM

NOON

1 PM

2 PM

3 PM

4 PM

5 PM

6 PM

ON THIS DAY IN 1990: THE TOWER OF PISA CLOSED AFTER LEANING TOO FAR.

NOTES AND/OR DOODLES

08

YOUR WEEK AT A GLANCE

MONDAY	TUESDAY	WEDNESDAY	THURSDAY	FRIDAY	SATURDAY ☐
TODAY ☐	TODAY ☐	TODAY ☐	TODAY ☐	TODAY ☐	☐ SUNDAY

IT'S BUBBLE BATH DAY

MARILYN MONROE WAS KNOWN FOR BATHING IN CHAMPAGNE.

ELVIS PRESLEY WAS BORN IN 1935

DAVID BOWIE WAS BORN IN 1947

9 AM

10 AM

11 AM

NOON

1 PM

2 PM

3 PM

4 PM

5 PM

6 PM

ON THIS DAY IN 1998: MR. ROGERS RECEIVED A STAR ON THE WALK OF FAME.

NOTES AND/OR DOODLES

THINGS TO WRITE ON MY TOMBSTONE

OR SOME BORING TO-DO LIST

1
2
3
4
5
6
7
8
9
10
11
12

FAVORITE PROFANITY SUBSTITUTES

OR A GROCERY LIST OR SOMETHING

1
2
3
4
5
6
7
8
9
10
11
12

A DRAWING OF WORLD PEACE

(OR SOME SUPER BUSINESSY STUFF)

WORST ADVICE I'VE EVER RECEIVED

OR A MORE USEFUL (BUT STUPID) LIST

1
2
3
4
5
6
7
8
9
10
11
12

BEST ADVICE I'VE EVER IGNORED

OR A LIST OF LITERALLY ANYTHING ELSE

1
2
3
4
5
6
7
8
9
10
11
12

JANUARY

:YEAR

09

YOUR WEEK AT A GLANCE

MONDAY	TUESDAY	WEDNESDAY	THURSDAY	FRIDAY	SATURDAY ☐
TODAY ☐	TODAY ☐	TODAY ☐	TODAY ☐	TODAY ☐	☐ SUNDAY

IT'S NATIONAL STATIC ELECTRICITY DAY

AROUND SEVENTY PERCENT OF THOSE STRUCK BY LIGHTING SURVIVE.

KATE MIDDLETON WAS BORN IN 1982

MUGGSY BOGUES WAS BORN IN 1965

9 AM

10 AM

11 AM

NOON

1 PM

2 PM

3 PM

4 PM

5 PM

6 PM

ON THIS DAY IN 2007: STEVE JOBS ANNOUNCED THE FIRST IPHONE.

NOTES AND/OR DOODLES

10

YOUR WEEK AT A GLANCE

MONDAY	TUESDAY	WEDNESDAY	THURSDAY	FRIDAY	SATURDAY ☐
TODAY ☐	TODAY ☐	TODAY ☐	TODAY ☐	TODAY ☐	☐ SUNDAY

IT'S HOUSEPLANT APPRECIATION DAY

A SOUTHERN-FACING WINDOW PROVIDES THE MOST AMOUNT OF LIGHT.

(IN THE NORTHERN HEMISPHERE, OF COURSE)

GEORGE FOREMAN WAS BORN IN 1949

PAT BENATAR WAS BORN IN 1953

9 AM

10 AM

11 AM

NOON

1 PM

2 PM

3 PM

4 PM

5 PM

6 PM

ON THIS DAY IN 1983: FRAGGLE ROCK PREMIERED ON HBO.

NOTES AND/OR DOODLES

YEAR: JANUARY

YOUR WEEK AT A GLANCE

MONDAY ☐ TODAY | TUESDAY ☐ TODAY | WEDNESDAY ☐ TODAY | THURSDAY ☐ TODAY | FRIDAY ☐ TODAY | SATURDAY ☐ | ☐ SUNDAY

11

NOTES AND/OR DOODLES

IT'S NATIONAL HOT TODDY DAY

ROBERT TODD INVENTED THE BEVERAGE TO WARD OFF ILLNESS (MAYBE).

MARY J. BLIGE WAS BORN IN 1971

AMANDA PEET WAS BORN IN 1972

9 AM

10 AM

11 AM

NOON

1 PM

2 PM

3 PM

4 PM

5 PM

6 PM

ON THIS DAY IN 1970: THE KANSAS CITY CHIEFS WON SUPER BOWL IV.

YOUR WEEK AT A GLANCE

MONDAY ☐ TODAY | TUESDAY ☐ TODAY | WEDNESDAY ☐ TODAY | THURSDAY ☐ TODAY | FRIDAY ☐ TODAY | SATURDAY ☐ | ☐ SUNDAY

12

NOTES AND/OR DOODLES

IT'S WORK HARDER DAY

PROCRASTINATING ON A PROJECT CAN INCREASE FOCUS AND EFFICIENCY.

JOE FRAZIER WAS BORN IN 1944

ROB ZOMBIE WAS BORN IN 1965

9 AM

10 AM

11 AM

NOON

1 PM

2 PM

3 PM

4 PM

5 PM

6 PM

ON THIS DAY IN 2019: MISSY ELLIOTT JOINED THE SONGWRITERS HALL OF FAME.

LISTS, NOTES & MEMOIRS

DRAWBACKS TO BEING SO ATTRACTIVE

OR A LIST OF LITERALLY ANYTHING ELSE

1
2
3
4
5
6
7
8
9
10
11
12

DEAD PEOPLE I'D HAVE LUNCH WITH

OR A MORE USEFUL (BUT STUPID) LIST

1
2
3
4
5
6
7
8
9
10
11
12

A DRAWING OF MY NEXT TATTOO

(OR SOME SUPER BUSINESSY STUFF)

TYPES OF CO-WORKERS AT EVERY JOB

OR SOME BORING TO-DO LIST

1
2
3
4
5
6
7
8
9
10
11
12

WORST IDEAS FOR OLYMPIC EVENTS

OR A GROCERY LIST OR SOMETHING

1
2
3
4
5
6
7
8
9
10
11
12

YEAR: **JANUARY**

YOUR WEEK AT A GLANCE

MONDAY	TUESDAY	WEDNESDAY	THURSDAY	FRIDAY	SATURDAY ☐
☐ TODAY	☐ TODAY	☐ TODAY	☐ TODAY	☐ TODAY	☐ SUNDAY

13

NOTES AND/OR DOODLES

IT'S NATIONAL CLEAN OFF YOUR DESK DAY

AKA: TAKE EVERYTHING AND SHOVE IT IN A DRAWER.

LIAM HEMSWORTH WAS BORN IN 1990

ORLANDO BLOOM WAS BORN IN 1977

9 AM
10 AM
11 AM
NOON
1 PM
2 PM
3 PM
4 PM
5 PM
6 PM

ON THIS DAY IN 1999: MICHAEL JORDAN RETIRED (FOR THE SECOND TIME).

YOUR WEEK AT A GLANCE

MONDAY	TUESDAY	WEDNESDAY	THURSDAY	FRIDAY	SATURDAY ☐
☐ TODAY	☐ TODAY	☐ TODAY	☐ TODAY	☐ TODAY	☐ SUNDAY

14

NOTES AND/OR DOODLES

IT'S NATIONAL DRESS UP YOUR PET DAY

DOGS SEND MESSAGES WITH THEIR URINE...LIKE GROSS EMAIL.

SLICK RICK WAS BORN IN 1965

DAVE GROHL WAS BORN IN 1969

9 AM
10 AM
11 AM
NOON
1 PM
2 PM
3 PM
4 PM
5 PM
6 PM

ON THIS DAY IN 1954: MARILYN MONROE MARRIED JOE DIMAGGIO.

JANUARY

:YEAR

15

YOUR WEEK AT A GLANCE

MONDAY	TUESDAY	WEDNESDAY	THURSDAY	FRIDAY	SATURDAY ☐
TODAY ☐	TODAY ☐	TODAY ☐	TODAY ☐	TODAY ☐	☐ SUNDAY

IT'S NATIONAL BAGEL DAY

BAGELS WENT TO SPACE IN 2008. THE CREAM CHEESE DIDN'T MAKE IT.

MARTIN LUTHER KING JR. WAS BORN IN 1929

PITBULL WAS BORN IN 1981

9 AM

10 AM

11 AM

NOON

1 PM

2 PM

3 PM

4 PM

5 PM

6 PM

ON THIS DAY IN 2009: SULLY SULLENBERGER LANDED A PLANE ON THE HUDSON.

NOTES AND/OR DOODLES

16

YOUR WEEK AT A GLANCE

MONDAY	TUESDAY	WEDNESDAY	THURSDAY	FRIDAY	SATURDAY ☐
TODAY ☐	TODAY ☐	TODAY ☐	TODAY ☐	TODAY ☐	☐ SUNDAY

IT'S NATIONAL FIG NEWTON DAY

OVER 1 BILLION ARE EATEN EVERY YEAR, AND YET WE'VE NEVER HAD ONE.

KATE MOSS WAS BORN IN 1974

AALIYAH WAS BORN IN 1979

9 AM

10 AM

11 AM

NOON

1 PM

2 PM

3 PM

4 PM

5 PM

6 PM

ON THIS DAY IN 1939: THE SUPERMAN DAILY COMIC STRIP DEBUTED.

NOTES AND/OR DOODLES

YEAR: **JANUARY**

YOUR WEEK AT A GLANCE

MONDAY	TUESDAY	WEDNESDAY	THURSDAY	FRIDAY	SATURDAY ☐
☐ TODAY	☐ TODAY	☐ TODAY	☐ TODAY	☐ TODAY	☐ SUNDAY

17

NOTES AND/OR DOODLES

IT'S NATIONAL BOOTLEGGER'S DAY

DURING PROHIBITION, CONGRESS HAD ITS OWN PRIVATE SMUGGLER.

JAMES EARL JONES WAS BORN IN 1931

ZOOEY DESCHANEL WAS BORN IN 1980

9 AM

10 AM

11 AM

NOON

1 PM

2 PM

3 PM

4 PM

5 PM

6 PM

ON THIS DAY IN 1949: THE 1ST VW BEETLE ARRIVED IN THE U.S. FROM GERMANY.

YOUR WEEK AT A GLANCE

MONDAY	TUESDAY	WEDNESDAY	THURSDAY	FRIDAY	SATURDAY ☐
☐ TODAY	☐ TODAY	☐ TODAY	☐ TODAY	☐ TODAY	☐ SUNDAY

18

NOTES AND/OR DOODLES

IT'S NATIONAL PEKING DUCK DAY

THE CHARACTER DONALD DUCK WAS BASED ON A PEKIN DUCK.

KEVIN COSTNER WAS BORN IN 1955

DAVE BAUTISTA WAS BORN IN 1969

9 AM

10 AM

11 AM

NOON

1 PM

2 PM

3 PM

4 PM

5 PM

6 PM

ON THIS DAY IN 1993: MARTIN LUTHER KING JR. DAY BECAME A FEDERAL HOLIDAY.

19

YOUR WEEK AT A GLANCE

MONDAY	TUESDAY	WEDNESDAY	THURSDAY	FRIDAY	SATURDAY ☐
TODAY ☐	TODAY ☐	TODAY ☐	TODAY ☐	TODAY ☐	☐ SUNDAY

IT'S NATIONAL POPCORN DAY

KERNELS CAN POP UPWARDS OF THREE FEET HIGH.

DOLLY PARTON WAS BORN IN 1946

ROBERT PALMER WAS BORN IN 1949

9 AM

10 AM

11 AM

NOON

1 PM

2 PM

3 PM

4 PM

5 PM

6 PM

ON THIS DAY IN 2013: LANCE ARMSTRONG ADMITTED TO DOPING.

NOTES AND/OR DOODLES

20

YOUR WEEK AT A GLANCE

MONDAY	TUESDAY	WEDNESDAY	THURSDAY	FRIDAY	SATURDAY ☐
TODAY ☐	TODAY ☐	TODAY ☐	TODAY ☐	TODAY ☐	☐ SUNDAY

IT'S NATIONAL CHEESE LOVERS DAY

MICE DON'T REALLY EVEN LIKE CHEESE. WE DO THOUGH.

BUZZ ALDRIN WAS BORN IN 1930

QUESTLOVE WAS BORN IN 1971

9 AM

10 AM

11 AM

NOON

1 PM

2 PM

3 PM

4 PM

5 PM

6 PM

ON THIS DAY IN 2009: BARACK OBAMA BECAME THE 44TH PRESIDENT.

NOTES AND/OR DOODLES

LISTS, NOTES & MEMOIRS

MY DEGREES TO KEVIN BACON
OR SOME BORING TO-DO LIST

1
2
3
4
5
6
7
8
9
10
11
12

MY DEGREES TO ACTUAL BACON
OR A GROCERY LIST OR SOMETHING

1
2
3
4
5
6
7
8
9
10
11
12

A DRAWING OF QUESTIONABLE TAXIDERMY

(OR SOME SUPER BUSINESSY STUFF)

THINGS THAT I'VE LOST FOREVER
OR A MORE USEFUL (BUT STUPID) LIST

1
2
3
4
5
6
7
8
9
10
11
12

TO DO (AFTER TIME TRAVELING)
OR A LIST OF LITERALLY ANYTHING ELSE

1
2
3
4
5
6
7
8
9
10
11
12

21

YOUR WEEK AT A GLANCE

MONDAY	TUESDAY	WEDNESDAY	THURSDAY	FRIDAY	SATURDAY ☐
TODAY ☐	TODAY ☐	TODAY ☐	TODAY ☐	TODAY ☐	☐ SUNDAY

IT'S ONE-LINERS DAY

SOMEONE STOLE OUR PLANNER. THEY GOT TWELVE MONTHS.

GEENA DAVIS WAS BORN IN 1956

JAM MASTER JAY WAS BORN IN 1965

9 AM

10 AM

11 AM

NOON

1 PM

2 PM

3 PM

4 PM

5 PM

6 PM

ON THIS DAY IN 1796: THE SMALLPOX VACCINE WAS INTRODUCED.

NOTES AND/OR DOODLES

22

YOUR WEEK AT A GLANCE

MONDAY	TUESDAY	WEDNESDAY	THURSDAY	FRIDAY	SATURDAY ☐
TODAY ☐	TODAY ☐	TODAY ☐	TODAY ☐	TODAY ☐	☐ SUNDAY

IT'S NATIONAL HOT SAUCE DAY

GENERALLY, THE SMALLER THE CHILI, THE HOTTER IT IS.

SAM COOKE WAS BORN IN 1931

GUY FIERI WAS BORN IN 1968

9 AM

10 AM

11 AM

NOON

1 PM

2 PM

3 PM

4 PM

5 PM

6 PM

ON THIS DAY IN 2003: CHAPPELLE'S SHOW DEBUTED ON COMEDY CENTRAL.

NOTES AND/OR DOODLES

YEAR: **JANUARY**

YOUR WEEK AT A GLANCE

MONDAY	TUESDAY	WEDNESDAY	THURSDAY	FRIDAY	SATURDAY ☐
☐ TODAY	☐ TODAY	☐ TODAY	☐ TODAY	☐ TODAY	☐ SUNDAY

23

NOTES AND/OR DOODLES

IT'S NATIONAL HANDWRITING DAY

SMALL HANDWRITING CAN INDICATE SHYNESS IN A PERSON.

MARISKA HARGITAY WAS BORN IN 1964

ANITA POINTER WAS BORN IN 1948

9 AM

10 AM

11 AM

NOON

1 PM

2 PM

3 PM

4 PM

5 PM

6 PM

ON THIS DAY IN 1979: WILLIE MAYS JOINED THE BASEBALL HALL OF FAME.

YOUR WEEK AT A GLANCE

MONDAY	TUESDAY	WEDNESDAY	THURSDAY	FRIDAY	SATURDAY ☐
☐ TODAY	☐ TODAY	☐ TODAY	☐ TODAY	☐ TODAY	☐ SUNDAY

24

NOTES AND/OR DOODLES

IT'S BELLY LAUGH DAY

LAUGHING FOR FIFTEEN MINUTES A DAY CAN HELP YOU LOSE WEIGHT.

MARY LOU RETTON WAS BORN IN 1968

ED HELMS WAS BORN IN 1974

9 AM

10 AM

11 AM

NOON

1 PM

2 PM

3 PM

4 PM

5 PM

6 PM

ON THIS DAY IN 2011: ADELE RELEASED THE ALBUM '21.'

LISTS, NOTES & MEMOIRS

POTENTIAL VANITY LICENSE PLATES
OR A LIST OF LITERALLY ANYTHING ELSE

1
2
3
4
5
6
7
8
9
10
11
12

PLACES WORSE THAN THE DMV
OR A MORE USEFUL (BUT STUPID) LIST

1
2
3
4
5
6
7
8
9
10
11
12

A DRAWING OF THE LAST THING I BOUGHT ONLINE

(OR SOME SUPER BUSINESSY STUFF)

RESOLUTIONS THAT I'LL KEEP
OR SOME BORING TO-DO LIST

1
2
3
4
5
6
7
8
9
10
11
12

RESOLUTIONS THAT I ALREADY BROKE
OR A GROCERY LIST OR SOMETHING

1
2
3
4
5
6
7
8
9
10
11
12

YEAR: JANUARY

YOUR WEEK AT A GLANCE

MONDAY	TUESDAY	WEDNESDAY	THURSDAY	FRIDAY	SATURDAY ☐
☐ TODAY	☐ TODAY	☐ TODAY	☐ TODAY	☐ TODAY	☐ SUNDAY

25

NOTES AND/OR DOODLES

IT'S NATIONAL OPPOSITE DAY

OPPOSITES RARELY ATTRACT—UNLESS YOU'RE PAULA ABDUL APPARENTLY.

DEAN JONES WAS BORN IN 1931

ALICIA KEYS WAS BORN IN 1981

9 AM

10 AM

11 AM

NOON

1 PM

2 PM

3 PM

4 PM

5 PM

6 PM

ON THIS DAY IN 2003: SERENA WILLIAMS WON A 5TH GRAND SLAM SINGLES TITLE.

YOUR WEEK AT A GLANCE

MONDAY	TUESDAY	WEDNESDAY	THURSDAY	FRIDAY	SATURDAY ☐
☐ TODAY	☐ TODAY	☐ TODAY	☐ TODAY	☐ TODAY	☐ SUNDAY

26

NOTES AND/OR DOODLES

IT'S NATIONAL PEANUT BRITTLE DAY

CREATED BY MISTAKE IN 1890, BY A WOMAN TRYING TO MAKE TAFFY.

MARIA VON TRAPP WAS BORN IN 1905

MICHAEL SAYRE WAS BORN IN 1980

9 AM

10 AM

11 AM

NOON

1 PM

2 PM

3 PM

4 PM

5 PM

6 PM

ON THIS DAY IN 1998: BILL CLINTON DENIED HAVING SEX W/ MONICA LEWINSKY.

27

YOUR WEEK AT A GLANCE

MONDAY	TUESDAY	WEDNESDAY	THURSDAY	FRIDAY	SATURDAY ☐
TODAY ☐	TODAY ☐	TODAY ☐	TODAY ☐	TODAY ☐	☐ SUNDAY

IT'S BUBBLE WRAP APPRECIATION DAY

IT WAS ORIGINALLY INTENDED TO A BE A TEXTURED WALLPAPER.

DONNA REED WAS BORN IN 1921

PATTON OSWALT WAS BORN IN 1969

9 AM

10 AM

11 AM

NOON

1 PM

2 PM

3 PM

4 PM

5 PM

6 PM

ON THIS DAY IN 1948: THE FIRST AUDIO TAPE RECORDER WAS SOLD.

NOTES AND/OR DOODLES

28

YOUR WEEK AT A GLANCE

MONDAY	TUESDAY	WEDNESDAY	THURSDAY	FRIDAY	SATURDAY ☐
TODAY ☐	TODAY ☐	TODAY ☐	TODAY ☐	TODAY ☐	☐ SUNDAY

IT'S NATIONAL KAZOO DAY

THERE'S A MUSEUM DEDICATED TO THEM IN BEAUFORT, SOUTH CAROLINA.

RICK ROSS WAS BORN IN 1976

ELIJAH WOOD WAS BORN IN 1981

9 AM

10 AM

11 AM

NOON

1 PM

2 PM

3 PM

4 PM

5 PM

6 PM

ON THIS DAY IN 1986: THE SPACE SHUTTLE CHALLENGER EXPLODED.

NOTES AND/OR DOODLES

YEAR: **JANUARY**

YOUR WEEK AT A GLANCE

MONDAY	TUESDAY	WEDNESDAY	THURSDAY	FRIDAY	SATURDAY ☐
☐ TODAY	☐ TODAY	☐ TODAY	☐ TODAY	☐ TODAY	☐ SUNDAY

29

NOTES AND/OR DOODLES

IT'S NATIONAL PUZZLE DAY

PEOPLE WHO ENJOY PUZZLES ARE KNOWN AS DISSECTOLOGISTS.

OPRAH WINFREY WAS BORN IN 1954

TOM SELLECK WAS BORN IN 1945

9 AM

10 AM

11 AM

NOON

1 PM

2 PM

3 PM

4 PM

5 PM

6 PM

ON THIS DAY IN 1959: WALT DISNEY'S 'SLEEPING BEAUTY' WAS RELEASED.

YOUR WEEK AT A GLANCE

MONDAY	TUESDAY	WEDNESDAY	THURSDAY	FRIDAY	SATURDAY ☐
☐ TODAY	☐ TODAY	☐ TODAY	☐ TODAY	☐ TODAY	☐ SUNDAY

30

NOTES AND/OR DOODLES

IT'S YODEL FOR YOUR NEIGHBORS DAY

BLAME IT ON US.

PHIL COLLINS WAS BORN IN 1951

CHRISTIAN BALE WAS BORN IN 1974

9 AM

10 AM

11 AM

NOON

1 PM

2 PM

3 PM

4 PM

5 PM

6 PM

ON THIS DAY IN 1973: KISS PLAYED THEIR FIRST SHOW IN QUEENS, NEW YORK.

JANUARY

:YEAR

31

YOUR WEEK AT A GLANCE

MONDAY	TUESDAY	WEDNESDAY	THURSDAY	FRIDAY	SATURDAY ☐
TODAY ☐	TODAY ☐	TODAY ☐	TODAY ☐	TODAY ☐	☐ SUNDAY

IT'S HELL IS FREEZING OVER DAY

IN JANUARY, THE AVERAGE TEMPERATURE OF HELL, MICHIGAN IS 23°.

KERRY WASHINGTON WAS BORN IN 1977

MARCUS MUMFORD WAS BORN IN 1987

9 AM

10 AM

11 AM

NOON

1 PM

2 PM

3 PM

4 PM

5 PM

6 PM

ON THIS DAY IN 1865: CONGRESS PASSED THE 13TH AMENDMENT.

NOTES AND/OR DOODLES

A DRAWING OF A FLEA CIRCUS

(OR FLEA AT THE CIRCUS)

UNCONVENTIONALLY ATTRACTIVE CELEBRITIES

OR A GROCERY LIST OR SOMETHING

1

2

3

4

5

6

7

8

9

10

11

12

13

14

15

16

17

18

JANUARY IN REVIEW

MY JANUARY ACCOMPLISHMENTS:

- ☐ TOOK DOWN THE TREE. FINALLY
- ☐ BAILED ON A NEW YEAR'S RESOLUTION
- ☐ ACTUALLY STUCK WITH ONE
- ☐ MADE A SNOWMAN, WOMAN, OR CHILD
- ☐ SELF-DIAGNOSED FROSTBITE
- ☐ REALIZED THAT WINTER JUST STARTED
- ☐ WORE SHORTS ON A 'WARM' DAY
- ☐ SAW DAYLIGHT DURING A WORK DAY
- ☐ SCRAPED ICE WITH A CREDIT CARD
- ☐ AVOIDED DRIVING INTO A DITCH
- ☐ JK, DROVE INTO A DITCH
- ☐ POSSIBLE VITAMIN D DEFICIENCY
- ☐ SAW A COLOR OTHER THAN GRAY
- ☐ LOST A SINGLE GLOVE
- ☐ ABSTAINED FROM TRYING THEMED LATTES

REASONS THAT JANUARY WAS GREAT

'IT ENDED' IS A VALID ANSWER

1
2
3
4
5
6
7
8
9
10
11
12

IF JANUARY WAS PERSONIFIED, PROVIDE ITS MUG SHOT

REASONS THAT I'M GLAD JANUARY IS OVER

USE ADDITIONAL PAPER IF NEEDED

1
2
3
4
5
6
7
8
9
10
11
12
13
14

CLICHÉS OVERHEARD THIS MONTH

- 'SURE IS COMING DOWN OUT THERE' ☐
- 'THANKS, IT WAS ON SALE' ☐
- 'SNOWPOCALYPSE' ☐
- 'I HAVEN'T SEEN YOU SINCE LAST YEAR' ☐
- 'NEW YEAR, NEW ME' ☐
- 'I NEED A VACATION FROM MY VACATION' ☐
- 'YOU WOULD TOTALLY LOVE CROSS FIT ☐
- 'HOW ARE THE ROADS?' ☐
- 'WE'RE JUST KEEPING THINGS CASUAL' ☐
- 'HERE COMES TROUBLE' ☐
- 'I LITERALLY DIED' ☐
- 'MONDAYS, AM I RIGHT?' ☐
- 'I'M NEVER DRINKING AGAIN' ☐
- 'LET'S DO A JUICE CLEANSE TOGETHER' ☐
- 'YOLO' ☐
- 'I FORGOT HOW TO WORK, LOL' ☐
- 'COLD ENOUGH FOR YA?' ☐

THE ONLY MONTH THAT CAN PASS WITHOUT HAVING A FULL MOON.

WELCOME TO

× FEBRUARY ×

OF WHATEVER YEAR
YOU SAY IT IS.

LET'S GO WITH:

NAMED AFTER THE ROMAN PURIFICATION FESTIVAL OF FEBRUARIUS.

FEBRUARY AT A GLANCE :YEAR

YOU MADE IT
TO FEBRUARY

✖

CELEBRATE, IT'S:

AFRICAN-AMERICAN HISTORY MONTH

NATIONAL CAT HEALTH MONTH

NATIONAL HOT BREAKFAST MONTH

GREAT AMERICAN PIE MONTH

NATIONAL SNACK FOOD MONTH

✖

OFFICIAL SYMBOLS:

BIRTHSTONE: AMETHYST

FLOWERS: VIOLET & PRIMROSE

TREES: POPLAR, CEDAR, & PINE

AQUARIUS (JAN 20 / FEB 18)

PISCES (FEB 19 / MAR 20)

DATES TO KNOW*
LIKE, IMPORTANT ONES

✖

GROUNDHOG DAY
FEBRUARY 2ND

PURIM
(JUDAISM)
14TH DAY OF ADAR IN THE JEWISH CALENDAR (MAY FALL IN MARCH)

VALENTINE'S DAY
FEBRUARY 14TH

SUSAN B. ANTHONY DAY
FEBRUARY 15TH

PRESIDENTS' DAY
THIRD MONDAY IN FEBRUARY

MARDI GRAS
47 DAYS BEFORE EASTER (SORRY)

ASH WEDNESDAY
(CHRISTIANITY)
46 DAYS BEFORE EASTER (SORRY AGAIN)

LEAP DAY
(APPROX. EVERY 4 YEARS)
FEBRUARY 29TH
(SEE OUR 'GET STARTED' PAGE FOR THE RULES)

THINGS TO ACCOMPLISH THIS MONTH
FOR EXAMPLE: FILL OUT A TO-DO LIST

1
2
3
4
5
6
7
8
9
10
11
12
13
14
15

THINGS THAT ARE NEVER GOING TO HAPPEN
THERE'S ALWAYS MARCH (OR APRIL)

1
2
3
4
5
6
7
8
9
10
11
12
13
14
15

*A DISCLAIMER OF SORTS

HEY THERE. WE HERE AT BRASS MONKEY LIKE TO JOKE AROUND...BUT WE ALSO WANT TO TAKE A MINUTE TO RECOGNIZE JUST A FEW OF THE MANY HOLIDAYS & EVENTS THAT ARE IMPORTANT TO OUR FRIENDS AROUND THE GLOBE (AND AT HOME). YOU MAY BE DIFFERENT THAN US. WE MAY HAVE NEVER MET. BUT WE LOVE YOU ALL THE SAME.

SO IF YOU HAVEN'T HEARD OF A DAY, LOOK IT UP. LEARNING ABOUT & APPRECIATING CULTURES DIFFERENT THAN YOURS IS IMPORTANT...WAY MORE THAN POSTING A FEW 'STRAWBERRY JAM DAY' SELFIES.

FEBRUARY AT A GLANCE

YEAR:

IT'S FEBRUARY

START PLANNING

×

GROUNDHOG DAY
FEBRUARY 2ND

VALENTINE'S DAY
FEBRUARY 14TH

PRESIDENTS' DAY*
THIRD MONDAY IN FEBRUARY

×

BIRTHDAYS

TO REMEMBER

....

....

....

....

....

....

*PSST: SINCE THIS HOLIDAY MOVES AROUND EACH YEAR (AND WE DON'T KNOW WHEN IN THE FUTURE YOU'RE USING THIS), HELP US OUT AND ADD IT TO THE CALENDAR.

ALSO, ARE THERE JET PACKS YET? OUR FINGERS ARE CROSSED.

DAY OF WEEK S M T W T F S	DAY OF WEEK S M T W T F S	DAY OF WEEK S M T W T F S	DAY OF WEEK S M T W T F S	DAY OF WEEK S M T W T F S	DAY OF WEEK S M T W T F S	DAY OF WEEK S M T W T F S
01	GROUNDHOG DAY 02	03	04	05	06	07
08	09	10	11	12	13	VALENTINE'S DAY 14
15	16	17	18	19	20	21
22	23	24	25	26	27	28
29						

NOTES:

FEBRUARY, AS EXPRESSED IN A DRAWING

LISTS, NOTES & MEMOIRS

ILLEGAL THINGS THAT I'VE DONE

OR A LIST OF LITERALLY ANYTHING ELSE

1
2
3
4
5
6
7
8
9
10
11
12

SONGS CURRENTLY STUCK IN MY HEAD

OR A MORE USEFUL (BUT STUPID) LIST

1
2
3
4
5
6
7
8
9
10
11
12

A DRAWING OF A TOURIST TRAP

(OR SOME SUPER BUSINESSY STUFF)

CHEESES THAT I CURRENTLY OWN

OR SOME BORING TO-DO LIST

1
2
3
4
5
6
7
8
9
10
11
12

PROBABLE REASONS WHY I'M LIKE THIS

OR A GROCERY LIST OR SOMETHING

1
2
3
4
5
6
7
8
9
10
11
12

YEAR: **FEBRUARY**

YOUR WEEK AT A GLANCE

MONDAY	TUESDAY	WEDNESDAY	THURSDAY	FRIDAY	SATURDAY ☐
☐ TODAY	☐ TODAY	☐ TODAY	☐ TODAY	☐ TODAY	☐ SUNDAY

01

NOTES AND/OR DOODLES

IT'S CHANGE YOUR PASSWORD DAY

THIRTY PERCENT OF ALL PHISHING EMAILS ARE OPENED.

BRANDON LEE WAS BORN IN 1965 HARRY STYLES WAS BORN IN 1994

9 AM
10 AM
11 AM
NOON
1 PM
2 PM
3 PM
4 PM
5 PM
6 PM

ON THIS DAY IN 1982: 'LATE NIGHT WITH DAVID LETTERMAN' DEBUTED.

YOUR WEEK AT A GLANCE

MONDAY	TUESDAY	WEDNESDAY	THURSDAY	FRIDAY	SATURDAY ☐
☐ TODAY	☐ TODAY	☐ TODAY	☐ TODAY	☐ TODAY	☐ SUNDAY

02

NOTES AND/OR DOODLES

IT'S GROUNDHOG DAY

THE GROUNDHOG BIT BILL MURRAY 3 TIMES DURING FILMING.

FARRAH FAWCETT WAS BORN IN 1947 SHIKIRA WAS BORN IN 1977

9 AM
10 AM
11 AM
NOON
1 PM
2 PM
3 PM
4 PM
5 PM
6 PM

ON THIS DAY IN 2020: THE KANSAS CITY CHIEFS WON THE SUPER BOWL.

FEBRUARY

:YEAR

03

YOUR WEEK AT A GLANCE

MONDAY	TUESDAY	WEDNESDAY	THURSDAY	FRIDAY	SATURDAY ☐
TODAY ☐	TODAY ☐	TODAY ☐	TODAY ☐	TODAY ☐	☐ SUNDAY

IT'S INTERNATIONAL GOLDEN RETRIEVER DAY

THEY WERE DEVELOPED BY LORD TWEEDMOUTH IN THE LATE 1800s.

(YES, THAT'S ACTUALLY A REAL PERSON)

ISLA FISHER WAS BORN IN 1976 | SEAN KINGSTON WAS BORN IN 1990

9 AM

10 AM

11 AM

NOON

1 PM

2 PM

3 PM

4 PM

5 PM

6 PM

ON THIS DAY IN 1959: BUDDY HOLLY (& OTHERS) DIED IN A PLANE CRASH.

NOTES AND/OR DOODLES

04

YOUR WEEK AT A GLANCE

MONDAY	TUESDAY	WEDNESDAY	THURSDAY	FRIDAY	SATURDAY ☐
TODAY ☐	TODAY ☐	TODAY ☐	TODAY ☐	TODAY ☐	☐ SUNDAY

IT'S ROSA PARKS DAY

THE FOUNDER OF LITTLE CAESARS PAID HER RENT FOR MANY YEARS.

ROSA PARKS WAS BORN IN 1913 | ALICE COOPER WAS BORN IN 1948

9 AM

10 AM

11 AM

NOON

1 PM

2 PM

3 PM

4 PM

5 PM

6 PM

ON THIS DAY IN 2004: MARK ZUCKERBERG LAUNCHED FACEBOOK.

NOTES AND/OR DOODLES

YEAR: **FEBRUARY**

YOUR WEEK AT A GLANCE

MONDAY	TUESDAY	WEDNESDAY	THURSDAY	FRIDAY	SATURDAY ☐
☐ TODAY	☐ TODAY	☐ TODAY	☐ TODAY	☐ TODAY	☐ SUNDAY

05

NOTES AND/OR DOODLES

IT'S NATIONAL FART DAY

FART JOKES HAVE EXISTED SINCE AT LEAST 1900 BCE.

TIM MEADOWS WAS BORN IN 1961

CHRIS PARNELL WAS BORN IN 1967

9 AM

10 AM

11 AM

NOON

1 PM

2 PM

3 PM

4 PM

5 PM

6 PM

ON THIS DAY IN 1971: THE APOLLO 14 ASTRONAUTS LANDED ON THE MOON.

YOUR WEEK AT A GLANCE

MONDAY	TUESDAY	WEDNESDAY	THURSDAY	FRIDAY	SATURDAY ☐
☐ TODAY	☐ TODAY	☐ TODAY	☐ TODAY	☐ TODAY	☐ SUNDAY

06

NOTES AND/OR DOODLES

IT'S PAY A COMPLIMENT DAY

YOU ARE REALLY GREAT AT CHOOSING PLANNERS, BTW.

KATHY NAJIMY WAS BORN IN 1957

AXL ROSE WAS BORN IN 1962

9 AM

10 AM

11 AM

NOON

1 PM

2 PM

3 PM

4 PM

5 PM

6 PM

ON THIS DAY IN 1943: FRANK SINATRA MADE HIS RADIO SINGING DEBUT.

07

YOUR WEEK AT A GLANCE

MONDAY	TUESDAY	WEDNESDAY	THURSDAY	FRIDAY	SATURDAY ☐
TODAY ☐	TODAY ☐	TODAY ☐	TODAY ☐	TODAY ☐	☐ SUNDAY

IT'S NATIONAL PERIODIC TABLE DAY

LESS THAN THIRTY GRAMS OF FRANCIUM EXIST ON EARTH AT ANY TIME.

JAMES SPADER WAS BORN IN 1960

CHRIS ROCK WAS BORN IN 1965

9 AM

10 AM

11 AM

NOON

1 PM

2 PM

3 PM

4 PM

5 PM

6 PM

ON THIS DAY IN 1985: 'NEW YORK, NEW YORK' BECAME NYC'S OFFICIAL SONG.

NOTES AND/OR DOODLES

08

YOUR WEEK AT A GLANCE

MONDAY	TUESDAY	WEDNESDAY	THURSDAY	FRIDAY	SATURDAY ☐
TODAY ☐	TODAY ☐	TODAY ☐	TODAY ☐	TODAY ☐	☐ SUNDAY

IT'S MOLASSES BAR DAY

IN 1919, 2 MILLION GALLONS OF IT FLOODED BOSTON'S NORTH END.

GARY COLEMAN WAS BORN IN 1968

SETH GREEN WAS BORN IN 1974

9 AM

10 AM

11 AM

NOON

1 PM

2 PM

3 PM

4 PM

5 PM

6 PM

ON THIS DAY IN 1992: THE SONG 'I'M TOO SEXY' TOPPED THE U.S. CHARTS.

NOTES AND/OR DOODLES

LISTS, NOTES & MEMOIRS

BEST EUPHEMISMS FOR POOPING

OR SOME BORING TO-DO LIST

1
2
3
4
5
6
7
8
9
10
11
12

ANIMALS THAT LOOK LIKE PRESIDENTS

OR A GROCERY LIST OR SOMETHING

1
2
3
4
5
6
7
8
9
10
11
12

A DRAWING OF MY JOB (AS AN 8-BIT VIDEO GAME)

(OR SOME SUPER BUSINESSY STUFF)

ONE SENTENCE MOVIE SUMMARIES

OR A MORE USEFUL (BUT STUPID) LIST

1
2
3
4
5
6
7
8
9
10
11
12

SATISFYING THINGS TO SET ON FIRE

OR A LIST OF LITERALLY ANYTHING ELSE

1
2
3
4
5
6
7
8
9
10
11
12

FEBRUARY

09

YOUR WEEK AT A GLANCE

MONDAY	TUESDAY	WEDNESDAY	THURSDAY	FRIDAY	SATURDAY ☐
TODAY ☐	TODAY ☐	TODAY ☐	TODAY ☐	TODAY ☐	☐ SUNDAY

IT'S PIZZA PIE DAY

AMERICANS EAT ABOUT 100 ACRES OF IT EVERY DAY.

(CUMULATIVELY—DON'T TRY TO DO THIS ALONE)

JOE PESCI WAS BORN IN 1943

TOM HIDDLESTON WAS BORN IN 1981

9 AM

10 AM

11 AM

NOON

1 PM

2 PM

3 PM

4 PM

5 PM

6 PM

ON THIS DAY IN 1895: VOLLEYBALL WAS INVENTED BY WILLIAM G. MORGAN.

NOTES AND/OR DOODLES

10

YOUR WEEK AT A GLANCE

MONDAY	TUESDAY	WEDNESDAY	THURSDAY	FRIDAY	SATURDAY ☐
TODAY ☐	TODAY ☐	TODAY ☐	TODAY ☐	TODAY ☐	☐ SUNDAY

IT'S NATIONAL FLANNEL DAY

THE UNOFFICIAL UNIFORM OF THE 1990s.

EMMA ROBERTS WAS BORN IN 1991

CHLOË MORETZ WAS BORN IN 1997

9 AM

10 AM

11 AM

NOON

1 PM

2 PM

3 PM

4 PM

5 PM

6 PM

ON THIS DAY IN 1993: 90M WATCHED AS OPRAH INTERVIEWED MICHAEL JACKSON.

NOTES AND/OR DOODLES

YOUR WEEK AT A GLANCE

MONDAY	TUESDAY	WEDNESDAY	THURSDAY	FRIDAY	SATURDAY ☐
☐ TODAY	☐ TODAY	☐ TODAY	☐ TODAY	☐ TODAY	☐ SUNDAY

11

NOTES AND/OR DOODLES

IT'S GET OUT YOUR GUITAR DAY

A BAR FIGHT INSPIRED B.B. KING TO NAME HIS GUITAR 'LUCILLE.'

JENNIFER ANISTON WAS BORN IN 1969

KELLY ROWLAND WAS BORN IN 1981

9 AM

10 AM

11 AM

NOON

1 PM

2 PM

3 PM

4 PM

5 PM

6 PM

ON THIS DAY IN 1990: NELSON MANDELA WAS RELEASED FROM PRISON.

YOUR WEEK AT A GLANCE

MONDAY	TUESDAY	WEDNESDAY	THURSDAY	FRIDAY	SATURDAY ☐
☐ TODAY	☐ TODAY	☐ TODAY	☐ TODAY	☐ TODAY	☐ SUNDAY

12

NOTES AND/OR DOODLES

IT'S NATIONAL LOST PENNY DAY

COPPER PENNIES (PRE-1983 TO BE SPECIFIC) WILL REPEL SLUGS.

CHRISTINA RICCI WAS BORN IN 1980

GUCCI MANE WAS BORN IN 1980

9 AM

10 AM

11 AM

NOON

1 PM

2 PM

3 PM

4 PM

5 PM

6 PM

ON THIS DAY IN 2004: MATTEL ANNOUNCED THE SPLIT OF BARBIE AND KEN.

LISTS, NOTES & MEMOIRS

TATTOOS THAT I'LL LATER REGRET

OR A LIST OF LITERALLY ANYTHING ELSE

1
2
3
4
5
6
7
8
9
10
11
12

WORST NAMES FOR A PET CAT

OR A MORE USEFUL (BUT STUPID) LIST

1
2
3
4
5
6
7
8
9
10
11
12

A DRAWING OF THE LAST PLANT I MURDERED

(OR SOME SUPER BUSINESSY STUFF)

REASONS THAT I'M STILL SINGLE

OR SOME BORING TO-DO LIST

1
2
3
4
5
6
7
8
9
10
11
12

REASONS I WISH I WERE STILL SINGLE

OR A GROCERY LIST OR SOMETHING

1
2
3
4
5
6
7
8
9
10
11
12

YOUR WEEK AT A GLANCE

MONDAY	TUESDAY	WEDNESDAY	THURSDAY	FRIDAY	SATURDAY ☐
☐ TODAY	☐ TODAY	☐ TODAY	☐ TODAY	☐ TODAY	☐ SUNDAY

13

NOTES AND/OR DOODLES

IT'S NATIONAL CRAB RANGOON DAY

LIKELY INVENTED BY VICTOR BERGERON, FOUNDER OF TRADER VIC'S.

JERRY SPRINGER WAS BORN IN 1944

ROBBIE WILLIAMS WAS BORN IN 1974

9 AM

10 AM

11 AM

NOON

1 PM

2 PM

3 PM

4 PM

5 PM

6 PM

ON THIS DAY IN 2000: THE LAST 'PEANUTS' COMIC STRIP WAS PUBLISHED.

YOUR WEEK AT A GLANCE

MONDAY	TUESDAY	WEDNESDAY	THURSDAY	FRIDAY	SATURDAY ☐
☐ TODAY	☐ TODAY	☐ TODAY	☐ TODAY	☐ TODAY	☐ SUNDAY

14

NOTES AND/OR DOODLES

IT'S VALENTINE'S DAY

OH, AND IT'S NATIONAL ORGAN DONOR DAY.

(A HEART SEEMS APPROPRIATE)

GREGORY HINES WAS BORN IN 1946

ROB THOMAS WAS BORN IN 1972

9 AM

10 AM

11 AM

NOON

1 PM

2 PM

3 PM

4 PM

5 PM

6 PM

ON THIS DAY IN 2005: YOUTUBE WAS LAUNCHED (AND PEWDIEPIE WAS SIX).

15

YOUR WEEK AT A GLANCE

MONDAY	TUESDAY	WEDNESDAY	THURSDAY	FRIDAY	SATURDAY
TODAY	TODAY	TODAY	TODAY	TODAY	SUNDAY

IT'S NATIONAL HIPPO DAY

CONSIDERED THE WORLD'S DEADLIEST (& HUNGRIEST) LAND MAMMAL.

CHRIS FARLEY WAS BORN IN 1964

JANE SEYMOUR WAS BORN IN 1951

9 AM

10 AM

11 AM

NOON

1 PM

2 PM

3 PM

4 PM

5 PM

6 PM

ON THIS DAY IN 1965: JOHN LENNON PASSED HIS DRIVING TEST.

NOTES AND/OR DOODLES

16

YOUR WEEK AT A GLANCE

MONDAY	TUESDAY	WEDNESDAY	THURSDAY	FRIDAY	SATURDAY
TODAY	TODAY	TODAY	TODAY	TODAY	SUNDAY

IT'S NATIONAL INNOVATION DAY

SAMUEL THOMAS HOUGHTON RECEIVED A PATENT AT THE AGE OF 5.

ICE-T WAS BORN IN 1958

LUPE FIASCO WAS BORN IN 1982

9 AM

10 AM

11 AM

NOON

1 PM

2 PM

3 PM

4 PM

5 PM

6 PM

ON THIS DAY IN 1968: THE FIRST 911 EMERGENCY CALL WAS PLACED.

NOTES AND/OR DOODLES

YEAR: **FEBRUARY**

YOUR WEEK AT A GLANCE

MONDAY	TUESDAY	WEDNESDAY	THURSDAY	FRIDAY	SATURDAY ☐ / ☐ SUNDAY
☐ TODAY	☐ TODAY	☐ TODAY	☐ TODAY	☐ TODAY	

17

NOTES AND/OR DOODLES

IT'S RANDOM ACT OF KINDNESS DAY

IF YOU COULD 'RANDOMLY' SEND US COOKIES, THAT WOULD BE GREAT.

(1107 HICKORY ST. KANSAS CITY, MO 64101)

ED SHEERAN WAS BORN IN 1991

MICHAEL JORDAN WAS BORN IN 1963

9 AM

10 AM

11 AM

NOON

1 PM

2 PM

3 PM

4 PM

5 PM

6 PM

ON THIS DAY IN 2014: JIMMY FALLON DEBUTED AS HOST OF 'THE TONIGHT SHOW.'

YOUR WEEK AT A GLANCE

MONDAY	TUESDAY	WEDNESDAY	THURSDAY	FRIDAY	SATURDAY ☐ / ☐ SUNDAY
☐ TODAY	☐ TODAY	☐ TODAY	☐ TODAY	☐ TODAY	

18

NOTES AND/OR DOODLES

IT'S NATIONAL DRINK WINE DAY

1 ACRE OF GRAPEVINES PRODUCE APPROX. 800 GALLONS OF WINE.

DR. DRE WAS BORN IN 1965

MOLLY RINGWALD WAS BORN IN 1968

9 AM

10 AM

11 AM

NOON

1 PM

2 PM

3 PM

4 PM

5 PM

6 PM

ON THIS DAY IN 1986: THE FIRST ANTI-SMOKING AD AIRED ON TELEVISION.

19

YOUR WEEK AT A GLANCE

MONDAY	TUESDAY	WEDNESDAY	THURSDAY	FRIDAY	SATURDAY ☐
TODAY ☐	TODAY ☐	TODAY ☐	TODAY ☐	TODAY ☐	☐ SUNDAY

IT'S INTERNATIONAL TUG OF WAR DAY

IT WAS AN OFFICIAL OLYMPIC SPORT FROM 1900 TO 1920.

BENICIO DEL TORO WAS BORN IN 1967

MILLIE BROWN WAS BORN IN 2004

9 AM

10 AM

11 AM

NOON

1 PM

2 PM

3 PM

4 PM

5 PM

6 PM

ON THIS DAY IN 1985: CHERRY COKE WAS INTRODUCED BY COCA-COLA.

NOTES AND/OR DOODLES

20

YOUR WEEK AT A GLANCE

MONDAY	TUESDAY	WEDNESDAY	THURSDAY	FRIDAY	SATURDAY ☐
TODAY ☐	TODAY ☐	TODAY ☐	TODAY ☐	TODAY ☐	☐ SUNDAY

IT'S LOVE YOUR PET DAY

FLEAS CAN JUMP OVER 350 TIMES THEIR BODY LENGTH.

KURT COBAIN WAS BORN IN 1967

RIHANNA WAS BORN IN 1988

9 AM

10 AM

11 AM

NOON

1 PM

2 PM

3 PM

4 PM

5 PM

6 PM

ON THIS DAY IN 1962: JOHN GLENN MADE THE 1ST AMERICAN ORBIT OF EARTH.

NOTES AND/OR DOODLES

LISTS, NOTES & MEMOIRS

WORST SUBJECT LINES FOR EMAILS

OR SOME BORING TO-DO LIST

1
2
3
4
5
6
7
8
9
10
11
12

SMELLS THAT I CAN'T STAND

OR A GROCERY LIST OR SOMETHING

1
2
3
4
5
6
7
8
9
10
11
12

A DRAWING OF A CUCKOO CLOCK

(OR SOME SUPER BUSINESSY STUFF)

MOVIES THAT DESCRIBE MY JOB

OR A MORE USEFUL (BUT STUPID) LIST

1
2
3
4
5
6
7
8
9
10
11
12

SONGS THAT DESCRIBE MY SEX LIFE

OR A LIST OF LITERALLY ANYTHING ELSE

1
2
3
4
5
6
7
8
9
10
11
12

FEBRUARY

:YEAR

21

YOUR WEEK AT A GLANCE

MONDAY	TUESDAY	WEDNESDAY	THURSDAY	FRIDAY	SATURDAY ☐
TODAY ☐	TODAY ☐	TODAY ☐	TODAY ☐	TODAY ☐	☐ SUNDAY

IT'S NATIONAL STICKY BUN DAY

GERMAN SETTLERS IN PENNSYLVANIA ARE TO THANK FOR THEM.

NINA SIMONE WAS BORN IN 1933

KELSEY GRAMMER WAS BORN IN 1955

9 AM

10 AM

11 AM

NOON

1 PM

2 PM

3 PM

4 PM

5 PM

6 PM

ON THIS DAY IN 1986: THE FIRST 'LEGEND OF ZELDA' GAME WAS RELEASED.

NOTES AND/OR DOODLES

22

YOUR WEEK AT A GLANCE

MONDAY	TUESDAY	WEDNESDAY	THURSDAY	FRIDAY	SATURDAY ☐
TODAY ☐	TODAY ☐	TODAY ☐	TODAY ☐	TODAY ☐	☐ SUNDAY

IT'S NATIONAL MARGARITA DAY

THE WORD MARGARITA MEANS DAISY IN SPANISH.

STEVE IRWIN WAS BORN IN 1962

DREW BARRYMORE WAS BORN IN 1975

9 AM

10 AM

11 AM

NOON

1 PM

2 PM

3 PM

4 PM

5 PM

6 PM

ON THIS DAY IN 2009: 'SLUMDOG MILLIONAIRE' WON EIGHT OSCARS.

NOTES AND/OR DOODLES

YEAR:

FEBRUARY

YOUR WEEK AT A GLANCE

MONDAY	TUESDAY	WEDNESDAY	THURSDAY	FRIDAY	SATURDAY ☐
☐ TODAY	☐ TODAY	☐ TODAY	☐ TODAY	☐ TODAY	☐ SUNDAY

23

NOTES AND/OR DOODLES

IT'S CURLING IS COOL DAY

CURLING STONES ARE MADE FROM A RARE TYPE OF MICRO-GRANITE.

EMILY BLUNT WAS BORN IN 1983

DAKOTA FANNING WAS BORN IN 1994

9 AM

10 AM

11 AM

NOON

1 PM

2 PM

3 PM

4 PM

5 PM

6 PM

ON THIS DAY IN 1997: NBC AIRED 'SCHINDLER'S LIST' COMPLETELY UNCENSORED.

YOUR WEEK AT A GLANCE

MONDAY	TUESDAY	WEDNESDAY	THURSDAY	FRIDAY	SATURDAY ☐
☐ TODAY	☐ TODAY	☐ TODAY	☐ TODAY	☐ TODAY	☐ SUNDAY

24

NOTES AND/OR DOODLES

IT'S NATIONAL TORTILLA CHIP DAY

MOST TORTILLA CHIPS ARE NATURALLY GLUTEN FREE.

STEVE JOBS WAS BORN IN 1955

FLOYD MAYWEATHER WAS BORN IN 1977

9 AM

10 AM

11 AM

NOON

1 PM

2 PM

3 PM

4 PM

5 PM

6 PM

ON THIS DAY IN 1972: RICHARD NIXON VISITED THE GREAT WALL OF CHINA.

LISTS, NOTES & MEMOIRS

REASONS THAT I'M NOT A REAL ADULT

OR A LIST OF LITERALLY ANYTHING ELSE

1
2
3
4
5
6
7
8
9
10
11
12

EMOJIS, RANKED BEST TO WORST

OR A MORE USEFUL (BUT STUPID) LIST

1
2
3
4
5
6
7
8
9
10
11
12

A DRAWING OF MY 100TH BIRTHDAY

(OR SOME SUPER BUSINESSY STUFF)

BRANDS THAT COULD SPONSOR MY LIFE

OR SOME BORING TO-DO LIST

1
2
3
4
5
6
7
8
9
10
11
12

THINGS I'VE PURCHASED WHILE DRUNK

OR A GROCERY LIST OR SOMETHING

1
2
3
4
5
6
7
8
9
10
11
12

YOUR WEEK AT A GLANCE

MONDAY	TUESDAY	WEDNESDAY	THURSDAY	FRIDAY	SATURDAY ☐ / ☐ SUNDAY
☐ TODAY	☐ TODAY	☐ TODAY	☐ TODAY	☐ TODAY	

25

NOTES AND/OR DOODLES

IT'S NATIONAL CLAM CHOWDER DAY

CLAMS WERE SOMETIMES USED AS CURRENCY AMONG NATIVE AMERICANS.

RIC FLAIR WAS BORN IN 1949

CHELSEA HANDLER WAS BORN IN 1975

9 AM

10 AM

11 AM

NOON

1 PM

2 PM

3 PM

4 PM

5 PM

6 PM

ON THIS DAY IN 1964: CASSIUS CLAY BECAME THE HEAVYWEIGHT CHAMPION.

YOUR WEEK AT A GLANCE

MONDAY	TUESDAY	WEDNESDAY	THURSDAY	FRIDAY	SATURDAY ☐ / ☐ SUNDAY
☐ TODAY	☐ TODAY	☐ TODAY	☐ TODAY	☐ TODAY	

26

NOTES AND/OR DOODLES

IT'S NATIONAL PISTACHIO DAY

THEIR GREEN AND PURPLE HUES ARE DUE TO ANTIOXIDANTS.

JOHNNY CASH WAS BORN IN 1932

ERYKAH BADU WAS BORN IN 1971

9 AM

10 AM

11 AM

NOON

1 PM

2 PM

3 PM

4 PM

5 PM

6 PM

ON THIS DAY IN 1970: NATIONAL PUBLIC RADIO WAS FOUNDED.

27

YOUR WEEK AT A GLANCE

MONDAY	TUESDAY	WEDNESDAY	THURSDAY	FRIDAY	SATURDAY ☐
TODAY ☐	TODAY ☐	TODAY ☐	TODAY ☐	TODAY ☐	☐ SUNDAY

IT'S NATIONAL RETRO DAY

EACH KOOSH BALL IS MADE FROM OVER 2,000 RUBBER STRANDS.

CHELSEA CLINTON WAS BORN IN 1980

JOSH GROBAN WAS BORN IN 1981

9 AM

10 AM

11 AM

NOON

1 PM

2 PM

3 PM

4 PM

5 PM

6 PM

ON THIS DAY IN 1984: CARL LEWIS SET THE INDOOR LONG JUMP WORLD RECORD.

NOTES AND/OR DOODLES

28

YOUR WEEK AT A GLANCE

MONDAY	TUESDAY	WEDNESDAY	THURSDAY	FRIDAY	SATURDAY ☐
TODAY ☐	TODAY ☐	TODAY ☐	TODAY ☐	TODAY ☐	☐ SUNDAY

IT'S NATIONAL TOOTH FAIRY DAY

TOOTH ENAMEL IS THE HARDEST PART OF THE HUMAN BODY.

JOHN TURTURRO WAS BORN IN 1957

ALI LARTER WAS BORN IN 1976

9 AM

10 AM

11 AM

NOON

1 PM

2 PM

3 PM

4 PM

5 PM

6 PM

ON THIS DAY IN 2016: LEONARDO DICAPRIO WON AN OSCAR. FINALLY.

NOTES AND/OR DOODLES

YEAR: **FEBRUARY**

YOUR WEEK AT A GLANCE

MONDAY	TUESDAY	WEDNESDAY	THURSDAY	FRIDAY	SATURDAY ☐
☐ TODAY	☐ TODAY	☐ TODAY	☐ TODAY	☐ TODAY	☐ SUNDAY

29

NOTES AND/OR DOODLES

IT'S LEAP DAY (DEPENDING ON THE YEAR)

OH, AND IT'S ALSO RARE DISEASE DAY. FUN.

JA RULE WAS BORN IN 1976

ANTHONY ROBBINS WAS BORN IN 1960

9 AM

10 AM

11 AM

NOON

1 PM

2 PM

3 PM

4 PM

5 PM

6 PM

ON THIS DAY IN 1960: THE FIRST PLAYBOY CLUB OPENED IN CHICAGO.

PUBLIC FIGURES MORE POLARIZING THAN CILANTRO

OR A GROCERY LIST OR SOMETHING

1
2
3
4
5
6
7
8
9
10
11
12
13
14
15
16
17
18

A DRAWING OF 'AN APPLE A DAY'

(OR UNEMPLOYED DOCTORS)

FEBRUARY IN REVIEW

REASONS THAT FEBRUARY WAS GREAT

'IT ENDED' IS A VALID ANSWER

1
2
3
4
5
6
7
8
9
10
11
12

MY FEBRUARY ACCOMPLISHMENTS

- [ ] BOUGHT CANDY ON CLEARANCE
- [ ] SAID A GROUND HOG'S NAME IN VAIN
- [ ] SPELLED FEBRUARY CORRECTLY
- [ ] REGRETTED BEING SINGLE
- [ ] REGRETTED NOT BEING SINGLE
- [ ] GOOGLED 'WHY DO WE HAVE LEAP DAY?'
- [ ] HAD A PARTY TO WATCH COMMERCIALS
- [ ] SAW ZERO OSCAR NOMINATED FILMS
- [ ] WATCHED 'LOVE ACTUALLY' 10 TIMES
- [ ] GASPED AT THE COST OF GREETING CARDS
- [ ] TEXTED A PHOTO OF A GREETING CARD
- [ ] SAW AN AD FOR HEART SHAPED PIZZA
- [ ] CONTEMPLATED MOVING TO HAWAII
- [ ] LOOKED UP THE COST TO LIVE IN HAWAII
- [ ] BOUGHT A PARKA INSTEAD

IF FEBRUARY WAS PERSONIFIED, PROVIDE A COURTROOM SKETCH

CLICHES OVERHEARD THIS MONTH

- [ ] 'GALENTINE'S DAY'
- [ ] 'OH, I DON'T NEED A GIFT THIS YEAR'
- [ ] 'IS IT SPRING YET?'
- [ ] 'MY CAT IS MY DATE TONIGHT'
- [ ] 'I'M JUST LIVING THE DREAM'
- [ ] 'CHOCOHOLIC'
- [ ] 'I HEAR THE ROADS ARE GETTING SLICK'
- [ ] 'IT'S JUST ANOTHER DAY'
- [ ] 'WE SHOULD HAVE STAYED HOME'
- [ ] 'SOMEONE'S GOT A SECRET ADMIRER'
- [ ] 'MY FLOWERS MUST HAVE GOTTEN LOST'
- [ ] 'IT FEELS LIKE GROUNDHOG DAY'
- [ ] 'I ONLY WATCHED THE HALFTIME SHOW'
- [ ] 'I CHOO-CHOO-CHOOSE YOU'
- [ ] 'OH SHIT, THAT'S TODAY?'
- [ ] 'IT'S ACTUALLY SINGLES AWARENESS DAY'
- [ ] 'HE'S TOTALLY GONNA PROPOSE!'

REASONS THAT I'M GLAD IT'S OVER

USE ADDITIONAL PAPER IF NEEDED

1
2
3
4
5
6
7
8
9
10
11
12
13
14

FEBRUARY IN REVIEW

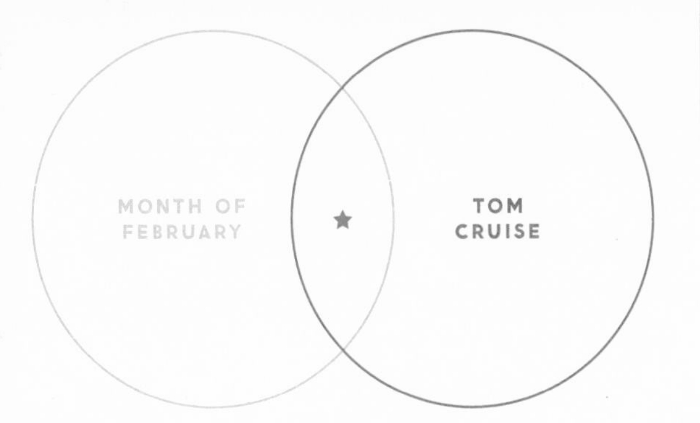

A FEBRUARY VENN DIAGRAM

WHAT DID THEY HAVE IN COMMON?

SHORTER THAN AVERAGE 1

2

3

4

5

6

7

8

AWKWARD THINGS THAT HAPPENED

(AND WILL KEEP ME UP AT NIGHT)

1

2

3

4

5

6

7

8

9

10

11

12

13

14

15

16

17

A DRAWING OF JA RULE'S BIRTHDAY PARTY

(IT'S ON LEAP DAY)

ENJOYMENT OVER TIME

CHOOSE A COLOR KEY

LINE	ITEM
——	FULL PRICED CHOCOLATE
– –	DISCOUNT CHOCOLATE
	GROUNDHOGS
	COLD WEATHER
	BEING IN A RELATIONSHIP
	SPENDING MONEY
	THINGS THAT ARE RED
	DRINKING (BOOZE)
	DRINKING (WATER)
	GREETING CARDS

FEBRUARY ENJOYMENT INDEX

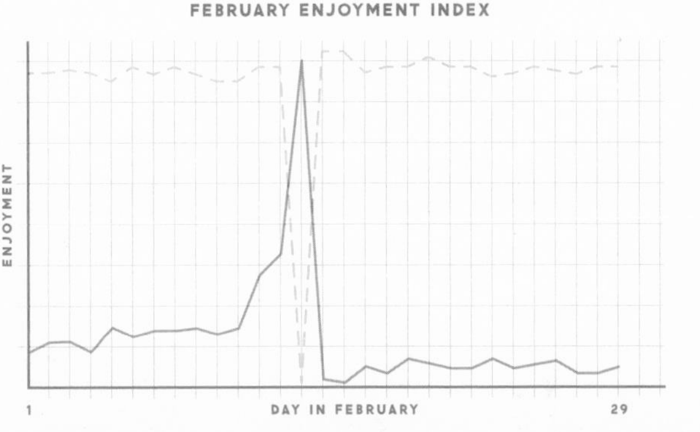

ORIGINALLY THE FIRST MONTH OF THE YEAR (IN THE ROMAN CALENDAR).

WELCOME TO

× MARCH ×

OF WHATEVER YEAR YOU SAY IT IS.

LET'S GO WITH:

NAMED AFTER MARS, THE ROMAN GOD OF WAR.

MARCH AT A GLANCE :YEAR

YOU MADE IT
TO MARCH

✖

CELEBRATE, IT'S:

NATIONAL FROZEN FOOD MONTH

IRISH-AMERICAN HERITAGE MONTH

NATIONAL NOODLE MONTH

NATIONAL NUTRITION MONTH

NATIONAL CRAFT MONTH

✖

OFFICIAL SYMBOLS:

BIRTHSTONE: AQUAMARINE

FLOWERS: DAFFODIL & JONQUIL

TREES: WEEPING WILLOW & OAK

PISCES (FEB 20 / MAR 20)

ARIES (MAR 21 / APR 20)

DATES TO KNOW*
LIKE, IMPORTANT ONES

✖

DAYLIGHT SAVING TIME
FIRST SUNDAY OF MARCH

INTERNATIONAL WOMEN'S DAY
MARCH 8TH

PURIM
(JUDAISM)
14TH DAY OF ADAR IN THE JEWISH CALENDAR (MAY FALL IN FEB.)

IDES OF MARCH
MARCH 15TH

ST. PATRICK'S DAY
MARCH 17TH

INTERNATIONAL DAY FOR THE ELIMINATION OF RACIAL DISCRIMINATION
MARCH 21ST

HOLI
(HINDUISM)
ON THE FULL MOON DAY OF PHALGUNA (OFTEN IN MARCH)

START OF SPRING
(SPRING EQUINOX)
MARCH 19TH (OR 20TH)

THINGS TO ACCOMPLISH THIS MONTH
FOR EXAMPLE: FILL OUT A TO-DO LIST

1
2
3
4
5
6
7
8
9
10
11
12
13
14
15

THINGS THAT ARE NEVER GOING TO HAPPEN
THERE'S ALWAYS APRIL (OR MAY)

1
2
3
4
5
6
7
8
9
10
11
12
13
14
15

*A DISCLAIMER OF SORTS

HEY THERE, WE HERE AT BRASS MONKEY LIKE TO JOKE AROUND...BUT WE ALSO WANT TO TAKE A MINUTE TO RECOGNIZE JUST A FEW OF THE MANY HOLIDAYS & EVENTS THAT ARE IMPORTANT TO OUR FRIENDS AROUND THE GLOBE (AND AT HOME). YOU MAY BE DIFFERENT THAN US. WE MAY HAVE NEVER MET. BUT WE LOVE YOU ALL THE SAME.

SO IF YOU HAVEN'T HEARD OF A DAY, LOOK IT UP. LEARNING ABOUT & APPRECIATING CULTURES DIFFERENT THAN YOURS IS IMPORTANT...WAY MORE THAN POSTING A FEW 'STRAWBERRY JAM DAY' SELFIES.

YEAR: MARCH AT A GLANCE

IT'S MARCH
START PLANNING

×

DAYLIGHT SAVING TIME*
2ND SUNDAY IN MARCH

ST. PATRICK'S DAY
MARCH 17TH

START OF SPRING*
MARCH 19TH (OR 20TH)

×

BIRTHDAYS
TO REMEMBER

*PSST: SINCE THIS HOLIDAY MOVES AROUND EACH YEAR (AND WE DON'T KNOW WHEN IN THE FUTURE YOU'RE USING THIS), HELP US OUT AND ADD IT TO THE CALENDAR.

ALSO, ARE THERE JET PACKS YET? OUR FINGERS ARE CROSSED.

S M T W T F S	S M T W T F S	S M T W T F S	S M T W T F S	S M T W T F S	S M T W T F S	S M T W T F S
01	02	03	04	05	06	07
08	09	10	11	12	13	14
15	16	ST. PATRICK'S DAY 17	18	19	20	21
22	23	24	25	26	27	28
29	30	31				

NOTES:

MARCH, AS EXPRESSED IN A DRAWING

MARCH PREVIEW

A MARCH VENN DIAGRAM
WHAT DO THEY HAVE IN COMMON?

1 USUALLY SMELLS LIKE BOOZE
2
3
4
5
6
7
8

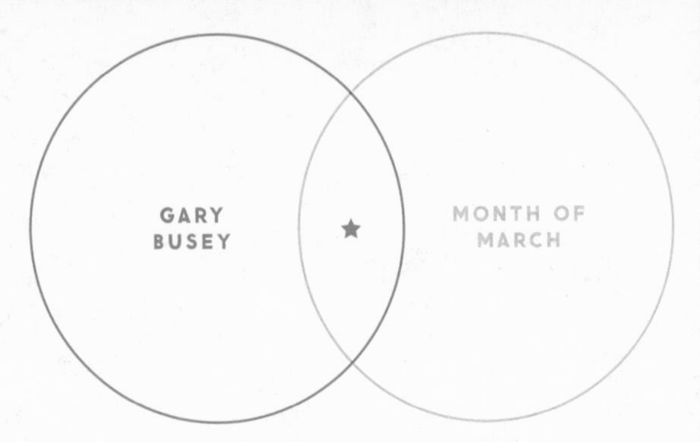

A DRAWING OF ST. PATRICK'S DAY

(IT'S A BLACKOUT)

SUPPLIES NEEDED FOR THE MONTH
ALCOHOL, AND OTHER NECESSITIES

1
2
3
4
5
6
7
8
9
10
11
12
13
14
15
16
17

MARCH ENJOYMENT INDEX

ENJOYMENT OVER TIME
CHOOSE A COLOR KEY

LINE	ITEM
——	GREEN BEER
– –	BEER OF OTHER COLORS
	IBUPROFEN
	MARCH MADNESS
	COW MADNESS
	TRADITIONAL IRISH FOODS
	LUCKY CHARMS
	BITCHING ABOUT CLOCKS
	FAKE IRISH ACCENTS
	SAYING 'ET TU, BRUTE?'

YEAR: MARCH

YOUR WEEK AT A GLANCE

MONDAY	TUESDAY	WEDNESDAY	THURSDAY	FRIDAY	SATURDAY ☐
☐ TODAY	☐ TODAY	☐ TODAY	☐ TODAY	☐ TODAY	☐ SUNDAY

01

NOTES AND/OR DOODLES

IT'S NATIONAL PIG DAY

PIGS DON'T HAVE SWEAT GLANDS (HENCE THE MUD).

JAMIE DORNAN WAS BORN IN 1982 TIM MCGRAW WAS BORN IN 1967

9 AM

10 AM

11 AM

NOON

1 PM

2 PM

3 PM

4 PM

5 PM

6 PM

ON THIS DAY IN 2020: MIKE AND MELANIE STARTED BRASS MONKEY.

YOUR WEEK AT A GLANCE

MONDAY	TUESDAY	WEDNESDAY	THURSDAY	FRIDAY	SATURDAY ☐
☐ TODAY	☐ TODAY	☐ TODAY	☐ TODAY	☐ TODAY	☐ SUNDAY

02

NOTES AND/OR DOODLES

IT'S OLD STUFF DAY

THAT UNIVERSAL 'THRIFT STORE SMELL' COMES FROM OUR BODY OILS.

REBEL WILSON WAS BORN IN 1980 REGGIE BUSH WAS BORN IN 1985

9 AM

10 AM

11 AM

NOON

1 PM

2 PM

3 PM

4 PM

5 PM

6 PM

ON THIS DAY IN 1933: 'KING KONG' PREMIERED IN NEW YORK CITY.

03

YOUR WEEK AT A GLANCE

MONDAY	TUESDAY	WEDNESDAY	THURSDAY	FRIDAY	SATURDAY ☐
TODAY ☐	TODAY ☐	TODAY ☐	TODAY ☐	TODAY ☐	☐ SUNDAY

IT'S TALK IN THIRD PERSON DAY

A PERSON WHO SPEAKS IN THIRD PERSON IS CALLED AN ILLEIST.

(WE ALSO HAVE A FEW OTHER TERMS FOR THEM)

TONE-LOC WAS BORN IN 1966

CAMILA CABELLO WAS BORN IN 1997

9 AM

10 AM

11 AM

NOON

1 PM

2 PM

3 PM

4 PM

5 PM

6 PM

NOTES AND/OR DOODLES

ON THIS DAY IN 1997: THE FIRST ISSUE OF 'TIME' APPEARED ON NEWSSTANDS.

04

YOUR WEEK AT A GLANCE

MONDAY	TUESDAY	WEDNESDAY	THURSDAY	FRIDAY	SATURDAY ☐
TODAY ☐	TODAY ☐	TODAY ☐	TODAY ☐	TODAY ☐	☐ SUNDAY

IT'S NATIONAL SNACK DAY

46 PERCENT OF WOMEN PREFER RIBBED CHIPS. *WINK*

ED ROTH WAS BORN IN 1932

LEN WISEMAN WAS BORN IN 1973

9 AM

10 AM

11 AM

NOON

1 PM

2 PM

3 PM

4 PM

5 PM

6 PM

NOTES AND/OR DOODLES

ON THIS DAY IN 1837: THE CITY OF CHICAGO WAS INCORPORATED.

YOUR WEEK AT A GLANCE

MONDAY	TUESDAY	WEDNESDAY	THURSDAY	FRIDAY	SATURDAY ☐
☐ TODAY	☐ TODAY	☐ TODAY	☐ TODAY	☐ TODAY	☐ SUNDAY

05

NOTES AND/OR DOODLES

IT'S NATIONAL POUTINE DAY

'POUTINE' IS QUEBEC SLANG FOR 'A MESS.'

ASSIF MANDVI WAS BORN IN 1966

EVA MENDES WAS BORN IN 1974

9 AM

10 AM

11 AM

NOON

1 PM

2 PM

3 PM

4 PM

5 PM

6 PM

ON THIS DAY IN 2004: MARTHA STEWART WAS CONVICTED.

YOUR WEEK AT A GLANCE

MONDAY	TUESDAY	WEDNESDAY	THURSDAY	FRIDAY	SATURDAY ☐
☐ TODAY	☐ TODAY	☐ TODAY	☐ TODAY	☐ TODAY	☐ SUNDAY

06

NOTES AND/OR DOODLES

IT'S NATIONAL FROZEN FOOD DAY

DESPITE THE MYTH, FREEZING FOOD DOES NOT REMOVE NUTRIENTS.

SHAQUILLE O'NEAL WAS BORN IN 1972

TYLER THE CREATOR WAS BORN IN 1991

9 AM

10 AM

11 AM

NOON

1 PM

2 PM

3 PM

4 PM

5 PM

6 PM

ON THIS DAY IN 2012: A 3-YEAR-OLD MCNUGGET SOLD FOR $8,100 ON EBAY.

07

YOUR WEEK AT A GLANCE

MONDAY	TUESDAY	WEDNESDAY	THURSDAY	FRIDAY	SATURDAY ☐
TODAY ☐	TODAY ☐	TODAY ☐	TODAY ☐	TODAY ☐	☐ SUNDAY

IT'S NATIONAL CEREAL DAY

ASTRONAUTS ATE KELLOGG'S CORN FLAKES ABOARD APOLLO 11.

BRYAN CRANSTON WAS BORN IN 1956

RACHEL WEISZ WAS BORN IN 1970

9 AM

10 AM

11 AM

NOON

1 PM

2 PM

3 PM

4 PM

5 PM

6 PM

ON THIS DAY IN 1985: THE SONG 'WE ARE THE WORLD' WAS RELEASED.

NOTES AND/OR DOODLES

08

YOUR WEEK AT A GLANCE

MONDAY	TUESDAY	WEDNESDAY	THURSDAY	FRIDAY	SATURDAY ☐
TODAY ☐	TODAY ☐	TODAY ☐	TODAY ☐	TODAY ☐	☐ SUNDAY

IT'S NATIONAL PROOFREADING DAY

THAT REMINDS US, WE REALLY TO HIRE ONE.

BORIS KODJOE WAS BORN IN 1973

LESTER HOLT WAS BORN IN 1959

9 AM

10 AM

11 AM

NOON

1 PM

2 PM

3 PM

4 PM

5 PM

6 PM

ON THIS DAY IN 1993: BEAVIS AND BUTT-HEAD PREMIERED ON MTV.

NOTES AND/OR DOODLES

LISTS, NOTES & MEMOIRS

MILLION DOLLAR IDEAS

OR SOME BORING TO-DO LIST

1
2
3
4
5
6
7
8
9
10
11
12

TEN DOLLAR IDEAS

OR A GROCERY LIST OR SOMETHING

1
2
3
4
5
6
7
8
9
10
11
12

A DRAWING OF HOW THE DINOSAURS REALLY DIED

(OR SOME SUPER BUSINESSY STUFF)

THINGS I'D DO IF I HAD EXTRA LIMBS

OR A MORE USEFUL (BUT STUPID) LIST

1
2
3
4
5
6
7
8
9
10
11
12

WORST FILLINGS FOR A BURRITO

OR A LIST OF LITERALLY ANYTHING ELSE

1
2
3
4
5
6
7
8
9
10
11
12

09

YOUR WEEK AT A GLANCE

MONDAY	TUESDAY	WEDNESDAY	THURSDAY	FRIDAY	SATURDAY ☐
TODAY ☐	TODAY ☐	TODAY ☐	TODAY ☐	TODAY ☐	☐ SUNDAY

IT'S NATIONAL MEATBALL DAY

THE LARGEST MEATBALL EVER MADE WAS 1,707 POUNDS.

(SOUNDS LIKE A CHALLENGE TO US)

LIL' BOW WOW WAS BORN IN 1987

EMMANUEL LEWIS WAS BORN IN 1971

9 AM

10 AM

11 AM

NOON

1 PM

2 PM

3 PM

4 PM

5 PM

6 PM

ON THIS DAY IN 1997: NOTORIOUS B.I.G. WAS SHOT & KILLED AT A STOPLIGHT.

NOTES AND/OR DOODLES

10

YOUR WEEK AT A GLANCE

MONDAY	TUESDAY	WEDNESDAY	THURSDAY	FRIDAY	SATURDAY ☐
TODAY ☐	TODAY ☐	TODAY ☐	TODAY ☐	TODAY ☐	☐ SUNDAY

IT'S INTERNATIONAL BAGPIPE DAY

BAGPIPES WERE ORIGINALLY USED TO SCARE ENEMIES DURING BATTLE.

CHUCK NORRIS WAS BORN IN 1940

JON HAMM WAS BORN IN 1971

9 AM

10 AM

11 AM

NOON

1 PM

2 PM

3 PM

4 PM

5 PM

6 PM

ON THIS DAY IN 1977: ASTRONOMERS DISCOVER THE RINGS OF URANUS (GROW UP).

NOTES AND/OR DOODLES

YOUR WEEK AT A GLANCE

MONDAY	TUESDAY	WEDNESDAY	THURSDAY	FRIDAY	SATURDAY ☐
☐ TODAY	☐ TODAY	☐ TODAY	☐ TODAY	☐ TODAY	☐ SUNDAY

11

NOTES AND/OR DOODLES

IT'S DEBUNKING DAY

WE'LL START: TWINKIES ONLY HAVE A SHELF LIFE OF 45 DAYS. SORRY.

THORA BIRCH WAS BORN IN 1982

TERRANCE HOWARD WAS BORN IN 1969

9 AM

10 AM

11 AM

NOON

1 PM

2 PM

3 PM

4 PM

5 PM

6 PM

ON THIS DAY IN 1986: THE NFL ADOPTED THE INSTANT REPLAY RULE.

YOUR WEEK AT A GLANCE

MONDAY	TUESDAY	WEDNESDAY	THURSDAY	FRIDAY	SATURDAY ☐
☐ TODAY	☐ TODAY	☐ TODAY	☐ TODAY	☐ TODAY	☐ SUNDAY

12

NOTES AND/OR DOODLES

IT'S NATIONAL BAKED SCALLOPS DAY

SCALLOPS SWIM BY OPENING AND CLOSING THEIR SHELLS.

LIZA MINNELLI WAS BORN IN 1946

DAVE EGGERS WAS BORN IN 1970

9 AM

10 AM

11 AM

NOON

1 PM

2 PM

3 PM

4 PM

5 PM

6 PM

ON THIS DAY IN 1894: COCA-COLA IS SOLD IN BOTTLES FOR THE 1ST TIME.

LISTS, NOTES & MEMOIRS

WHY DAYLIGHT SAVING TIME IS STUPID

OR A LIST OF LITERALLY ANYTHING ELSE

1
2
3
4
5
6
7
8
9
10
11
12

CELEBRITIES I COULD TOTALLY BEAT UP

OR A MORE USEFUL (BUT STUPID) LIST

1
2
3
4
5
6
7
8
9
10
11
12

A DRAWING OF WHERE BABIES COME FROM

(OR SOME SUPER BUSINESSY STUFF)

KNOCK-OFF BRANDS

OR SOME BORING TO-DO LIST

1
2
3
4
5
6
7
8
9
10
11
12

KNOCK-OFF BANDS

OR A GROCERY LIST OR SOMETHING

1
2
3
4
5
6
7
8
9
10
11
12

YOUR WEEK AT A GLANCE

MONDAY	TUESDAY	WEDNESDAY	THURSDAY	FRIDAY	SATURDAY ☐
☐ TODAY	☐ TODAY	☐ TODAY	☐ TODAY	☐ TODAY	☐ SUNDAY

13

NOTES AND/OR DOODLES

IT'S EARMUFF DAY

CHESTER GREENWOOD WAS 15 YEARS OLD WHEN HE INVENTED THEM.

WILLIAM H. MACY WAS BORN IN 1950

EMILE HIRSCH WAS BORN IN 1985

9 AM

10 AM

11 AM

NOON

1 PM

2 PM

3 PM

4 PM

5 PM

6 PM

ON THIS DAY IN 1969: THE DISNEY MOVIE 'THE LOVE BUG' WAS RELEASED.

YOUR WEEK AT A GLANCE

MONDAY	TUESDAY	WEDNESDAY	THURSDAY	FRIDAY	SATURDAY ☐
☐ TODAY	☐ TODAY	☐ TODAY	☐ TODAY	☐ TODAY	☐ SUNDAY

14

NOTES AND/OR DOODLES

IT'S GENIUS DAY

MENSA WAS FOUNDED TO HELP PEOPLE WITH HIGH IQs CONNECT.

QUINCY JONES JR WAS BORN IN 1933

KIRBY PUCKETT WAS BORN IN 1960

9 AM

10 AM

11 AM

NOON

1 PM

2 PM

3 PM

4 PM

5 PM

6 PM

ON THIS DAY IN 1794: ELI WHITNEY RECEIVED A PATENT FOR THE COTTON GIN.

15

YOUR WEEK AT A GLANCE

MONDAY	TUESDAY	WEDNESDAY	THURSDAY	FRIDAY	SATURDAY ☐
TODAY ☐	TODAY ☐	TODAY ☐	TODAY ☐	TODAY ☐	☐ SUNDAY

IT'S DUMBSTRUCK DAY

WE'RE SPEECHLESS.

BRET MICHAELS WAS BORN IN 1963 EVA LONGORIA WAS BORN IN 1975

9 AM

10 AM

11 AM

NOON

1 PM

2 PM

3 PM

4 PM

5 PM

6 PM

ON THIS DAY IN 1985: THE 1ST DOMAIN NAME WAS REGISTERED (SYMBOLICS.COM).

NOTES AND/OR DOODLES

16

YOUR WEEK AT A GLANCE

MONDAY	TUESDAY	WEDNESDAY	THURSDAY	FRIDAY	SATURDAY ☐
TODAY ☐	TODAY ☐	TODAY ☐	TODAY ☐	TODAY ☐	☐ SUNDAY

IT'S LIP APPRECIATION DAY

THEY'RE PRETTY GREAT—HOLDING FOOD IN AND ALL OF THAT.

PATTY GRIFFIN WAS BORN IN 1964 ERIK ESTRADA WAS BORN IN 1949

9 AM

10 AM

11 AM

NOON

1 PM

2 PM

3 PM

4 PM

5 PM

6 PM

ON THIS DAY IN 1994: TONYA HARDING PLED GUILTY TO ATTACK ON KERRIGAN.

NOTES AND/OR DOODLES

YEAR: MARCH

YOUR WEEK AT A GLANCE

MONDAY	TUESDAY	WEDNESDAY	THURSDAY	FRIDAY	SATURDAY ☐
☐ TODAY	☐ TODAY	☐ TODAY	☐ TODAY	☐ TODAY	☐ SUNDAY

17

NOTES AND/OR DOODLES

IT'S ST. PATRICK'S DAY

OH, AND IT'S ALSO NATIONAL PANDA DAY.

NAT KING COLE WAS BORN IN 1919

ROB LOWE WAS BORN IN 1964

9 AM

10 AM

11 AM

NOON

1 PM

2 PM

3 PM

4 PM

5 PM

6 PM

ON THIS DAY IN 1762: NYC HELD ITS FIRST ST. PATRICK'S DAY PARADE.

YOUR WEEK AT A GLANCE

MONDAY	TUESDAY	WEDNESDAY	THURSDAY	FRIDAY	SATURDAY ☐
☐ TODAY	☐ TODAY	☐ TODAY	☐ TODAY	☐ TODAY	☐ SUNDAY

18

NOTES AND/OR DOODLES

IT'S AWKWARD MOMENTS DAY

CELEBRATE THE THINGS THAT KEEP YOU UP AT NIGHT.

VANESSA WILLIAMS WAS BORN IN 1963

QUEEN LATIFA WAS BORN IN 1970

9 AM

10 AM

11 AM

NOON

1 PM

2 PM

3 PM

4 PM

5 PM

6 PM

ON THIS DAY IN 1991: THE '76ERS RETIRED WILT CHAMBERLAIN'S JERSEY.

19

YOUR WEEK AT A GLANCE

MONDAY	TUESDAY	WEDNESDAY	THURSDAY	FRIDAY	SATURDAY ☐
TODAY ☐	TODAY ☐	TODAY ☐	TODAY ☐	TODAY ☐	☐ SUNDAY

IT'S LET'S LAUGH DAY

ADULTS LAUGH AROUND 15-30 TIMES PER DAY. BABIES? 300.

ANDY REID WAS BORN IN 1958

GLEN CLOSE WAS BORN IN 1947

9 AM

10 AM

11 AM

NOON

1 PM

2 PM

3 PM

4 PM

5 PM

6 PM

ON THIS DAY IN 1918: CONGRESS APPROVED DAYLIGHT SAVING TIME. JERKS.

NOTES AND/OR DOODLES

20

YOUR WEEK AT A GLANCE

MONDAY	TUESDAY	WEDNESDAY	THURSDAY	FRIDAY	SATURDAY ☐
TODAY ☐	TODAY ☐	TODAY ☐	TODAY ☐	TODAY ☐	☐ SUNDAY

IT'S ALIEN ABDUCTION DAY

THE MOVIE 'ALIEN' WAS ORIGINALLY TITLED 'STAR BEAST.'

FRED ROGERS WAS BORN IN 1928

SPIKE LEE WAS BORN IN 1957

9 AM

10 AM

11 AM

NOON

1 PM

2 PM

3 PM

4 PM

5 PM

6 PM

ON THIS DAY IN 1969: JOHN LENNON MARRIED YOKO ONO.

NOTES AND/OR DOODLES

LISTS, NOTES & MEMOIRS

NAME IDEAS FOR MY IMAGINARY BOAT

OR SOME BORING TO-DO LIST

1
2
3
4
5
6
7
8
9
10
11
12

RULES THAT WOULD IMPROVE FOOTBALL

OR A GROCERY LIST OR SOMETHING

1
2
3
4
5
6
7
8
9
10
11
12

A DRAWING OF CATS PLOTTING A MURDER (SO LIKE, JUST CATS)

(OR SOME SUPER BUSINESSY STUFF)

GREETINGS SUPERIOR TO HELLO

OR A MORE USEFUL (BUT STUPID) LIST

1
2
3
4
5
6
7
8
9
10
11
12

FITTING THEME SONGS FOR MY EXES

OR A LIST OF LITERALLY ANYTHING ELSE

1
2
3
4
5
6
7
8
9
10
11
12

MARCH

:YEAR

21

YOUR WEEK AT A GLANCE

MONDAY	TUESDAY	WEDNESDAY	THURSDAY	FRIDAY	SATURDAY ☐
TODAY ☐	TODAY ☐	TODAY ☐	TODAY ☐	TODAY ☐	☐ SUNDAY

IT'S NATIONAL CORNDOG DAY

THE TEXAS STATE FAIR SELLS 630,000 OF THEM PER SEASON.

GARY OLDMAN WAS BORN IN 1958

RONALDINHO WAS BORN IN 1980

9 AM

10 AM

11 AM

NOON

1 PM

2 PM

3 PM

4 PM

5 PM

6 PM

ON THIS DAY IN 2006: TWITTER WAS FOUNDED.

NOTES AND/OR DOODLES

22

YOUR WEEK AT A GLANCE

MONDAY	TUESDAY	WEDNESDAY	THURSDAY	FRIDAY	SATURDAY ☐
TODAY ☐	TODAY ☐	TODAY ☐	TODAY ☐	TODAY ☐	☐ SUNDAY

IT'S NATIONAL GOOF-OFF DAY

IF WE MADE AN OFF-BRAND 'GOO GONE,' WE'D CALL IT GOOF-OFF.

REESE WITHERSPOON WAS BORN IN 1976

CONSTANCE WU WAS BORN IN 1982

9 AM

10 AM

11 AM

NOON

1 PM

2 PM

3 PM

4 PM

5 PM

6 PM

ON THIS DAY IN 1894: THE 1ST STANLEY CUP CHAMPIONSHIP GAME WAS PLAYED.

NOTES AND/OR DOODLES

YEAR: **MARCH**

YOUR WEEK AT A GLANCE

MONDAY	TUESDAY	WEDNESDAY	THURSDAY	FRIDAY	SATURDAY ☐
☐ TODAY	☐ TODAY	☐ TODAY	☐ TODAY	☐ TODAY	☐ SUNDAY

23

NOTES AND/OR DOODLES

IT'S NATIONAL PUPPY DAY

THEY CAN SPEND 15 TO 20 HOURS A DAY SLEEPING.

(THE REST IS SPENT CHEWING ON THINGS)

CHAKA KHAN WAS BORN IN 1953

JOAN CRAWFORD WAS BORN IN 1904

9 AM

10 AM

11 AM

NOON

1 PM

2 PM

3 PM

4 PM

5 PM

6 PM

ON THIS DAY IN 1987: THE SOAP OPERA 'THE BOLD & THE BEAUTIFUL' PREMIERED.

YOUR WEEK AT A GLANCE

MONDAY	TUESDAY	WEDNESDAY	THURSDAY	FRIDAY	SATURDAY ☐
☐ TODAY	☐ TODAY	☐ TODAY	☐ TODAY	☐ TODAY	☐ SUNDAY

24

NOTES AND/OR DOODLES

IT'S NATIONAL COCKTAIL DAY

THE MOVIE 'COCKTAIL' WAS REWRITTEN 40 TIMES.

DOROTHY HEIGHT WAS BORN IN 1912

JIM PARSONS WAS BORN IN 1973

9 AM

10 AM

11 AM

NOON

1 PM

2 PM

3 PM

4 PM

5 PM

6 PM

ON THIS DAY IN 1958: ELVIS PRESLEY JOINED THE UNITED STATES ARMY.

LISTS, NOTES & MEMOIRS

SONGS RUINED BY ADVERTISEMENTS

OR A LIST OF LITERALLY ANYTHING ELSE

1
2
3
4
5
6
7
8
9
10
11
12

THINGS I MISUNDERSTOOD AS A CHILD

OR A MORE USEFUL (BUT STUPID) LIST

1
2
3
4
5
6
7
8
9
10
11
12

MY SELF-PORTRAIT, AS A PUPPET

(OR SOME SUPER BUSINESSY STUFF)

TWO-WORD PIECES OF ADVICE

OR SOME BORING TO-DO LIST

1
2
3
4
5
6
7
8
9
10
11
12

HATS THAT I COULD NEVER PULL OFF

OR A GROCERY LIST OR SOMETHING

1
2
3
4
5
6
7
8
9
10
11
12

YEAR: **MARCH**

YOUR WEEK AT A GLANCE

MONDAY	TUESDAY	WEDNESDAY	THURSDAY	FRIDAY	SATURDAY ☐
☐ TODAY	☐ TODAY	☐ TODAY	☐ TODAY	☐ TODAY	☐ SUNDAY

25

NOTES AND/OR DOODLES

IT'S INTERNATIONAL WAFFLE DAY

NIKE'S FIRST RUNNING SHOES WERE MADE IN A WAFFLE IRON.

ARETHA FRANKLIN WAS BORN IN 1942

ELTON JOHN WAS BORN IN 1947

9 AM
10 AM
11 AM
NOON
1 PM
2 PM
3 PM
4 PM
5 PM
6 PM

ON THIS DAY IN 2001: BJORK WORE A SWAN DRESS TO THE OSCARS.

YOUR WEEK AT A GLANCE

MONDAY	TUESDAY	WEDNESDAY	THURSDAY	FRIDAY	SATURDAY ☐
☐ TODAY	☐ TODAY	☐ TODAY	☐ TODAY	☐ TODAY	☐ SUNDAY

26

NOTES AND/OR DOODLES

IT'S NATIONAL MAKE UP YOUR OWN HOLIDAY DAY

AKA: 'GIVE MELANIE BRIDGES TONS OF COMPLIMENTS DAY.'

(MELANIE@BRASSMONKEYGOODS.COM)

DIANA ROSS WAS BORN IN 1944

KEIRA KNIGHTLY WAS BORN IN 1985

9 AM
10 AM
11 AM
NOON
1 PM
2 PM
3 PM
4 PM
5 PM
6 PM

ON THIS DAY IN 1953: DR. JONAS SALK ANNOUNCED THE POLIO VACCINE.

27

YOUR WEEK AT A GLANCE

MONDAY	TUESDAY	WEDNESDAY	THURSDAY	FRIDAY	SATURDAY ☐
TODAY ☐	TODAY ☐	TODAY ☐	TODAY ☐	TODAY ☐	☐ SUNDAY

IT'S INTERNATIONAL SCRIBBLE DAY

IF ONLY YOU HAD A PLACE TO DO THAT.

QUENTIN TARANTINO WAS BORN IN 1963

MARIAH CAREY WAS BORN IN 1970

9 AM

10 AM

11 AM

NOON

1 PM

2 PM

3 PM

4 PM

5 PM

6 PM

ON THIS DAY IN 1948: BILLIE HOLIDAY PERFORMED AT CARNEGIE HALL.

NOTES AND/OR SCRIBBLES

28

YOUR WEEK AT A GLANCE

MONDAY	TUESDAY	WEDNESDAY	THURSDAY	FRIDAY	SATURDAY ☐
TODAY ☐	TODAY ☐	TODAY ☐	TODAY ☐	TODAY ☐	☐ SUNDAY

IT'S NATIONAL SOMETHING ON A STICK DAY

EACH SUMMER, 50 PERCENT OF ALL MARSHMALLOWS SOLD ARE ROASTED.

LADY GAGA WAS BORN IN 1986

REBA MCENTIRE WAS BORN IN 1955

9 AM

10 AM

11 AM

NOON

1 PM

2 PM

3 PM

4 PM

5 PM

6 PM

ON THIS DAY IN 1995: JULIA ROBERTS AND LYLE LOVETTE SPLIT UP.

NOTES AND/OR DOODLES

YOUR WEEK AT A GLANCE

MONDAY	TUESDAY	WEDNESDAY	THURSDAY	FRIDAY	SATURDAY ☐
☐ TODAY	☐ TODAY	☐ TODAY	☐ TODAY	☐ TODAY	☐ SUNDAY

29

NOTES AND/OR DOODLES

IT'S VIETNAM VETERANS DAY

MORE THAN 3 MILLION PEOPLE WERE KILLED DURING THE WAR.

AMY SEDARIS WAS BORN IN 1961

SCOTT WILSON WAS BORN IN 1942

9 AM

10 AM

11 AM

NOON

1 PM

2 PM

3 PM

4 PM

5 PM

6 PM

ON THIS DAY IN 2007: RIHANNA RELEASED THE SONG 'UMBRELLA.'

YOUR WEEK AT A GLANCE

MONDAY	TUESDAY	WEDNESDAY	THURSDAY	FRIDAY	SATURDAY ☐
☐ TODAY	☐ TODAY	☐ TODAY	☐ TODAY	☐ TODAY	☐ SUNDAY

30

NOTES AND/OR DOODLES

IT'S NATIONAL VIRTUAL VACATION DAY

THE FUTURE IS HERE, AND IT'S STUPID.

VINCENT VAN GOGH WAS BORN IN 1953

CELINE DION WAS BORN IN 1968

9 AM

10 AM

11 AM

NOON

1 PM

2 PM

3 PM

4 PM

5 PM

6 PM

ON THIS DAY IN 1987: VAN GOGH'S 'SUNFLOWERS' PAINTING SOLD FOR $39.7M.

MARCH :YEAR

31

YOUR WEEK AT A GLANCE

MONDAY	TUESDAY	WEDNESDAY	THURSDAY	FRIDAY	SATURDAY
TODAY	TODAY	TODAY	TODAY	TODAY	SUNDAY

IT'S NATIONAL TATER DAY

CAN WE ALL JUST AGREE TO STOP SAYING TATER? UGH.

EWAN MCGREGOR WAS BORN IN 1971 RHEA PERLMAN WAS BORN IN 1948

9 AM

10 AM

11 AM

NOON

1 PM

2 PM

3 PM

4 PM

5 PM

6 PM

ON THIS DAY IN 1988: TONI MORRISON'S 'BELOVED' WON A PULITZER PRIZE.

NOTES AND/OR DOODLES

A DRAWING OF A SQUARE MEAL

(OR A ROUND DESSERT)

JOBS I WOULD ACCEPT, REGARDLESS OF SALARY

OR A GROCERY LIST OR SOMETHING

1
2
3
4
5
6
7
8
9
10
11
12
13
14
15
16
17
18

MARCH IN REVIEW

MY MARCH ACCOMPLISHMENTS

- [ ] BLAMED SOMETHING ON THE TIME CHANGE
- [ ] WORE GREEN ON ACCIDENT
- [ ] INCORRECT CLOCK NOW CORRECT AGAIN
- [ ] THOUGHT A PUB CRAWL WAS A GREAT IDEA
- [ ] SAW A PARADE FOR SOME DUMB REASON
- [ ] PUT AWAY THE WINTER CLOTHES
- [ ] SHOVELED SNOW THE NEXT DAY
- [ ] WASTED MONEY ON A NCAA BRACKET
- [ ] PICKED THE WINNERS BASED ON MASCOTS
- [ ] PRODUCED GREEN VOMIT
- [ ] PRODUCED NORMAL COLORED VOMIT
- [ ] TOOK BREATHING FOR GRANTED
- [ ] GOT SUPER HIGH (ON ANTIHISTAMINES)
- [ ] STARTED SPRING CLEANING
- [ ] REALIZED THAT IT CAN WAIT

REASONS THAT MARCH WAS GREAT

'IT ENDED' IS A VALID ANSWER

1
2
3
4
5
6
7
8
9
10
11
12

IF MARCH WAS PERSONIFIED, DRAW ITS TINDER PROFILE

REASONS THAT I'M GLAD MARCH IS OVER

USE ADDITIONAL PAPER IF NEEDED

1
2
3
4
5
6
7
8
9
10
11
12
13
14

CLICHÉS OVERHEARD THIS MONTH

- [ ] 'WHERE'S ME POT O' GOLD?'
- [ ] 'BRACKETOLOGY'
- [ ] 'ENJOY THE ONE WEEK OF SPRING'
- [ ] 'I'M NEVER DRINKING AGAIN'
- [ ] 'WOOOOOOOOOO! SPRING BREAK!'
- [ ] 'TOP O' THE MORNING TO YA'
- [ ] 'UH OH, SOMEBODY'S GETTING PINCHED'
- [ ] 'KISS ME, I'M IRISH'
- [ ] 'I THINK I'M ALLERGIC TO WORK'
- [ ] 'THERE'S NO PRICE TAG, MUST BE FREE'
- [ ] 'LET'S PLAY IT BY EAR'
- [ ] 'I'M ACTUALLY LIKE 1/8TH IRISH'
- [ ] 'RAIN? I'LL TAKE THE FREE CAR WASH'
- [ ] 'THAT'S WHY THEY PAY ME THE BIG BUCKS'
- [ ] 'LET ME SNEAK RIGHT PAST YA'
- [ ] 'I WOULDN'T REALLY CALL IT A *BREAK*'
- [ ] 'IS IT SUMMER YET?'

DERIVED FROM THE LATIN WORD APERIRE, WHICH MEANS TO OPEN.

WELCOME TO

× APRIL ×

OF WHATEVER YEAR
YOU SAY IT IS.

LET'S GO WITH:

□□□□

. . . .

. . . .

. . . .

NAMED AFTER THE GREEK GODDESS OF LOVE, APHRODITE.

APRIL AT A GLANCE :YEAR

YOU MADE IT
TO APRIL

×

CELEBRATE, IT'S:

NATIONAL WELDING MONTH

KEEP AMERICA BEAUTIFUL MONTH

NATIONAL SOFT PRETZEL MONTH

INTERNATIONAL GUITAR MONTH

NATIONAL HUMOR MONTH

×

OFFICIAL SYMBOLS:

BIRTHSTONE: DIAMOND

FLOWERS: DAISY & SWEET PEA

TREES: ROWAN, MAPLE, & WALNUT

ARIES (MAR 21 / APR 19)

TAURUS (APR 20 / MAY 20)

DATES TO KNOW*
LIKE, IMPORTANT ONES

×

APRIL FOOLS' DAY
APRIL 1ST

EASTER
FIRST SUNDAY AFTER THE FULL MOON (ON OR AFTER MARCH 21ST)

PALM SUNDAY
THE SUNDAY BEFORE EASTER (COULD FALL IN MARCH)

NATIONAL TARTAN DAY
APRIL 6TH

HANUMAN JAYANTI
(HINDUISM)
15TH DAY OF SHUKLA PAKSHA (WAXING MOON PHASE) DURING THE MONTH OF CHITRA (OFTEN APRIL)

THERAVADA NEW YEAR
(BUDDHISM)
FIRST FULL MOON OF APRIL

PASSOVER BEGINS
(JUDAISM)
15TH DAY OF THE HEBREW MONTH OF NISAN (MARCH OR APRIL)

DAY OF SILENCE
SECOND FRIDAY OF APRIL (WITH EXCEPTIONS)

THINGS TO ACCOMPLISH THIS MONTH
FOR EXAMPLE: FILL OUT A TO-DO LIST

1
2
3
4
5
6
7
8
9
10
11
12
13
14
15

THINGS THAT ARE NEVER GOING TO HAPPEN
THERE'S ALWAYS MAY (OR JUNE)

1
2
3
4
5
6
7
8
9
10
11
12
13
14
15

*A DISCLAIMER OF SORTS

HEY THERE. WE HERE AT BRASS MONKEY LIKE TO JOKE AROUND...BUT WE ALSO WANT TO TAKE A MINUTE TO RECOGNIZE JUST A FEW OF THE MANY HOLIDAYS & EVENTS THAT ARE IMPORTANT TO OUR FRIENDS AROUND THE GLOBE (AND AT HOME). YOU MAY BE DIFFERENT THAN US. WE MAY HAVE NEVER MET. BUT WE LOVE YOU ALL THE SAME.

SO IF YOU HAVEN'T HEARD OF A DAY, LOOK IT UP. LEARNING ABOUT & APPRECIATING CULTURES DIFFERENT THAN YOURS IS IMPORTANT...WAY MORE THAN POSTING A FEW 'STRAWBERRY JAM DAY' SELFIES.

YEAR: APRIL AT A GLANCE

IT'S APRIL
START PLANNING

×

APRIL FOOLS' DAY
APRIL 1ST
(A HOLIDAY WE LOVE TO HATE)

EASTER*
1ST SUNDAY AFTER THE FULL MOON (ON OR AFTER MAR. 21ST)

NOTE: THIS MAY FALL IN MARCH

×

BIRTHDAYS
TO REMEMBER

*PSST: SINCE THIS HOLIDAY MOVES AROUND EACH YEAR (AND WE DON'T KNOW WHEN IN THE FUTURE YOU'RE USING THIS), HELP US OUT AND ADD IT TO THE CALENDAR.

ALSO, ARE THERE JET PACKS YET? OUR FINGERS ARE CROSSED.

DAY OF WEEK S M T W T F S	DAY OF WEEK S M T W T F S	DAY OF WEEK S M T W T F S	DAY OF WEEK S M T W T F S	DAY OF WEEK S M T W T F S	DAY OF WEEK S M T W T F S	DAY OF WEEK S M T W T F S
APRIL FOOLS' DAY 01	02	03	04	05	06	07
08	09	10	11	12	13	14
15	16	17	18	19	20	21
22	23	24	25	26	27	28
29	30	NOTES:				

APRIL, AS EXPRESSED IN A DRAWING

LISTS, NOTES & MEMOIRS

MOVIES SO BAD THEY'RE GOOD

OR A LIST OF LITERALLY ANYTHING ELSE

1
2
3
4
5
6
7
8
9
10
11
12

MOVIES SO BAD THEY'RE STILL BAD

OR A MORE USEFUL (BUT STUPID) LIST

1
2
3
4
5
6
7
8
9
10
11
12

A DRAWING OF MY LIFE (AS A BROADWAY MUSICAL)

(OR SOME SUPER BUSINESSY STUFF)

THINGS TO DO OUT OF SPITE

OR SOME BORING TO-DO LIST

1
2
3
4
5
6
7
8
9
10
11
12

THE MOST DELICIOUS ANIMALS

OR A GROCERY LIST OR SOMETHING

1
2
3
4
5
6
7
8
9
10
11
12

YEAR: **APRIL**

YOUR WEEK AT A GLANCE

MONDAY	TUESDAY	WEDNESDAY	THURSDAY	FRIDAY	SATURDAY ☐ / ☐ SUNDAY
☐ TODAY	☐ TODAY	☐ TODAY	☐ TODAY	☐ TODAY	

01

NOTES AND/OR DOODLES

IT'S APRIL FOOLS' DAY

OH, AND IT'S ALSO NATIONAL TROMBONE PLAYERS DAY.

SUSAN BOYLE WAS BORN IN 1961

ASA BUTTERFIELD WAS BORN IN 1997

9 AM

10 AM

11 AM

NOON

1 PM

2 PM

3 PM

4 PM

5 PM

6 PM

ON THIS DAY IN 2007: A PYTHON GOT LOOSE INSIDE GOOGLE'S NYC OFFICE.

YOUR WEEK AT A GLANCE

MONDAY	TUESDAY	WEDNESDAY	THURSDAY	FRIDAY	SATURDAY ☐ / ☐ SUNDAY
☐ TODAY	☐ TODAY	☐ TODAY	☐ TODAY	☐ TODAY	

02

NOTES AND/OR DOODLES

IT'S NATIONAL BURRITO DAY

THE WORD BURRITO MEANS 'LITTLE DONKEY' IN SPANISH.

MARVIN GAYE WAS BORN IN 1939

LINDA HUNT WAS BORN IN 1945

9 AM

10 AM

11 AM

NOON

1 PM

2 PM

3 PM

4 PM

5 PM

6 PM

ON THIS DAY IN 1986: ED KOCH SIGNED THE NYC GAY RIGHTS BILL INTO EFFECT.

03

YOUR WEEK AT A GLANCE

MONDAY	TUESDAY	WEDNESDAY	THURSDAY	FRIDAY	SATURDAY ☐
TODAY ☐	TODAY ☐	TODAY ☐	TODAY ☐	TODAY ☐	☐ SUNDAY

IT'S TWEED DAY

YOU CAN CELEBRATE JEFF TWEEDY TOO.

EDDIE MURPHY WAS BORN IN 1961

JANE GOODALL WAS BORN IN 1934

9 AM

10 AM

11 AM

NOON

1 PM

2 PM

3 PM

4 PM

5 PM

6 PM

ON THIS DAY IN 1953: THE FIRST CELL PHONE CALL WAS MADE.

NOTES AND/OR DOODLES

04

YOUR WEEK AT A GLANCE

MONDAY	TUESDAY	WEDNESDAY	THURSDAY	FRIDAY	SATURDAY ☐
TODAY ☐	TODAY ☐	TODAY ☐	TODAY ☐	TODAY ☐	☐ SUNDAY

IT'S INTERNATIONAL CARROT DAY

CARROTS WERE FIRST GROWN AS MEDICINE, NOT FOOD.

MUDDY WATERS WAS BORN IN 1913

MAYA ANGELOU WAS BORN IN 1928

9 AM

10 AM

11 AM

NOON

1 PM

2 PM

3 PM

4 PM

5 PM

6 PM

ON THIS DAY IN 1968: MARTIN LUTHER KING JR. WAS ASSASSINATED.

NOTES AND/OR DOODLES

YEAR: **APRIL**

YOUR WEEK AT A GLANCE

MONDAY	TUESDAY	WEDNESDAY	THURSDAY	FRIDAY	SATURDAY ☐
☐ TODAY	☐ TODAY	☐ TODAY	☐ TODAY	☐ TODAY	☐ SUNDAY

05

NOTES AND/OR DOODLES

IT'S BELL BOTTOMS DAY

SAILORS IN THE U.S. NAVY WORE THEM AS EARLY AS THE 19TH CENTURY.

PHARRELL WILLIAMS WAS BORN IN 1973

LILY JAMES WAS BORN IN 1989

9 AM

10 AM

11 AM

NOON

1 PM

2 PM

3 PM

4 PM

5 PM

6 PM

ON THIS DAY IN 1994: KURT COBAIN COMMITTED SUICIDE.

YOUR WEEK AT A GLANCE

MONDAY	TUESDAY	WEDNESDAY	THURSDAY	FRIDAY	SATURDAY ☐
☐ TODAY	☐ TODAY	☐ TODAY	☐ TODAY	☐ TODAY	☐ SUNDAY

06

NOTES AND/OR DOODLES

IT'S NATIONAL SIAMESE CAT DAY

JAMES DEAN WAS GIVEN ONE BY ELIZABETH TAYLOR.

PAUL RUDD WAS BORN IN 1969

ZACH BRAFF WAS BORN IN 1975

9 AM

10 AM

11 AM

NOON

1 PM

2 PM

3 PM

4 PM

5 PM

6 PM

ON THIS DAY IN 1957: TROLLEY CARS STOPPED SERVICE IN NYC.

YOUR WEEK AT A GLANCE

07

MONDAY	TUESDAY	WEDNESDAY	THURSDAY	FRIDAY	SATURDAY ☐
TODAY ☐	TODAY ☐	TODAY ☐	TODAY ☐	TODAY ☐	☐ SUNDAY

IT'S NATIONAL BEER DAY

HUMANS CONSUME OVER 50 BILLION GALLONS OF BEER EVERY YEAR.

BILLIE HOLIDAY WAS BORN IN 1915

RUSSELL CROWE WAS BORN IN 1964

9 AM

10 AM

11 AM

NOON

1 PM

2 PM

3 PM

4 PM

5 PM

6 PM

ON THIS DAY IN 1933: BEER COULD ONCE AGAIN BE PURCHASED IN THE U.S.

NOTES AND/OR DOODLES

YOUR WEEK AT A GLANCE

08

MONDAY	TUESDAY	WEDNESDAY	THURSDAY	FRIDAY	SATURDAY ☐
TODAY ☐	TODAY ☐	TODAY ☐	TODAY ☐	TODAY ☐	☐ SUNDAY

IT'S DRAW A PICTURE OF A BIRD DAY

SCIENTISTS BELIEVE THAT BIRDS EVOLVED FROM THEROPOD DINOSAURS.

BETTY FORD WAS BORN IN 1918

ROBIN WRIGHT WAS BORN IN 1966

9 AM

10 AM

11 AM

NOON

1 PM

2 PM

3 PM

4 PM

5 PM

6 PM

ON THIS DAY IN 1879: MILK WAS SOLD IN GLASS BOTTLES FOR THE FIRST TIME.

NOTES AND/OR DOODLES

LISTS, NOTES & MEMOIRS

POTENTIAL WAYS TO AVOID JURY DUTY

OR SOME BORING TO-DO LIST

1
2
3
4
5
6
7
8
9
10
11
12

HOLIDAYS THAT SHOULD EXIST

OR A GROCERY LIST OR SOMETHING

1
2
3
4
5
6
7
8
9
10
11
12

A DRAWING OF A BETTER MOUSE TRAP

(OR SOME SUPER BUSINESSY STUFF)

WORDS THAT RHYME WITH MY NAME

OR A MORE USEFUL (BUT STUPID) LIST

1
2
3
4
5
6
7
8
9
10
11
12

REJECTED THEME RESTAURANT IDEAS

OR A LIST OF LITERALLY ANYTHING ELSE

1
2
3
4
5
6
7
8
9
10
11
12

09

YOUR WEEK AT A GLANCE

MONDAY	TUESDAY	WEDNESDAY	THURSDAY	FRIDAY	SATURDAY ☐
TODAY ☐	TODAY ☐	TODAY ☐	TODAY ☐	TODAY ☐	☐ SUNDAY

IT'S NATIONAL GIN AND TONIC DAY

SOME SAY IT WAS A MALARIA TREATMENT. WE SAY IT'S DELICIOUS.

CYNTHIA NIXON WAS BORN IN 1966 LIL NAS X WAS BORN IN 1999

9 AM

10 AM

11 AM

NOON

1 PM

2 PM

3 PM

4 PM

5 PM

6 PM

ON THIS DAY IN 2009: THE SHOW 'PARKS AND RECREATION' DEBUTED ON NBC.

NOTES AND/OR DOODLES

10

YOUR WEEK AT A GLANCE

MONDAY	TUESDAY	WEDNESDAY	THURSDAY	FRIDAY	SATURDAY ☐
TODAY ☐	TODAY ☐	TODAY ☐	TODAY ☐	TODAY ☐	☐ SUNDAY

IT'S NATIONAL HUG YOUR DOG DAY

YOU SHOULD DO IT EVERY DAY THOUGH.

MANDY MOORE WAS BORN IN 1984 STEVEN SEAGAL WAS BORN IN 1952

9 AM

10 AM

11 AM

NOON

1 PM

2 PM

3 PM

4 PM

5 PM

6 PM

ON THIS DAY IN 1970: PAUL MCCARTNEY ANNOUNCED THE BEATLES BROKE UP.

NOTES AND/OR DOODLES

YEAR: APRIL

YOUR WEEK AT A GLANCE

MONDAY	TUESDAY	WEDNESDAY	THURSDAY	FRIDAY	SATURDAY ☐
☐ TODAY	☐ TODAY	☐ TODAY	☐ TODAY	☐ TODAY	☐ SUNDAY

11

NOTES AND/OR DOODLES

IT'S BARBERSHOP QUARTET DAY

IT SHOULD BE HANDLEBAR MUSTACHE DAY TOO, JUST BY PROXY.

JOSS STONE WAS BORN IN 1987

JENNIFER ESPOSITO WAS BORN IN 1973

9 AM

10 AM

11 AM

NOON

1 PM

2 PM

3 PM

4 PM

5 PM

6 PM

ON THIS DAY IN 1921: IOWA BECAME THE 1ST STATE TO TAX CIGARETTES.

YOUR WEEK AT A GLANCE

MONDAY	TUESDAY	WEDNESDAY	THURSDAY	FRIDAY	SATURDAY ☐
☐ TODAY	☐ TODAY	☐ TODAY	☐ TODAY	☐ TODAY	☐ SUNDAY

12

NOTES AND/OR DOODLES

IT'S NATIONAL GRILLED CHEESE SANDWICH DAY

THE MOST EXPENSIVE ONE IN THE WORLD SOLD FOR $214.

DAVID LETTERMAN WAS BORN IN 1947

SAOIRSE RONAN WAS BORN IN 1994

9 AM

10 AM

11 AM

NOON

1 PM

2 PM

3 PM

4 PM

5 PM

6 PM

ON THIS DAY IN 1995: DREW BARRYMORE FLASHED DAVID LETTERMAN ON AIR.

LISTS, NOTES & MEMOIRS

WORDS THAT I CAN'T SPELL

OR A LIST OF LITERALLY ANYTHING ELSE

1
2
3
4
5
6
7
8
9
10
11
12

MOVIE TITLES THAT SUMMARIZE MY LIFE

OR A MORE USEFUL (BUT STUPID) LIST

1
2
3
4
5
6
7
8
9
10
11
12

AN ELABORATE PLAN FOR A HEIST

(OR SOME SUPER BUSINESSY STUFF)

THINGS I NEVER WANT TO SEE AGAIN

OR SOME BORING TO-DO LIST

1
2
3
4
5
6
7
8
9
10
11
12

FAVORITE NAMES TO SAY IN VAIN

OR A GROCERY LIST OR SOMETHING

1
2
3
4
5
6
7
8
9
10
11
12

YOUR WEEK AT A GLANCE

MONDAY	TUESDAY	WEDNESDAY	THURSDAY	FRIDAY	SATURDAY ☐
☐ TODAY	☐ TODAY	☐ TODAY	☐ TODAY	☐ TODAY	☐ SUNDAY

13

NOTES AND/OR DOODLES

IT'S SCRABBLE DAY

THE GAME WAS INVENTED IN 1931 BY AN UNEMPLOYED ARCHITECT.

(THAT STILL DOESN'T EXCUSE THOSE BULLSHIT TWO LETTER WORDS THOUGH)

RON PERLMAN WAS BORN IN 1950

RICKY SCHRODER WAS BORN IN 1970

9 AM
10 AM
11 AM
NOON
1 PM
2 PM
3 PM
4 PM
5 PM
6 PM

ON THIS DAY IN 1979: THE LONGEST DOUBLES PING PONG GAME ENDED (101 HRS).

YOUR WEEK AT A GLANCE

MONDAY	TUESDAY	WEDNESDAY	THURSDAY	FRIDAY	SATURDAY ☐
☐ TODAY	☐ TODAY	☐ TODAY	☐ TODAY	☐ TODAY	☐ SUNDAY

14

NOTES AND/OR DOODLES

IT'S NATIONAL PECAN DAY

PECANS AREN'T TECHNICALLY NUTS. THEY ARE A TYPE OF 'DRUPE.'

ADRIEN BRODY WAS BORN IN 1973

ABIGAIL BRESLIN WAS BORN IN 1996

9 AM
10 AM
11 AM
NOON
1 PM
2 PM
3 PM
4 PM
5 PM
6 PM

ON THIS DAY IN 1912: THE TITANIC STRUCK AN ICEBERG AT 11:40 PM.

15

YOUR WEEK AT A GLANCE

MONDAY	TUESDAY	WEDNESDAY	THURSDAY	FRIDAY	SATURDAY ☐
TODAY ☐	TODAY ☐	TODAY ☐	TODAY ☐	TODAY ☐	☐ SUNDAY

IT'S NATIONAL THAT SUCKS DAY

SO WHEN YOUR TACO SHELL BREAKS DOWN THE MIDDLE, CELEBRATE.

EMMA THOMPSON WAS BORN IN 1959

ANDY DALY WAS BORN IN 1971

9 AM

10 AM

11 AM

NOON

1 PM

2 PM

3 PM

4 PM

5 PM

6 PM

ON THIS DAY IN 1955: MCDONALD'S OPENED ITS 1ST FRANCHISED RESTAURANT.

NOTES AND/OR DOODLES

16

YOUR WEEK AT A GLANCE

MONDAY	TUESDAY	WEDNESDAY	THURSDAY	FRIDAY	SATURDAY ☐
TODAY ☐	TODAY ☐	TODAY ☐	TODAY ☐	TODAY ☐	☐ SUNDAY

IT'S NATIONAL BEAN COUNTERS' DAY

SO HONOR YOUR ACCOUNTANT FRIENDS...BY DISPARAGING THEM?

CHARLIE CHAPLIN WAS BORN IN 1889

SELENA WAS BORN IN 1971

9 AM

10 AM

11 AM

NOON

1 PM

2 PM

3 PM

4 PM

5 PM

6 PM

ON THIS DAY IN 2018: KENDRICK LAMAR RECEIVED A PULITZER FOR 'DAMN.'

NOTES AND/OR DOODLES

YEAR: **APRIL**

YOUR WEEK AT A GLANCE

MONDAY	TUESDAY	WEDNESDAY	THURSDAY	FRIDAY	SATURDAY ☐
☐ TODAY	☐ TODAY	☐ TODAY	☐ TODAY	☐ TODAY	☐ SUNDAY

17

NOTES AND/OR DOODLES

IT'S NATIONAL KICKBALL DAY

WHEN CREATED IN 1917, IT WAS KNOWN AS 'KICK BASEBALL.'

JENNIFER GARNER WAS BORN IN 1972

ROONEY MARA WAS BORN IN 1985

9 AM

10 AM

11 AM

NOON

1 PM

2 PM

3 PM

4 PM

5 PM

6 PM

ON THIS DAY IN 2011: 'GAME OF THRONES' PREMIERED ON HBO.

YOUR WEEK AT A GLANCE

MONDAY	TUESDAY	WEDNESDAY	THURSDAY	FRIDAY	SATURDAY ☐
☐ TODAY	☐ TODAY	☐ TODAY	☐ TODAY	☐ TODAY	☐ SUNDAY

18

NOTES AND/OR DOODLES

IT'S PIÑATA DAY

THEY WERE ORIGINALLY BUILT AROUND A CLAY POT CENTER.

(I MEAN, WHAT'S MORE FUN THAN SHRAPNEL?)

AMERICA FERRERA WAS BORN IN 1984

RICK MORANIS WAS BORN IN 1953

9 AM

10 AM

11 AM

NOON

1 PM

2 PM

3 PM

4 PM

5 PM

6 PM

ON THIS DAY IN 1999: WAYNE GRETZKY PLAYED HIS LAST GAME IN THE NHL.

19

YOUR WEEK AT A GLANCE

MONDAY	TUESDAY	WEDNESDAY	THURSDAY	FRIDAY	SATURDAY ☐
TODAY ☐	TODAY ☐	TODAY ☐	TODAY ☐	TODAY ☐	☐ SUNDAY

IT'S GO FLY A KITE DAY

THE CHINESE NAME FOR A KITE IS 'FEN ZHENG'—MEANING 'WIND HARP.'

JAMES FRANCO WAS BORN IN 1978

KATE HUDSON WAS BORN IN 1979

9 AM

10 AM

11 AM

NOON

1 PM

2 PM

3 PM

4 PM

5 PM

6 PM

ON THIS DAY IN 1897: THE FIRST BOSTON MARATHON WAS HELD.

NOTES AND/OR DOODLES

20

YOUR WEEK AT A GLANCE

MONDAY	TUESDAY	WEDNESDAY	THURSDAY	FRIDAY	SATURDAY ☐
TODAY ☐	TODAY ☐	TODAY ☐	TODAY ☐	TODAY ☐	☐ SUNDAY

IT'S NATIONAL LOOK-ALIKE DAY

THE TWIN STRANGERS PROJECT CAN HELP LOCATE YOUR DOPPELGANGER.

GEORGE TAKEI WAS BORN IN 1937

HARRIS WITTELS WAS BORN IN 1984

9 AM

10 AM

11 AM

NOON

1 PM

2 PM

3 PM

4 PM

5 PM

6 PM

ON THIS DAY IN 2008: DANICA PATRICK WON AN INDY CAR RACE (1ST WOMAN).

NOTES AND/OR DOODLES

LISTS, NOTES & MEMOIRS

WORST WORDS TO GET TATTOOED

OR SOME BORING TO-DO LIST

1
2
3
4
5
6
7
8
9
10
11
12

GREETINGS SUPERIOR TO HELLO

OR A GROCERY LIST OR SOMETHING

1
2
3
4
5
6
7
8
9
10
11
12

A DRAWING OF EVERYTHING WRONG WITH THE WORLD

(OR SOME SUPER BUSINESSY STUFF)

WAYS TO AVOID EYE CONTACT

OR A MORE USEFUL (BUT STUPID) LIST

1
2
3
4
5
6
7
8
9
10
11
12

THINGS THAT I'VE STOLEN

OR A LIST OF LITERALLY ANYTHING ELSE

1
2
3
4
5
6
7
8
9
10
11
12

21

YOUR WEEK AT A GLANCE

MONDAY	TUESDAY	WEDNESDAY	THURSDAY	FRIDAY	SATURDAY ☐
TODAY ☐	TODAY ☐	TODAY ☐	TODAY ☐	TODAY ☐	☐ SUNDAY

IT'S KEEP OFF THE GRASS DAY

OVER 1,400 SPECIES OF GRASSES EXIST IN THE UNITED STATES ALONE.

QUEEN ELIZABETH II WAS BORN IN 1926

ROB RIGGLE WAS BORN IN 1970

9 AM

10 AM

11 AM

NOON

1 PM

2 PM

3 PM

4 PM

5 PM

6 PM

ON THIS DAY IN 1984: 'AGAINST ALL ODDS' BY PHIL COLLINS HIT NUMBER ONE.

NOTES AND/OR DOODLES

22

YOUR WEEK AT A GLANCE

MONDAY	TUESDAY	WEDNESDAY	THURSDAY	FRIDAY	SATURDAY ☐
TODAY ☐	TODAY ☐	TODAY ☐	TODAY ☐	TODAY ☐	☐ SUNDAY

IT'S EARTH DAY

THIS SHOULDN'T BE TRIVIA, BUT HERE WE ARE: IT'S ROUND.

JACK NICHOLSON WAS BORN IN 1937

SHERRI SHEPHERD WAS BORN IN 1967

9 AM

10 AM

11 AM

NOON

1 PM

2 PM

3 PM

4 PM

5 PM

6 PM

ON THIS DAY IN 1970: THE FIRST EARTH DAY WAS OBSERVED.

NOTES AND/OR DOODLES

YEAR: **APRIL**

YOUR WEEK AT A GLANCE

MONDAY	TUESDAY	WEDNESDAY	THURSDAY	FRIDAY	SATURDAY ☐
☐ TODAY	☐ TODAY	☐ TODAY	☐ TODAY	☐ TODAY	☐ SUNDAY

23

NOTES AND/OR DOODLES

IT'S NATIONAL PICNIC DAY

THE FIRST PICNIC TABLE WAS CREATED IN THE LATE 1800s.

SHIRLEY TEMPLE WAS BORN IN 1928

KAL PENN WAS BORN IN 1977

9 AM

10 AM

11 AM

NOON

1 PM

2 PM

3 PM

4 PM

5 PM

6 PM

ON THIS DAY IN 1985: COCA-COLA CHANGED FORMULAS & RELEASED 'NEW COKE.'

YOUR WEEK AT A GLANCE

MONDAY	TUESDAY	WEDNESDAY	THURSDAY	FRIDAY	SATURDAY ☐
☐ TODAY	☐ TODAY	☐ TODAY	☐ TODAY	☐ TODAY	☐ SUNDAY

24

NOTES AND/OR DOODLES

IT'S NEW KIDS ON THE BLOCK DAY

THE BAND'S ORIGINAL NAME WAS NYNUK.

BARBRA STREISAND WAS BORN IN 1942

KELLY CLARKSON WAS BORN IN 1982

9 AM

10 AM

11 AM

NOON

1 PM

2 PM

3 PM

4 PM

5 PM

6 PM

ON THIS DAY IN 1800: THE LIBRARY OF CONGRESS WAS ESTABLISHED.

LISTS, NOTES & MEMOIRS

PIZZA TOPPINGS FROM HELL

OR A LIST OF LITERALLY ANYTHING ELSE

1
2
3
4
5
6
7
8
9
10
11
12

MORE ACCURATE NAMES FOR COCKTAILS

OR A MORE USEFUL (BUT STUPID) LIST

1
2
3
4
5
6
7
8
9
10
11
12

A DRAWING OF A BIRD THAT'S UP TO NO GOOD

(OR SOME SUPER BUSINESSY STUFF)

BEST WAYS TO START AN OBITUARY

OR SOME BORING TO-DO LIST

1
2
3
4
5
6
7
8
9
10
11
12

WORST WAYS TO END AN OBITUARY

OR A GROCERY LIST OR SOMETHING

1
2
3
4
5
6
7
8
9
10
11
12

YEAR: **APRIL**

YOUR WEEK AT A GLANCE

MONDAY	TUESDAY	WEDNESDAY	THURSDAY	FRIDAY	SATURDAY ☐
☐ TODAY	☐ TODAY	☐ TODAY	☐ TODAY	☐ TODAY	☐ SUNDAY

25

NOTES AND/OR DOODLES

IT'S WORLD PENGUIN DAY

EXPLORERS ORIGINALLY CALLED THEM 'STRANGE GEESE.' ACCURATE.

AL PACINO WAS BORN IN 1940

ELLA FITZGERALD WAS BORN IN 1917

9 AM

10 AM

11 AM

NOON

1 PM

2 PM

3 PM

4 PM

5 PM

6 PM

ON THIS DAY IN 1992: THE FINAL EPISODE OF 'GROWING PAINS' AIRED.

YOUR WEEK AT A GLANCE

MONDAY	TUESDAY	WEDNESDAY	THURSDAY	FRIDAY	SATURDAY ☐
☐ TODAY	☐ TODAY	☐ TODAY	☐ TODAY	☐ TODAY	☐ SUNDAY

26

NOTES AND/OR DOODLES

IT'S HUG A FRIEND DAY

ON AVERAGE, PEOPLE SPEND ONE HOUR A MONTH HUGGING.

CHANNING TATUM WAS BORN IN 1980

KEVIN JAMES WAS BORN IN 1965

9 AM

10 AM

11 AM

NOON

1 PM

2 PM

3 PM

4 PM

5 PM

6 PM

ON THIS DAY IN 1977: STUDIO 54 OPENED IN NEW YORK CITY.

27

YOUR WEEK AT A GLANCE

MONDAY	TUESDAY	WEDNESDAY	THURSDAY	FRIDAY	SATURDAY ☐
TODAY ☐	TODAY ☐	TODAY ☐	TODAY ☐	TODAY ☐	☐ SUNDAY

IT'S NATIONAL PRIME RIB DAY

ALSO KNOWN AS A 'STANDING RIB ROAST,' AS IT'S ROASTED UPRIGHT.

CASEY KASEM WAS BORN IN 1932

STAS MIKHAYLOV WAS BORN IN 1956

9 AM

10 AM

11 AM

NOON

1 PM

2 PM

3 PM

4 PM

5 PM

6 PM

ON THIS DAY IN 4977 BCE: THE UNIVERSE WAS CREATED (SAID JOHANNES KEPLER).

NOTES AND/OR DOODLES

28

YOUR WEEK AT A GLANCE

MONDAY	TUESDAY	WEDNESDAY	THURSDAY	FRIDAY	SATURDAY ☐
TODAY ☐	TODAY ☐	TODAY ☐	TODAY ☐	TODAY ☐	☐ SUNDAY

IT'S PAY IT FORWARD DAY

DO SOMETHING NICE FOR YOURSELF TOO...DON'T WATCH THE MOVIE.

PENÉLOPE CRUZ WAS BORN IN 1940

HARPER LEE WAS BORN IN 1926

9 AM

10 AM

11 AM

NOON

1 PM

2 PM

3 PM

4 PM

5 PM

6 PM

ON THIS DAY IN 2001: MILLIONAIRE DENNIS TITO BECAME THE 1ST SPACE TOURIST.

NOTES AND/OR DOODLES

YEAR: **APRIL**

YOUR WEEK AT A GLANCE

MONDAY	TUESDAY	WEDNESDAY	THURSDAY	FRIDAY	SATURDAY ☐
☐ TODAY	☐ TODAY	☐ TODAY	☐ TODAY	☐ TODAY	☐ SUNDAY

29

NOTES AND/OR DOODLES

IT'S ZIPPER DAY

90 PERCENT OF ALL ZIPPERS ARE PRODUCED BY ONE COMPANY—YKK.

WILLIE NELSON WAS BORN IN 1933

MASTER P WAS BORN IN 1970

9 AM

10 AM

11 AM

NOON

1 PM

2 PM

3 PM

4 PM

5 PM

6 PM

ON THIS DAY IN 2011: PRINCE WILLIAM MARRIED KATE MIDDLETON.

YOUR WEEK AT A GLANCE

MONDAY	TUESDAY	WEDNESDAY	THURSDAY	FRIDAY	SATURDAY ☐
☐ TODAY	☐ TODAY	☐ TODAY	☐ TODAY	☐ TODAY	☐ SUNDAY

30

NOTES AND/OR DOODLES

IT'S ADOPT A SHELTER PET DAY

OVER 3 MILLION SHELTER ANIMALS ARE ADOPTED EACH YEAR.

ISIAH THOMAS WAS BORN IN 1961

GAL GADOT WAS BORN IN 1985

9 AM

10 AM

11 AM

NOON

1 PM

2 PM

3 PM

4 PM

5 PM

6 PM

ON THIS DAY IN 1997: BIG BEN STOPPED WORKING AT 12:11 PM (FOR 54 MINUTES).

APRIL IN REVIEW

REASONS THAT APRIL WAS GREAT

'IT ENDED' IS A VALID ANSWER

1
2
3
4
5
6
7
8
9
10
11
12

MY APRIL ACCOMPLISHMENTS

- THOUGHT OF THE PERFECT PRANK ☐
- DETERMINED IT WAS TOO MUCH WORK ☐
- WENT TO CHURCH FOR THE YEAR ☐
- FOUND AN EASTER EGG FROM LAST YEAR ☐
- ATE THE EARS OFF A BUNNY ☐
- ATE THE EARS OFF A CHOCOLATE BUNNY ☐
- GOT 13 ITEMS THROUGH AN EXPRESS LANE ☐
- BOUGHT A NEW UMBRELLA ☐
- IMMEDIATELY LOST SAID UMBRELLA ☐
- DECORATED EASTER EGGS ☐
- PERMANENTLY STAINED HANDS PURPLE ☐
- DRANK WINE WITH EASTER DINNER ☐
- DRANK WINE WITH EVERY OTHER DINNER ☐
- TOOK APRIL 1ST OFF FROM WORK ☐
- PUT A PEEP IN THE MICROWAVE ☐

IF APRIL WAS PERSONIFIED, DRAW ITS DRIVERS LICENSE

CLICHES OVERHEARD THIS MONTH

- ☐ 'WE REALLY NEEDED THE RAIN'
- ☐ 'IS IT TOO COLD TO SIT OUTSIDE?'
- ☐ 'WE GOT YOU SO GOOD!'
- ☐ 'SERIOUSLY, WHEN'S OUR NEXT DAY OFF'
- ☐ 'I KEEP THINKING IT'S FRIDAY ALREADY'
- ☐ 'I DIDN'T KNOW BUNNIES LAID EGGS'
- ☐ 'I GUESS EVERYBODY HAD THE SAME IDEA'
- ☐ 'KNOCK KNOCK'
- ☐ 'HAVE YOU SIGNED THE CARD YET?'
- ☐ 'THERE'S A BUG GOING AROUND'
- ☐ 'THERE'S MY CARDIO FOR THE DAY'
- ☐ 'FEEL HOW COLD MY HANDS ARE'
- ☐ 'THE EASTER BUNNY BROUGHT IT'
- ☐ 'I CAN'T BELIEVE IT'S ALREADY APRIL'
- ☐ 'SOMEBODY SURE WAS HUNGRY'
- ☐ 'I CAN'T TODAY ANYMORE'
- ☐ 'TRY THESE CHIPS, THEY'RE DANGEROUS'

REASONS THAT I'M GLAD APRIL IS OVER

USE ADDITIONAL PAPER IF NEEDED

1
2
3
4
5
6
7
8
9
10
11
12
13
14

APRIL IN REVIEW

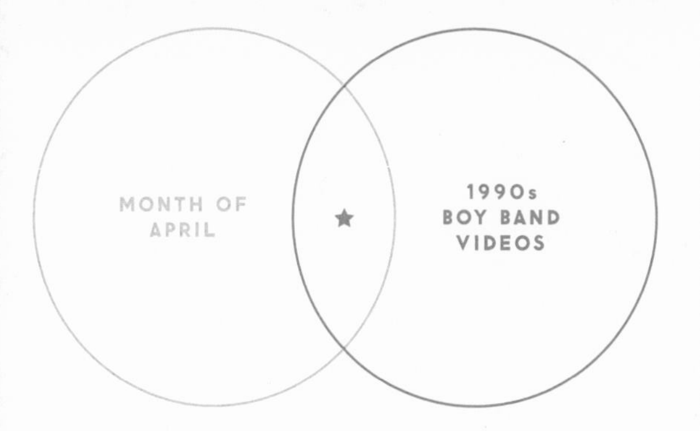

AN APRIL VENN DIAGRAM

WHAT DID THEY HAVE IN COMMON?

IT WAS ALWAYS RAINING 1
2
3
4
5
6
7
8

AWKWARD THINGS THAT HAPPENED

(AND WILL KEEP ME UP AT NIGHT)

1
2
3
4
5
6
7
8
9
10
11
12
13
14
15
16
17

A DRAWING OF AN ADULT EASTER BASKET
(JK, IT'S JUST BOOZE)

ENJOYMENT OVER TIME

CHOOSE A COLOR KEY

LINE	ITEM
——	PRANKS ON THE INTERNET
– –	PRANKS AT WORK
	HARD BOILED EGGS
	RAIN
	THE IDEA OF FLOWERS
	EATING ON PATIOS
	POLLEN ALLERGIES
	MONTHS BESIDES APRIL
	CHOCOLATE BUNNIES
	HIDING THINGS IN GRASS

APRIL ENJOYMENT INDEX

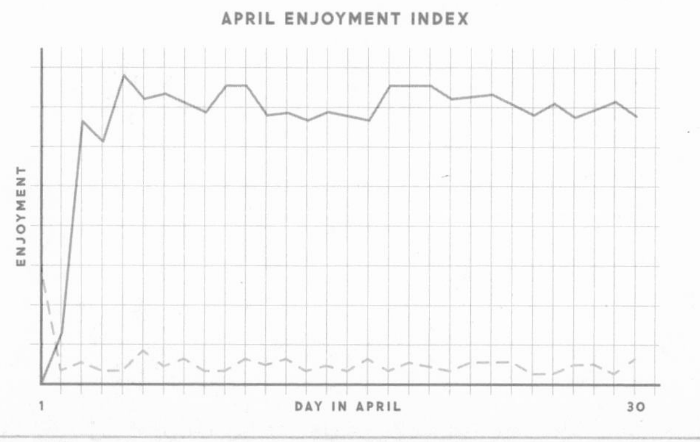

IN THE SOUTHERN HEMISPHERE, IT'S THE CLIMATE EQUIVALENT OF NOVEMBER.

WELCOME TO

OF WHATEVER YEAR
YOU SAY IT IS.

LET'S GO WITH:

☐☐☐☐

. . . .

. . . .

. . . .

NAMED AFTER THE GREEK GODDESS MAIA.

MAY AT A GLANCE :YEAR

YOU MADE IT
TO MAY

✖

CELEBRATE, IT'S:

NATIONAL BARBECUE MONTH

CORRECT YOUR POSTURE MONTH

NATIONAL CHAMBER MUSIC MONTH

AMERICAN CHEESE MONTH

NATIONAL WATER SAFETY MONTH

✖

OFFICIAL SYMBOLS:

BIRTHSTONE: EMERALD

FLOWER: HAWTHORN

TREES: CHESTNUT & ASH

TAURUS (APR 20 / MAY 20)

GEMINI (MAY 21 / JUN 20)

DATES TO KNOW*
LIKE, IMPORTANT ONES

✖

MAY DAY
MAY 1ST

CINCO DE MAYO
MAY 5TH

SHAVUOT
(JUDAISM)
6TH DAY OF THE HEBREW MONTH OF SIVAN (MAY OR JUNE)

RAMADAN
(ISLAMIC)
MOVES 11 DAYS EARLIER (IN RELATION TO OUR CALENDAR) EVERY YEAR. WE'D LOOK IT UP.

NATIONAL NURSES DAY
MAY 12TH

MEMORIAL DAY
THE LAST MONDAY IN MAY

AMNESTY INTERNATIONAL DAY
MAY 28TH

PENTECOST
(CHRISTIANITY)
7TH SUNDAY AFTER EASTER (USUALLY IN MAY)

THINGS TO ACCOMPLISH THIS MONTH
FOR EXAMPLE: FILL OUT A TO-DO LIST

1
2
3
4
5
6
7
8
9
10
11
12
13
14
15

THINGS THAT ARE NEVER GOING TO HAPPEN
THERE'S ALWAYS JUNE (OR JULY)

1
2
3
4
5
6
7
8
9
10
11
12
13
14
15

***A DISCLAIMER OF SORTS**

HEY THERE. WE HERE AT BRASS MONKEY LIKE TO JOKE AROUND...BUT WE ALSO WANT TO TAKE A MINUTE TO RECOGNIZE JUST A FEW OF THE MANY HOLIDAYS & EVENTS THAT ARE IMPORTANT TO OUR FRIENDS AROUND THE GLOBE (AND AT HOME). YOU MAY BE DIFFERENT THAN US. WE MAY HAVE NEVER MET, BUT WE LOVE YOU ALL THE SAME.

SO IF YOU HAVEN'T HEARD OF A DAY, LOOK IT UP. LEARNING ABOUT & APPRECIATING CULTURES DIFFERENT THAN YOURS IS IMPORTANT...WAY MORE THAN POSTING A FEW 'STRAWBERRY JAM DAY' SELFIES.

IT'S MAY
START PLANNING

×

MEMORIAL DAY*
OBSERVED ON THE LAST MONDAY IN MAY

CINCO DE MAYO
MAY 5TH
(OKAY, IT'S NOT REALLY A U.S. HOLIDAY, BUT IT MIGHT AS WELL BE)

×

BIRTHDAYS
TO REMEMBER

*PSST: SINCE THIS HOLIDAY MOVES AROUND EACH YEAR (AND WE DON'T KNOW WHEN IN THE FUTURE YOU'RE USING THIS), HELP US OUT AND ADD IT TO THE CALENDAR.

ALSO, ARE THERE JET PACKS YET? OUR FINGERS ARE CROSSED.

MAY AT A GLANCE

YEAR:

S M T W T F S	S M T W T F S	S M T W T F S	S M T W T F S	S M T W T F S	S M T W T F S	S M T W T F S
01	02	03	04	CINCO DE MAYO 05	06	07
08	09	10	11	12	13	14
15	16	17	18	19	20	21
22	23	24	25	26	27	28
29	30	31				

NOTES:

MAY, AS EXPRESSED IN A DRAWING

MAY PREVIEW

A MAY VENN DIAGRAM

WHAT DO THEY HAVE IN COMMON?

1 MOMS CAN'T GET ENOUGH
2
3
4
5
6
7
8

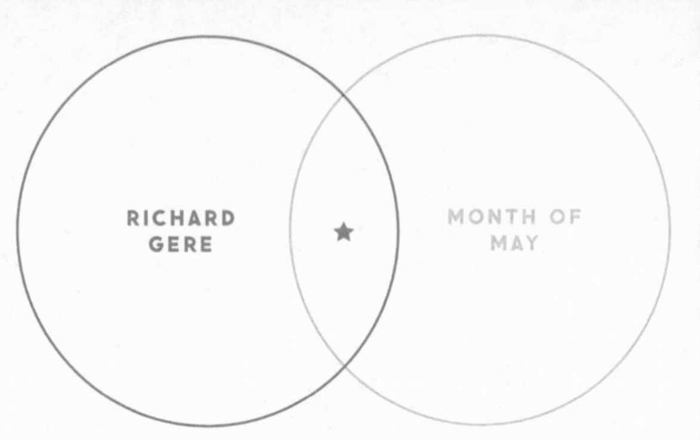

A DRAWING OF SEIS DE MAYO

SUPPLIES NEEDED FOR THE MONTH

ALCOHOL, AND OTHER NECESSITIES

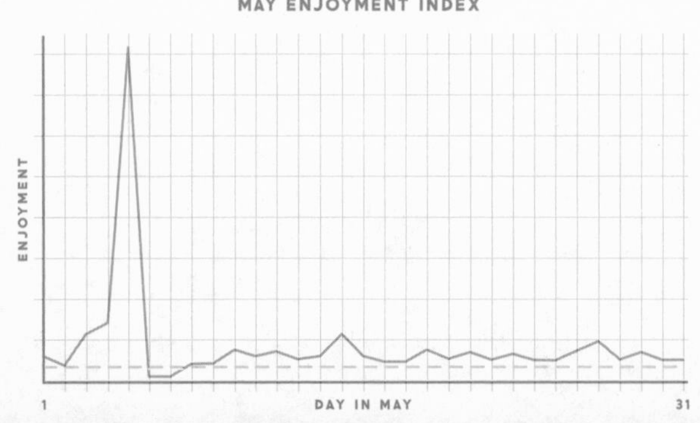

ENJOYMENT OVER TIME

CHOOSE A COLOR KEY

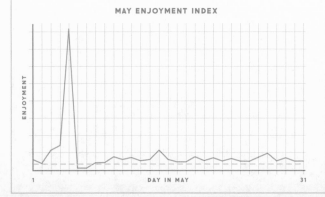

LINE	ITEM
—	CORONA BEER
– –	CORONA VIRUSES
	THE IDEA OF THE BEACH
	ACTUALLY SWIMMING
	CALLING MOM
	TALKING TO HER
	MEMORIAL DAY SALES
	HAVING THE WINDOW OPEN
	FLYING INSECTS
	THE THOUGHT OF WINTER

YOUR WEEK AT A GLANCE

MONDAY	TUESDAY	WEDNESDAY	THURSDAY	FRIDAY	SATURDAY ☐
☐ TODAY	☐ TODAY	☐ TODAY	☐ TODAY	☐ TODAY	☐ SUNDAY

01

NOTES AND/OR DOODLES

IT'S PHONE IN SICK DAY

PRO-TIP: START MENTIONING 'SYMPTOMS' THE DAY BEFORE.

JAMIE DORNAN WAS BORN IN 1982 WES ANDERSON WAS BORN IN 1969

9 AM
10 AM
11 AM
NOON
1 PM
2 PM
3 PM
4 PM
5 PM
6 PM

ON THIS DAY IN 1999: 'SPONGEBOB SQUAREPANTS' PREMIERED ON NICKELODEON.

YOUR WEEK AT A GLANCE

MONDAY	TUESDAY	WEDNESDAY	THURSDAY	FRIDAY	SATURDAY ☐
☐ TODAY	☐ TODAY	☐ TODAY	☐ TODAY	☐ TODAY	☐ SUNDAY

02

NOTES AND/OR DOODLES

IT'S NATIONAL TRUFFLE DAY

THESE MUSHROOMS CAN COST BETWEEN $800 AND $1,500 A POUND.

DWAYNE JOHNSON WAS BORN IN 1972 ELLIE KEMPER WAS BORN IN 1980

9 AM
10 AM
11 AM
NOON
1 PM
2 PM
3 PM
4 PM
5 PM
6 PM

ON THIS DAY IN 1956: THE WEATHER CHANNEL BEGAN BROADCASTING IN THE U.S.

03

YOUR WEEK AT A GLANCE

MONDAY	TUESDAY	WEDNESDAY	THURSDAY	FRIDAY	SATURDAY ☐
TODAY ☐	TODAY ☐	TODAY ☐	TODAY ☐	TODAY ☐	☐ SUNDAY

IT'S NATIONAL PARANORMAL DAY

'PARANORMAL ACTIVITY' IS THE 2ND MOST PROFITABLE FILM OF ALL TIME.

JAMES BROWN WAS BORN IN 1933

DAMON DASH WAS BORN IN 1971

9 AM

10 AM

11 AM

NOON

1 PM

2 PM

3 PM

4 PM

5 PM

6 PM

ON THIS DAY IN 1991: THE 356TH (& FINAL) EPISODE OF 'DALLAS' AIRED.

NOTES AND/OR DOODLES

04

YOUR WEEK AT A GLANCE

MONDAY	TUESDAY	WEDNESDAY	THURSDAY	FRIDAY	SATURDAY ☐
TODAY ☐	TODAY ☐	TODAY ☐	TODAY ☐	TODAY ☐	☐ SUNDAY

IT'S PETITE AND PROUD DAY

THE AVERAGE HEIGHT OF AN ADULT WOMAN IN THE U.S. IS 5'3".

AUDREY HEPBURN WAS BORN IN 1929

LANCE BASS WAS BORN IN 1979

9 AM

10 AM

11 AM

NOON

1 PM

2 PM

3 PM

4 PM

5 PM

6 PM

ON THIS DAY IN 1959: THE 1ST ANNUAL GRAMMY AWARDS WERE HELD.

NOTES AND/OR DOODLES

YEAR: MAY

YOUR WEEK AT A GLANCE

MONDAY	TUESDAY	WEDNESDAY	THURSDAY	FRIDAY	SATURDAY ☐
☐ TODAY	☐ TODAY	☐ TODAY	☐ TODAY	☐ TODAY	☐ SUNDAY

05

NOTES AND/OR DOODLES

IT'S CINCO DE MAYO

OH, AND IT'S ALSO HUG A SHED AND TAKE A SELFIE DAY.

(SERIOUSLY, TAG US. @BRASSMONKEYGOODS)

ADELE WAS BORN IN 1988

HENRY CAVILL WAS BORN IN 1983

9 AM

10 AM

11 AM

NOON

1 PM

2 PM

3 PM

4 PM

5 PM

6 PM

ON THIS DAY IN 1921: CHANEL NO. 5 WAS RELEASED.

YOUR WEEK AT A GLANCE

MONDAY	TUESDAY	WEDNESDAY	THURSDAY	FRIDAY	SATURDAY ☐
☐ TODAY	☐ TODAY	☐ TODAY	☐ TODAY	☐ TODAY	☐ SUNDAY

06

NOTES AND/OR DOODLES

IT'S NATIONAL BEVERAGE DAY

ENJOY CONSUMING LIQUIDS? WELL, YOU'RE IN LUCK.

WILLIE MAYS WAS BORN IN 1931

MEEK MILL WAS BORN IN 1987

9 AM

10 AM

11 AM

NOON

1 PM

2 PM

3 PM

4 PM

5 PM

6 PM

ON THIS DAY IN 1994: BOBCAT GOLDTHWAIT SET FIRE TO THE 'TONIGHT SHOW' COUCH.

07

YOUR WEEK AT A GLANCE

MONDAY	TUESDAY	WEDNESDAY	THURSDAY	FRIDAY	SATURDAY ☐
TODAY ☐	TODAY ☐	TODAY ☐	TODAY ☐	TODAY ☐	☐ SUNDAY

IT'S NATIONAL COSMOPOLITAN DAY

BLAME 'SEX AND THE CITY.'

AIDY BRYANT WAS BORN IN 1987

EVA PERÓN WAS BORN IN 1919

9 AM

10 AM

11 AM

NOON

1 PM

2 PM

3 PM

4 PM

5 PM

6 PM

ON THIS DAY IN 1994: EDVARD MUNCH'S 'THE SCREAM' WAS RECOVERED UNDAMAGED.

NOTES AND/OR DOODLES

08

YOUR WEEK AT A GLANCE

MONDAY	TUESDAY	WEDNESDAY	THURSDAY	FRIDAY	SATURDAY ☐
TODAY ☐	TODAY ☐	TODAY ☐	TODAY ☐	TODAY ☐	☐ SUNDAY

IT'S NATIONAL HAVE A COKE DAY

THE ORIGINAL GLASS BOTTLE WAS MODELED AFTER A COCOA POD.

PHILLIS WHEATLEY WAS BORN IN 1753

ENRIQUE IGLESIAS WAS BORN IN 1975

9 AM

10 AM

11 AM

NOON

1 PM

2 PM

3 PM

4 PM

5 PM

6 PM

ON THIS DAY IN 2010: BETTY WHITE HOSTED 'SATURDAY NIGHT LIVE.'

NOTES AND/OR DOODLES

PEOPLE I'D LIKE TO PUNCH IN THE FACE

OR SOME BORING TO-DO LIST

1
2
3
4
5
6
7
8
9
10
11
12

REASONS NOT TO EAT A SALAD

OR A GROCERY LIST OR SOMETHING

1
2
3
4
5
6
7
8
9
10
11
12

A DRAWING OF A BACKSEAT DRIVER

(OR SOME SUPER BUSINESSY STUFF)

THINGS NOT TO SAY AT JOB INTERVIEWS

OR A MORE USEFUL (BUT STUPID) LIST

1
2
3
4
5
6
7
8
9
10
11
12

POTENTIAL EXCUSES FOR BEING LATE

OR A LIST OF LITERALLY ANYTHING ELSE

1
2
3
4
5
6
7
8
9
10
11
12

09

YOUR WEEK AT A GLANCE

MONDAY	TUESDAY	WEDNESDAY	THURSDAY	FRIDAY	SATURDAY ☐
TODAY ☐	TODAY ☐	TODAY ☐	TODAY ☐	TODAY ☐	☐ SUNDAY

IT'S HOORAY FOR BUTTONS DAY

PREHISTORIC PEOPLE HELD THEIR GARMENTS IN PLACE WITH THORNS.

ROSARIO DAWSON WAS BORN IN 1979

BILLY JOEL WAS BORN IN 1949

9 AM

10 AM

11 AM

NOON

1 PM

2 PM

3 PM

4 PM

5 PM

6 PM

ON THIS DAY IN 1992: 'THE GOLDEN GIRLS' AIRED THEIR SERIES FINALE.

NOTES AND/OR DOODLES

10

YOUR WEEK AT A GLANCE

MONDAY	TUESDAY	WEDNESDAY	THURSDAY	FRIDAY	SATURDAY ☐
TODAY ☐	TODAY ☐	TODAY ☐	TODAY ☐	TODAY ☐	☐ SUNDAY

IT'S NATIONAL SHRIMP DAY

THE PISTOL SHRIMP CAN PRODUCE SOUNDS LOUDER THAN A GUNSHOT.

SID VICIOUS WAS BORN IN 1957

BONO WAS BORN IN 1960

9 AM

10 AM

11 AM

NOON

1 PM

2 PM

3 PM

4 PM

5 PM

6 PM

ON THIS DAY IN 1877: THE 1ST TELEPHONE WAS INSTALLED IN THE WHITE HOUSE.

NOTES AND/OR DOODLES

YEAR: MAY

YOUR WEEK AT A GLANCE

MONDAY	TUESDAY	WEDNESDAY	THURSDAY	FRIDAY	SATURDAY ☐
☐ TODAY	☐ TODAY	☐ TODAY	☐ TODAY	☐ TODAY	☐ SUNDAY

11

NOTES AND/OR DOODLES

IT'S EAT WHAT YOU WANT DAY

IN NYC? CHECK OUT SHOPSIN'S ON THE LOWER EAST SIDE.

SALVADOR DALI WAS BORN IN 1904

VALENTINO WAS BORN IN 1932

9 AM

10 AM

11 AM

NOON

1 PM

2 PM

3 PM

4 PM

5 PM

6 PM

ON THIS DAY IN 2000: AASTHA ARORA, INDIA'S 1 BILLIONTH BABY, WAS BORN.

YOUR WEEK AT A GLANCE

MONDAY	TUESDAY	WEDNESDAY	THURSDAY	FRIDAY	SATURDAY ☐
☐ TODAY	☐ TODAY	☐ TODAY	☐ TODAY	☐ TODAY	☐ SUNDAY

12

NOTES AND/OR DOODLES

IT'S LIMERICK DAY

FIRST COLLECTIONS OF LIMERICKS IN ENGLISH DATE FROM ABOUT 1820.

RAMI MALEK WAS BORN IN 1981

EMILIO ESTEVES WAS BORN IN 1962

9 AM

10 AM

11 AM

NOON

1 PM

2 PM

3 PM

4 PM

5 PM

6 PM

ON THIS DAY IN 1995: 'AS THE WORLD TURNS' AIRED THEIR 10,000TH EPISODE.

LISTS, NOTES & MEMOIRS

BAD MASCOTS FOR A RESTAURANT CHAIN

OR A LIST OF LITERALLY ANYTHING ELSE

1
2
3
4
5
6
7
8
9
10
11
12

THINGS CURRENTLY IN MY POCKETS

OR A MORE USEFUL (BUT STUPID) LIST

1
2
3
4
5
6
7
8
9
10
11
12

A DRAWING OF A BOOBY TRAP (OR A BRA)

(OR SOME SUPER BUSINESSY STUFF)

GOOD DECISIONS

OR SOME BORING TO-DO LIST

1
2
3
4
5
6
7
8
9
10
11
12

EXCELLENT MISTAKES

OR A GROCERY LIST OR SOMETHING

1
2
3
4
5
6
7
8
9
10
11
12

YOUR WEEK AT A GLANCE

MONDAY	TUESDAY	WEDNESDAY	THURSDAY	FRIDAY	SATURDAY ☐
☐ TODAY	☐ TODAY	☐ TODAY	☐ TODAY	☐ TODAY	☐ SUNDAY

13

NOTES AND/OR DOODLES

IT'S NATIONAL LEPRECHAUN DAY

THEY ARE A PROTECTED SPECIES UNDER EUROPEAN LAW.

STEVIE WONDER WAS BORN IN 1950

BEA ARTHUR WAS BORN IN 1922

9 AM

10 AM

11 AM

NOON

1 PM

2 PM

3 PM

4 PM

5 PM

6 PM

ON THIS DAY IN 1981: POPE JOHN PAUL II WAS SHOT BY MEHMET ALI AĞCA.

YOUR WEEK AT A GLANCE

MONDAY	TUESDAY	WEDNESDAY	THURSDAY	FRIDAY	SATURDAY ☐
☐ TODAY	☐ TODAY	☐ TODAY	☐ TODAY	☐ TODAY	☐ SUNDAY

14

NOTES AND/OR DOODLES

IT'S BUTTERMILK BISCUIT DAY

NORMAL MILK BISCUITS? GARBAGE.

GEORGE LUCAS WAS BORN IN 1944

CATE BLANCHETT WAS BORN IN 1969

9 AM

10 AM

11 AM

NOON

1 PM

2 PM

3 PM

4 PM

5 PM

6 PM

ON THIS DAY IN 1998: 76 MILLION PEOPLE WATCHED THE FINALE OF 'SEINFELD.'

15

YOUR WEEK AT A GLANCE

MONDAY	TUESDAY	WEDNESDAY	THURSDAY	FRIDAY	SATURDAY ☐
TODAY ☐	TODAY ☐	TODAY ☐	TODAY ☐	TODAY ☐	☐ SUNDAY

IT'S NYLON STOCKINGS DAY

UPON RELEASE IN 1940, DUPONT SOLD 4 MILLION PAIRS IN 2 DAYS.

EMMITT SMITH WAS BORN IN 1969

ANDY MURRAY WAS BORN IN 1987

9 AM

10 AM

11 AM

NOON

1 PM

2 PM

3 PM

4 PM

5 PM

6 PM

ON THIS DAY IN 1941: JOE DIMAGGIO BEGAN A 56-GAME HITTING STREAK.

NOTES AND/OR DOODLES

16

YOUR WEEK AT A GLANCE

MONDAY	TUESDAY	WEDNESDAY	THURSDAY	FRIDAY	SATURDAY ☐
TODAY ☐	TODAY ☐	TODAY ☐	TODAY ☐	TODAY ☐	☐ SUNDAY

IT'S NATIONAL SEA MONKEY DAY

THEY AREN'T MONKEYS, AND THEY DON'T LIVE IN THE SEA.

LIBERACE WAS BORN IN 1919

JANET JACKSON WAS BORN IN 1966

9 AM

10 AM

11 AM

NOON

1 PM

2 PM

3 PM

4 PM

5 PM

6 PM

ON THIS DAY IN 1875: ROOT BEER WAS INVENTED BY CHARLES ELMER HIRES.

NOTES AND/OR DOODLES

YEAR: MAY

YOUR WEEK AT A GLANCE

MONDAY	TUESDAY	WEDNESDAY	THURSDAY	FRIDAY	SATURDAY ☐
☐ TODAY	☐ TODAY	☐ TODAY	☐ TODAY	☐ TODAY	☐ SUNDAY

17

NOTES AND/OR DOODLES

IT'S NATIONAL MUSHROOM HUNTING DAY

THE LAETIPORUS VARIETY TASTES NEARLY IDENTICAL TO FRIED CHICKEN.

KANDI BURRUSS WAS BORN IN 1976

BOB SAGET WAS BORN IN 1956

9 AM

10 AM

11 AM

NOON

1 PM

2 PM

3 PM

4 PM

5 PM

6 PM

ON THIS DAY IN 1792: THE NEW YORK STOCK EXCHANGE WAS FORMED.

YOUR WEEK AT A GLANCE

MONDAY	TUESDAY	WEDNESDAY	THURSDAY	FRIDAY	SATURDAY ☐
☐ TODAY	☐ TODAY	☐ TODAY	☐ TODAY	☐ TODAY	☐ SUNDAY

18

NOTES AND/OR DOODLES

IT'S NATIONAL CHEESE SOUFFLÉ DAY

THE BIGGEST SOUFFLÉ EVER PRODUCED WAS 243 FEET LONG.

TINA FEY WAS BORN IN 1970

CHOW YUN-FAT WAS BORN IN 1955

9 AM

10 AM

11 AM

NOON

1 PM

2 PM

3 PM

4 PM

5 PM

6 PM

ON THIS DAY IN 1910: THE EARTH PASSED THROUGH THE TAIL OF HALLEY'S COMET.

19

YOUR WEEK AT A GLANCE

MONDAY	TUESDAY	WEDNESDAY	THURSDAY	FRIDAY	SATURDAY ☐
TODAY ☐	TODAY ☐	TODAY ☐	TODAY ☐	TODAY ☐	☐ SUNDAY

IT'S NATIONAL DEVIL'S FOOD CAKE DAY

IT'S JUST A REALLY DECADENT CAKE—NOT INHERENTLY EVIL.

KENNY SHOPSIN WAS BORN IN 1942

MALCOLM X WAS BORN IN 1925

9 AM

10 AM

11 AM

NOON

1 PM

2 PM

3 PM

4 PM

5 PM

6 PM

ON THIS DAY IN 1962: MARILYN MONROE SANG 'HAPPY BIRTHDAY' TO JFK.

NOTES AND/OR DOODLES

20

YOUR WEEK AT A GLANCE

MONDAY	TUESDAY	WEDNESDAY	THURSDAY	FRIDAY	SATURDAY ☐
TODAY ☐	TODAY ☐	TODAY ☐	TODAY ☐	TODAY ☐	☐ SUNDAY

IT'S WORLD BEE DAY

THEY FLY 55,000 MILES TO PRODUCE 1 POUND OF HONEY.

CHER WAS BORN IN 1946

BUSTA RHYMES WAS BORN IN 1972

9 AM

10 AM

11 AM

NOON

1 PM

2 PM

3 PM

4 PM

5 PM

6 PM

ON THIS DAY IN 2013: YAHOO PURCHASED TUMBLER FOR $1.1 BILLION.

NOTES AND/OR DOODLES

LISTS, NOTES & MEMOIRS

BEST FOODS TO USE IN A FOOD FIGHT

OR SOME BORING TO-DO LIST

1
2
3
4
5
6
7
8
9
10
11
12

BEST FOODS TO USE IN A KNIFE FIGHT

OR A GROCERY LIST OR SOMETHING

1
2
3
4
5
6
7
8
9
10
11
12

A DRAWING OF A FOUR-LETTER WORD

(OR SOME SUPER BUSINESSY STUFF)

WORST TIMES TO HAVE THE HICCUPS

OR A MORE USEFUL (BUT STUPID) LIST

1
2
3
4
5
6
7
8
9
10
11
12

WHAT MILKSHAKES BRING TO MY YARD

OR A LIST OF LITERALLY ANYTHING ELSE

1
2
3
4
5
6
7
8
9
10
11
12

21

YOUR WEEK AT A GLANCE

MONDAY	TUESDAY	WEDNESDAY	THURSDAY	FRIDAY	SATURDAY ☐
TODAY ☐	TODAY ☐	TODAY ☐	TODAY ☐	TODAY ☐	☐ SUNDAY

IT'S INTERNATIONAL TEA DAY

BLACK AND GREEN TEAS ARE MADE FROM THE SAME PLANT.

MR. T WAS BORN IN 1952

NOTORIOUS B.I.G. WAS BORN IN 1972

9 AM
10 AM
11 AM
NOON
1 PM
2 PM
3 PM
4 PM
5 PM
6 PM

ON THIS DAY IN 1980: THE COYOTE FINALLY CAUGHT THE ROAD RUNNER.

NOTES AND/OR DOODLES

22

YOUR WEEK AT A GLANCE

MONDAY	TUESDAY	WEDNESDAY	THURSDAY	FRIDAY	SATURDAY ☐
TODAY ☐	TODAY ☐	TODAY ☐	TODAY ☐	TODAY ☐	☐ SUNDAY

IT'S NATIONAL SOLITAIRE DAY

WINDOWS SOLITAIRE WAS DEVELOPED IN 1989 BY A BORED INTERN.

NAOMI CAMPBELL WAS BORN IN 1970

GINNIFER GOODWIN WAS BORN IN 1978

9 AM
10 AM
11 AM
NOON
1 PM
2 PM
3 PM
4 PM
5 PM
6 PM

ON THIS DAY IN 1986: CHER CALLED DAVID LETTERMAN AN ASSHOLE ON TV.

NOTES AND/OR DOODLES

YOUR WEEK AT A GLANCE

MONDAY	TUESDAY	WEDNESDAY	THURSDAY	FRIDAY	SATURDAY ☐
☐ TODAY	☐ TODAY	☐ TODAY	☐ TODAY	☐ TODAY	☐ SUNDAY

23

NOTES AND/OR DOODLES

IT'S LUCKY PENNY DAY

$62 MILLION IN PENNIES ARE LOST IN CIRCULATION EVERY YEAR.

JOAN COLLINS WAS BORN IN 1933

DREW CAREY WAS BORN IN 1958

9 AM

10 AM

11 AM

NOON

1 PM

2 PM

3 PM

4 PM

5 PM

6 PM

ON THIS DAY IN 2005: TOM CRUISE JUMPED AROUND ON OPRAH'S COUCH.

YOUR WEEK AT A GLANCE

MONDAY	TUESDAY	WEDNESDAY	THURSDAY	FRIDAY	SATURDAY ☐
☐ TODAY	☐ TODAY	☐ TODAY	☐ TODAY	☐ TODAY	☐ SUNDAY

24

NOTES AND/OR DOODLES

IT'S SCAVENGER HUNT DAY

TAKE A PICTURE OF A BRASS MONKEY AND TAG US.

(WE'LL GIVE YOU A PRIZE. @BRASSMONKEYGOODS)

PATTI LABELLE WAS BORN IN 1944

TOMMY CHONG WAS BORN IN 1938

9 AM

10 AM

11 AM

NOON

1 PM

2 PM

3 PM

4 PM

5 PM

6 PM

ON THIS DAY IN 1883: THE BROOKLYN BRIDGE OPENED TO THE PUBLIC.

LISTS, NOTES & MEMOIRS

PEOPLE I'D LIKE TO BE FOR A DAY

OR A LIST OF LITERALLY ANYTHING ELSE

1
2
3
4
5
6
7
8
9
10
11
12

PEOPLE I'D LIKE TO BE FOREVER

OR A MORE USEFUL (BUT STUPID) LIST

1
2
3
4
5
6
7
8
9
10
11
12

A DRAWING OF WHAT'S REALLY AT THE END OF THE RAINBOW

(OR SOME SUPER BUSINESSY STUFF)

BOOKS I HAVE READ MORE THAN ONCE

OR SOME BORING TO-DO LIST

1
2
3
4
5
6
7
8
9
10
11
12

LESSONS THAT I'LL NEVER LEARN

OR A GROCERY LIST OR SOMETHING

1
2
3
4
5
6
7
8
9
10
11
12

YEAR: **MAY**

YOUR WEEK AT A GLANCE

MONDAY	TUESDAY	WEDNESDAY	THURSDAY	FRIDAY	SATURDAY ☐ / ☐ SUNDAY
☐ TODAY	☐ TODAY	☐ TODAY	☐ TODAY	☐ TODAY	

25

NOTES AND/OR DOODLES

IT'S GEEK PRIDE DAY

STEVE URKEL WAS ONLY SUPPOSED TO BE IN ONE EPISODE. LUCKY US.

RALPH EMERSON WAS BORN IN 1803

MIKE MYERS WAS BORN IN 1963

9 AM

10 AM

11 AM

NOON

1 PM

2 PM

3 PM

4 PM

5 PM

6 PM

ON THIS DAY IN 1986: HANDS ACROSS AMERICA (KIND OF) TOOK PLACE.

YOUR WEEK AT A GLANCE

MONDAY	TUESDAY	WEDNESDAY	THURSDAY	FRIDAY	SATURDAY ☐ / ☐ SUNDAY
☐ TODAY	☐ TODAY	☐ TODAY	☐ TODAY	☐ TODAY	

26

NOTES AND/OR DOODLES

IT'S NATIONAL PAPER AIRPLANE DAY

THE FURTHEST THAT ONE HAS EVER BEEN THROWN IS 226' 10".

MILES DAVIS WAS BORN IN 1926

HELENA CARTER WAS BORN IN 1966

9 AM

10 AM

11 AM

NOON

1 PM

2 PM

3 PM

4 PM

5 PM

6 PM

ON THIS DAY IN 1978: THE 1ST LEGAL U.S. CASINO (OUTSIDE OF NV) OPENED.

27

YOUR WEEK AT A GLANCE

MONDAY	TUESDAY	WEDNESDAY	THURSDAY	FRIDAY	SATURDAY ☐
TODAY ☐	TODAY ☐	TODAY ☐	TODAY ☐	TODAY ☐	☐ SUNDAY

IT'S NATIONAL GRAPE POPSICLE DAY

INVENTED BY FRANK EPPERSON IN 1905, WHEN HE WAS 11 YEARS OLD.

ANDRÉ 3000 WAS BORN IN 1975

JACK MCBRAYER WAS BORN IN 1973

9 AM

10 AM

11 AM

NOON

1 PM

2 PM

3 PM

4 PM

5 PM

6 PM

ON THIS DAY IN 1930: MASKING TAPE WAS PATENTED.

NOTES AND/OR DOODLES

28

YOUR WEEK AT A GLANCE

MONDAY	TUESDAY	WEDNESDAY	THURSDAY	FRIDAY	SATURDAY ☐
TODAY ☐	TODAY ☐	TODAY ☐	TODAY ☐	TODAY ☐	☐ SUNDAY

IT'S NATIONAL BRISKET DAY

NO BREED OF COW IS ACTUALLY NATIVE TO AMERICA.

KYLIE MINOGUE WAS BORN IN 1968

JAKE JOHNSON WAS BORN IN 1978

9 AM

10 AM

11 AM

NOON

1 PM

2 PM

3 PM

4 PM

5 PM

6 PM

ON THIS DAY IN 1897: JELL-O WAS FIRST INTRODUCED.

NOTES AND/OR DOODLES

YEAR: **MAY**

YOUR WEEK AT A GLANCE

MONDAY	TUESDAY	WEDNESDAY	THURSDAY	FRIDAY	SATURDAY ☐ / ☐ SUNDAY
☐ TODAY	☐ TODAY	☐ TODAY	☐ TODAY	☐ TODAY	

29

NOTES AND/OR DOODLES

IT'S LEARN ABOUT COMPOSTING DAY

WELL? WHAT ARE YOU WAITING FOR?

JOHN F. KENNEDY WAS BORN IN 1917 LAVERNE COX WAS BORN IN 1972

9 AM

10 AM

11 AM

NOON

1 PM

2 PM

3 PM

4 PM

5 PM

6 PM

ON THIS DAY IN 1987: MICHAEL JACKSON TRIED TO BUY ELEPHANT MAN'S REMAINS.

YOUR WEEK AT A GLANCE

MONDAY	TUESDAY	WEDNESDAY	THURSDAY	FRIDAY	SATURDAY ☐ / ☐ SUNDAY
☐ TODAY	☐ TODAY	☐ TODAY	☐ TODAY	☐ TODAY	

30

NOTES AND/OR DOODLES

IT'S NATIONAL CREATIVITY DAY

72 PERCENT OF PEOPLE HAVE CREATIVE INSIGHTS IN THE SHOWER.

IDINA MENZEL WAS BORN IN 1971 TOM MORELLO WAS BORN IN 1964

9 AM

10 AM

11 AM

NOON

1 PM

2 PM

3 PM

4 PM

5 PM

6 PM

ON THIS DAY IN 1996: WENDY GUEY SPELLED 'VIVISEPULTURE' TO WIN THE NSB.

MAY

:YEAR

31

YOUR WEEK AT A GLANCE

MONDAY	TUESDAY	WEDNESDAY	THURSDAY	FRIDAY	SATURDAY
TODAY	TODAY	TODAY	TODAY	TODAY	SUNDAY

IT'S NATIONAL SMILE DAY

SMILING IS MORE CONTAGIOUS THAN THE FLU.

CLINT EASTWOOD WAS BORN IN 1930

BROOKE SHIELDS WAS BORN IN 1965

9 AM

10 AM

11 AM

NOON

1 PM

2 PM

3 PM

4 PM

5 PM

6 PM

ON THIS DAY IN 2017: U.S. PRESIDENT DONALD TRUMP TWEETED 'COVFEFE.'

NOTES AND/OR DOODLES

A DRAWING OF DOGS PLAYING POKER

(OR IN GAMBLERS ANONYMOUS)

SUBCATEGORIES OF PORN I'M WORRIED MIGHT EXIST

OR A GROCERY LIST OR SOMETHING

1
2
3
4
5
6
7
8
9
10
11
12
13
14
15
16
17
18

MAY IN REVIEW

MY MAY ACCOMPLISHMENTS

- ☐ ENJOYED A THREE DAY WEEKEND
- ☐ DID FIVE DAYS OF WORK IN FOUR DAYS
- ☐ APPRECIATED MOM FOR ALL THAT SHE DID
- ☐ STILL ALMOST FORGOT TO CALL
- ☐ UNOFFICIALLY STARTED SUMMER
- ☐ OFFICIALLY REGRETTED EATING SO MUCH
- ☐ HONORED OUR FALLEN SOLDIERS
- ☐ GOT 532 'MEMORIAL DAY SALE' EMAILS
- ☐ STEREOTYPICALLY CELEBRATED MEXICO
- ☐ SWORE OFF TEQUILA FOREVER
- ☐ WENT TO A POOL PARTY
- ☐ DRANK SOME MORE TEQUILA
- ☐ DIDN'T GET WITHIN 9 FEET OF THE POOL
- ☐ WAS INTRODUCED TO A NEW PERSON
- ☐ IMMEDIATELY FORGOT THEIR NAME

REASONS THAT MAY WAS GREAT

'IT ENDED' IS A VALID ANSWER

1
2
3
4
5
6
7
8
9
10
11
12

IF MAY WAS PERSONIFIED, DRAW ITS LAST INSTAGRAM POST

REASONS THAT I'M GLAD MAY IS OVER

USE ADDITIONAL PAPER IF NEEDED

1
2
3
4
5
6
7
8
9
10
11
12
13
14

CLICHÉS OVERHEARD THIS MONTH

- 'IT'S CINCO DE DRINKO' ☐
- 'I THINK WE'RE STILL NIBBLING ON IT' ☐
- 'MAY THE FOURTH BE WITH YOU' ☐
- 'WHEN IS CINCO DE MAYO THIS YEAR?' ☐
- 'WELL LOOK WHO DECIDED TO CALL' ☐
- 'WOW, THE YEAR'S ALMOST HALF OVER!' ☐
- 'SUN TIME, FUN TIME' ☐
- 'MY EYES CHANGE COLOR IN THE SUN' ☐
- 'GREAT MINDS THINK ALIKE' ☐
- 'PACK ME IN YOUR SUITCASE, PLEASE' ☐
- 'OMG, I'M SO JELLY' ☐
- 'THAT'S ENOUGH ADULTING FOR TODAY' ☐
- 'HAPPY HUMP DAY' ☐
- 'NOW LET'S TAKE A SILLY ONE' ☐
- 'BARBECUE? DON'T MIND IF I DO' ☐
- 'I NEED SOME MOMMY JUICE' ☐
- 'THANKS, I GOT IT AT TAR-JAY' ☐

NO OTHER MONTH IN THE YEAR BEGINS ON THE SAME DAY OF THE WEEK AS JUNE.

WELCOME TO

× JUNE ×

OF WHATEVER YEAR
YOU SAY IT IS.

LET'S GO WITH:

NAMED AFTER THE ROMAN GODDESS OF MARRIAGE, JUNO.

JUNE AT A GLANCE

:YEAR

YOU MADE IT
TO JUNE

✕

CELEBRATE, IT'S:

LGBTQIA PRIDE MONTH

NATIONAL HOMEOWNERSHIP MONTH

NATIONAL ICED TEA MONTH

TURKEY LOVERS MONTH

NATIONAL SOUL FOOD MONTH

✕

OFFICIAL SYMBOLS:

BIRTHSTONE: PEARL

FLOWERS: ROSE & HONEYSUCKLE

TREES: ASH, FIG, & APPLE

GEMINI (MAY 21 / JUN 20)

CANCER (JUN 21 / JUL 22)

DATES TO KNOW*
LIKE, IMPORTANT ONES

✕

WORLD ENVIRONMENT DAY
JUNE 5TH

D-DAY (WWII)
JUNE 6TH

FLAG DAY
JUNE 14TH

NATIVE AMERICAN CITIZENSHIP DAY
JUNE 15TH

ST. VLADIMIR DAY
(ROMAN CATHOLIC)
JUNE 15TH

MARTYRDOM OF GURU ARJAN DEV
(SIKHISM)
JUNE 16TH

JUNETEENTH
JUNE 19TH

START OF SUMMER
(SUMMER SOLSTICE)
JUNE 20TH (OR 21ST)

FORGIVENESS DAY
JUNE 26TH

THINGS TO ACCOMPLISH THIS MONTH
FOR EXAMPLE: FILL OUT A TO-DO LIST

1
2
3
4
5
6
7
8
9
10
11
12
13
14
15

THINGS THAT ARE NEVER GOING TO HAPPEN
THERE'S ALWAYS JULY (OR AUGUST)

1
2
3
4
5
6
7
8
9
10
11
12
13
14
15

*A DISCLAIMER OF SORTS

HEY THERE. WE HERE AT BRASS MONKEY LIKE TO JOKE AROUND...BUT WE ALSO WANT TO TAKE A MINUTE TO RECOGNIZE JUST A FEW OF THE MANY HOLIDAYS & EVENTS THAT ARE IMPORTANT TO OUR FRIENDS AROUND THE GLOBE (AND AT HOME). YOU MAY BE DIFFERENT THAN US. WE MAY HAVE NEVER MET. BUT WE LOVE YOU ALL THE SAME.

SO IF YOU HAVEN'T HEARD OF A DAY, LOOK IT UP. LEARNING ABOUT & APPRECIATING CULTURES DIFFERENT THAN YOURS IS IMPORTANT...WAY MORE THAN POSTING A FEW 'STRAWBERRY JAM DAY' SELFIES.

JUNE AT A GLANCE

YEAR:

IT'S JUNE
START PLANNING

×

FLAG DAY
JUNE 14TH

JUNETEENTH
JUNE 19TH

START OF SUMMER*
JUNE 20TH (OR 21ST)

×

BIRTHDAYS
TO REMEMBER

*PSST: SINCE THIS HOLIDAY MOVES AROUND EACH YEAR (AND WE DON'T KNOW WHEN IN THE FUTURE YOU'RE USING THIS), HELP US OUT AND ADD IT TO THE CALENDAR.

ALSO, ARE THERE JET PACKS YET? OUR FINGERS ARE CROSSED.

S M T W T F S	S M T W T F S	S M T W T F S	S M T W T F S	S M T W T F S	S M T W T F S	S M T W T F S
01	02	03	04	05	06	07
08	09	10	11	12	13	FLAG DAY 14
15	16	17	18	JUNETEENTH 19	20	21
22	23	24	25	26	27	28
29	30					

NOTES:

JUNE, AS EXPRESSED IN A DRAWING

LISTS, NOTES & MEMOIRS

ONE SENTENCE BOOK SUMMARIES

OR A LIST OF LITERALLY ANYTHING ELSE

1
2
3
4
5
6
7
8
9
10
11
12

BUMPER STICKERS THAT SHOULD EXIST

OR A MORE USEFUL (BUT STUPID) LIST

1
2
3
4
5
6
7
8
9
10
11
12

A DRAWING OF MINIATURE GOLF (OR GIGANTIC GOLF)

(OR SOME SUPER BUSINESSY STUFF)

WORST POSSIBLE SONGS FOR KARAOKE

OR SOME BORING TO-DO LIST

1
2
3
4
5
6
7
8
9
10
11
12

EVERYTHING THAT I'VE EVER RUINED

OR A GROCERY LIST OR SOMETHING

1
2
3
4
5
6
7
8
9
10
11
12

YEAR: **JUNE**

YOUR WEEK AT A GLANCE

MONDAY	TUESDAY	WEDNESDAY	THURSDAY	FRIDAY	SATURDAY ☐
☐ TODAY	☐ TODAY	☐ TODAY	☐ TODAY	☐ TODAY	☐ SUNDAY

01

NOTES AND/OR DOODLES

IT'S NATIONAL OLIVE DAY

THE OLDEST KNOWN OLIVE TREE IS OVER 4,000 YEARS OLD.

MARILYN MONROE WAS BORN IN 1926

MORGAN FREEMAN WAS BORN IN 1937

9 AM

10 AM

11 AM

NOON

1 PM

2 PM

3 PM

4 PM

5 PM

6 PM

ON THIS DAY IN 1974: THE HEIMLICH MANEUVER WAS FIRST PUBLISHED.

YOUR WEEK AT A GLANCE

MONDAY	TUESDAY	WEDNESDAY	THURSDAY	FRIDAY	SATURDAY ☐
☐ TODAY	☐ TODAY	☐ TODAY	☐ TODAY	☐ TODAY	☐ SUNDAY

02

NOTES AND/OR DOODLES

IT'S NATIONAL ROTISSERIE CHICKEN DAY

JOHN LEGEND REPORTEDLY EATS HALF OF ONE BEFORE EVERY SHOW.

(NO WORD ON WHO GETS THE OTHER HALF)

WAYNE BRADY WAS BORN IN 1972

AWKWAFINA WAS BORN IN 1988

9 AM

10 AM

11 AM

NOON

1 PM

2 PM

3 PM

4 PM

5 PM

6 PM

ON THIS DAY IN 1989: THE FILM 'DEAD POET'S SOCIETY' WAS RELEASED.

03

YOUR WEEK AT A GLANCE

MONDAY	TUESDAY	WEDNESDAY	THURSDAY	FRIDAY	SATURDAY ☐
TODAY ☐	TODAY ☐	TODAY ☐	TODAY ☐	TODAY ☐	☐ SUNDAY

IT'S NATIONAL EGG DAY

THE AVERAGE HEN LAYS 266 OF THEM PER YEAR.

JOSEPHINE BAKER WAS BORN IN 1906 ANDERSON COOPER WAS BORN IN 1967

9 AM

10 AM

11 AM

NOON

1 PM

2 PM

3 PM

4 PM

5 PM

6 PM

ON THIS DAY IN 1992: BILL CLINTON PLAYED SAX ON 'THE ARSENIO HALL SHOW.'

NOTES AND/OR DOODLES

04

YOUR WEEK AT A GLANCE

MONDAY	TUESDAY	WEDNESDAY	THURSDAY	FRIDAY	SATURDAY ☐
TODAY ☐	TODAY ☐	TODAY ☐	TODAY ☐	TODAY ☐	☐ SUNDAY

IT'S HUG YOUR CAT DAY

ALSO KNOWN AS: GET YOUR EYES CLAWED OUT DAY.

ANGELINA JOLIE WAS BORN IN 1975 BAR REFAELI WAS BORN IN 1985

9 AM

10 AM

11 AM

NOON

1 PM

2 PM

3 PM

4 PM

5 PM

6 PM

ON THIS DAY IN 1984: BRUCE SPRINGSTEEN'S 'BORN IN THE USA' WAS RELEASED.

NOTES AND/OR DOODLES

YEAR: JUNE

YOUR WEEK AT A GLANCE

MONDAY	TUESDAY	WEDNESDAY	THURSDAY	FRIDAY	SATURDAY ☐
☐ TODAY	☐ TODAY	☐ TODAY	☐ TODAY	☐ TODAY	☐ SUNDAY

05

NOTES AND/OR DOODLES

IT'S NATIONAL ATTITUDE DAY

'DON'T WORRY, BE HAPPY' IS PREFORMED ENTIRELY A CAPPELLA.

NICK KROLL WAS BORN IN 1978

MARK WAHLBERG WAS BORN IN 1971

9 AM

10 AM

11 AM

NOON

1 PM

2 PM

3 PM

4 PM

5 PM

6 PM

ON THIS DAY IN 1985: FERRIS BUELLER TOOK HIS FICTIONAL DAY OFF.

YOUR WEEK AT A GLANCE

MONDAY	TUESDAY	WEDNESDAY	THURSDAY	FRIDAY	SATURDAY ☐
☐ TODAY	☐ TODAY	☐ TODAY	☐ TODAY	☐ TODAY	☐ SUNDAY

06

NOTES AND/OR DOODLES

IT'S D-DAY

OH, AND IT'S ALSO DRIVE-IN MOVIE DAY.

PAUL GIAMATTI WAS BORN IN 1967

JASON ISAACS WAS BORN IN 1963

9 AM

10 AM

11 AM

NOON

1 PM

2 PM

3 PM

4 PM

5 PM

6 PM

ON THIS DAY IN 1983: 'READING RAINBOW' PREMIERED ON PBS.

07

YOUR WEEK AT A GLANCE

MONDAY	TUESDAY	WEDNESDAY	THURSDAY	FRIDAY	SATURDAY ☐
TODAY ☐	TODAY ☐	TODAY ☐	TODAY ☐	TODAY ☐	☐ SUNDAY

IT'S NATIONAL CHOCOLATE ICE CREAM DAY

SCIENTIFICALLY SPEAKING, IT TAKES ABOUT 50 LICKS TO FINISH A CONE.

PRINCE WAS BORN IN 1958

MICHAEL CERA WAS BORN IN 1988

9 AM

10 AM

11 AM

NOON

1 PM

2 PM

3 PM

4 PM

5 PM

6 PM

ON THIS DAY IN 1990: UNIVERSAL STUDIOS OPENED IN FLORIDA.

NOTES AND/OR DOODLES

08

YOUR WEEK AT A GLANCE

MONDAY	TUESDAY	WEDNESDAY	THURSDAY	FRIDAY	SATURDAY ☐
TODAY ☐	TODAY ☐	TODAY ☐	TODAY ☐	TODAY ☐	☐ SUNDAY

IT'S BEST FRIENDS DAY

ONLY 1 OUT OF EVERY 12 FRIENDSHIPS LAST.

(GOOD LUCK, I GUESS)

JOAN RIVERS WAS BORN IN 1933

JERRY STILLER WAS BORN IN 1927

9 AM

10 AM

11 AM

NOON

1 PM

2 PM

3 PM

4 PM

5 PM

6 PM

ON THIS DAY IN 1966: THE NFL AND AFL ANNOUNCED THEIR MERGER.

NOTES AND/OR DOODLES

LISTS, NOTES & MEMOIRS

THE ONE(S) THAT GOT AWAY
OR SOME BORING TO-DO LIST

1
2
3
4
5
6
7
8
9
10
11
12

THE ONE(S) I WISH HAD GOTTEN AWAY
OR A GROCERY LIST OR SOMETHING

1
2
3
4
5
6
7
8
9
10
11
12

A DRAWING OF A UNICYCLE GANG

(OR SOME SUPER BUSINESSY STUFF)

FAVORITE THINGS TO DO ON THE TOILET
OR A MORE USEFUL (BUT STUPID) LIST

1
2
3
4
5
6
7
8
9
10
11
12

ANIMALS I'M IRRATIONALLY SCARED OF
OR A LIST OF LITERALLY ANYTHING ELSE

1
2
3
4
5
6
7
8
9
10
11
12

09

YOUR WEEK AT A GLANCE

MONDAY	TUESDAY	WEDNESDAY	THURSDAY	FRIDAY	SATURDAY ☐
TODAY ☐	TODAY ☐	TODAY ☐	TODAY ☐	TODAY ☐	☐ SUNDAY

IT'S NATIONAL STRAWBERRY RHUBARB PIE DAY

THE LEAVES ATTACHED TO THE RHUBARB STALK ARE POISONOUS.

MICHAEL J. FOX WAS BORN IN 1961

JOHNNY DEPP WAS BORN IN 1963

9 AM

10 AM

11 AM

NOON

1 PM

2 PM

3 PM

4 PM

5 PM

6 PM

ON THIS DAY IN 1993: HEIDI FLEISS (THE HOLLYWOOD MADAM) WAS ARRESTED.

NOTES AND/OR DOODLES

10

YOUR WEEK AT A GLANCE

MONDAY	TUESDAY	WEDNESDAY	THURSDAY	FRIDAY	SATURDAY ☐
TODAY ☐	TODAY ☐	TODAY ☐	TODAY ☐	TODAY ☐	☐ SUNDAY

IT'S BALLPOINT PEN DAY

AN AVERAGE PEN CAN WRITE APPROXIMATELY 45,000 WORDS.

HATTIE MCDANIEL WAS BORN IN 1893

JUDY GARLAND WAS BORN IN 1922

9 AM

10 AM

11 AM

NOON

1 PM

2 PM

3 PM

4 PM

5 PM

6 PM

ON THIS DAY IN 1949: SAAB REVEALED ITS FIRST AUTOMOBILE.

NOTES AND/OR DOODLES

YEAR: **JUNE**

YOUR WEEK AT A GLANCE

MONDAY	TUESDAY	WEDNESDAY	THURSDAY	FRIDAY	SATURDAY ☐
☐ TODAY	☐ TODAY	☐ TODAY	☐ TODAY	☐ TODAY	☐ SUNDAY

11

NOTES AND/OR DOODLES

IT'S NATIONAL GERMAN CHOCOLATE CAKE DAY

THE MOST POPULAR WAY TO RUIN A PERFECTLY GOOD CAKE WITH COCONUT.

PETER DINKLAGE WAS BORN IN 1969

GENE WILDER WAS BORN IN 1933

9 AM

10 AM

11 AM

NOON

1 PM

2 PM

3 PM

4 PM

5 PM

6 PM

ON THIS DAY IN 1949: HANK WILLIAMS SR. DEBUTED AT THE GRAND OLE OPRY.

YOUR WEEK AT A GLANCE

MONDAY	TUESDAY	WEDNESDAY	THURSDAY	FRIDAY	SATURDAY ☐
☐ TODAY	☐ TODAY	☐ TODAY	☐ TODAY	☐ TODAY	☐ SUNDAY

12

NOTES AND/OR DOODLES

IT'S MAGIC DAY

BUT IT'S PROBABLY JUST MIRRORS OR SOMETHING.

ANNE FRANK WAS BORN IN 1929

ADRIANA LIMA WAS BORN IN 1981

9 AM

10 AM

11 AM

NOON

1 PM

2 PM

3 PM

4 PM

5 PM

6 PM

ON THIS DAY IN 1942: ANNE FRANK RECEIVED A DIARY FOR HER 13TH BIRTHDAY.

LISTS, NOTES & MEMOIRS

STATES THAT I'VE NEVER BEEN TO

OR A LIST OF LITERALLY ANYTHING ELSE

1
2
3
4
5
6
7
8
9
10
11
12

STATES THAT I WISH I HADN'T BEEN TO

OR A MORE USEFUL (BUT STUPID) LIST

1
2
3
4
5
6
7
8
9
10
11
12

A DRAWING OF TOMORROW'S NEWSPAPER

(OR SOME SUPER BUSINESSY STUFF)

REGRETTABLE YEARBOOK QUOTES

OR SOME BORING TO-DO LIST

1
2
3
4
5
6
7
8
9
10
11
12

WHAT I WAS WORRIED ABOUT AT AGE 12

OR A GROCERY LIST OR SOMETHING

1
2
3
4
5
6
7
8
9
10
11
12

YEAR: JUNE

YOUR WEEK AT A GLANCE

MONDAY	TUESDAY	WEDNESDAY	THURSDAY	FRIDAY	SATURDAY ☐	13
☐ TODAY	☐ TODAY	☐ TODAY	☐ TODAY	☐ TODAY	☐ SUNDAY	

NOTES AND/OR DOODLES

IT'S WORLD SOFTBALL DAY

IT WAS ORIGINALLY GOING TO BE CALLED 'KITTEN BALL.'

(GROSS)

KAT DENNINGS WAS BORN IN 1986 — CHRIS EVANS WAS BORN IN 1981

9 AM
10 AM
11 AM
NOON
1 PM
2 PM
3 PM
4 PM
5 PM
6 PM

ON THIS DAY IN 1920: THE USPS FORBID THE MAILING OF CHILDREN.

YOUR WEEK AT A GLANCE

MONDAY	TUESDAY	WEDNESDAY	THURSDAY	FRIDAY	SATURDAY ☐	14
☐ TODAY	☐ TODAY	☐ TODAY	☐ TODAY	☐ TODAY	☐ SUNDAY	

NOTES AND/OR DOODLES

IT'S NATIONAL BOURBON DAY

95 PERCENT OF ALL BOURBON IS PRODUCED IN KENTUCKY.

BOY GEORGE WAS BORN IN 1961 — HEATHER MCDONALD WAS BORN IN 1970

9 AM
10 AM
11 AM
NOON
1 PM
2 PM
3 PM
4 PM
5 PM
6 PM

ON THIS DAY IN 1989: CONSTRUCTION BEGAN ON THE MALL OF AMERICA IN MN.

15

YOUR WEEK AT A GLANCE

MONDAY	TUESDAY	WEDNESDAY	THURSDAY	FRIDAY	SATURDAY ☐
TODAY ☐	TODAY ☐	TODAY ☐	TODAY ☐	TODAY ☐	☐ SUNDAY

IT'S NATIONAL LOBSTER DAY

LOBSTERS SQUIRT URINE AT EACH OTHER DURING COURTSHIP.

(AND THEY SAY ROMANCE IS DEAD)

ICE CUBE WAS BORN IN 1969 COURTENEY COX WAS BORN IN 1964

9 AM

10 AM

11 AM

NOON

1 PM

2 PM

3 PM

4 PM

5 PM

6 PM

ON THIS DAY IN 1934: THE GREAT SMOKY MOUNTAINS NATL. PARK WAS FOUNDED.

NOTES AND/OR DOODLES

16

YOUR WEEK AT A GLANCE

MONDAY	TUESDAY	WEDNESDAY	THURSDAY	FRIDAY	SATURDAY ☐
TODAY ☐	TODAY ☐	TODAY ☐	TODAY ☐	TODAY ☐	☐ SUNDAY

IT'S NATIONAL FUDGE DAY

MACKINAC ISLAND, MI MAKES 10,000 LBS OF IT DAILY.

(DURING TOURIST SEASON ANYWAY)

GERONIMO WAS BORN IN 1829 TUPAC SHAKUR WAS BORN IN 1971

9 AM

10 AM

11 AM

NOON

1 PM

2 PM

3 PM

4 PM

5 PM

6 PM

ON THIS DAY IN 1884: THE 1ST ROLLER COASTER OPENED ON CONEY ISLAND.

NOTES AND/OR DOODLES

YEAR: **JUNE**

YOUR WEEK AT A GLANCE

MONDAY	TUESDAY	WEDNESDAY	THURSDAY	FRIDAY	SATURDAY ☐
☐ TODAY	☐ TODAY	☐ TODAY	☐ TODAY	☐ TODAY	☐ SUNDAY

17

NOTES AND/OR DOODLES

IT'S GLOBAL GARBAGE MAN DAY

THE JOB HAS A 7 TIMES HIGHER FATALITY RATE THAN FIRE FIGHTING.

VENUS WILLIAMS WAS BORN IN 1980 KENDRICK LAMAR WAS BORN IN 1987

9 AM

10 AM

11 AM

NOON

1 PM

2 PM

3 PM

4 PM

5 PM

6 PM

ON THIS DAY IN 1885: THE STATUE OF LIBERTY ARRIVED IN NEW YORK HARBOR.

YOUR WEEK AT A GLANCE

MONDAY	TUESDAY	WEDNESDAY	THURSDAY	FRIDAY	SATURDAY ☐
☐ TODAY	☐ TODAY	☐ TODAY	☐ TODAY	☐ TODAY	☐ SUNDAY

18

NOTES AND/OR DOODLES

IT'S GO FISHING DAY

THE WORD HALIBUT MEANS 'HOLY FLATFISH.'

PAUL MCCARTNEY WAS BORN IN 1942 BLAKE SHELTON WAS BORN IN 1976

9 AM

10 AM

11 AM

NOON

1 PM

2 PM

3 PM

4 PM

5 PM

6 PM

ON THIS DAY IN 1873: SUSAN B. ANTHONY WAS FINED $100 FOR TRYING TO VOTE.

19

YOUR WEEK AT A GLANCE

MONDAY	TUESDAY	WEDNESDAY	THURSDAY	FRIDAY	SATURDAY ☐
TODAY ☐	TODAY ☐	TODAY ☐	TODAY ☐	TODAY ☐	☐ SUNDAY

IT'S JUNETEENTH

TEXAS WAS THE FIRST STATE TO DECLARE IT A HOLIDAY.

PAULA ABDUL WAS BORN IN 1962

ZOE SALDANA WAS BORN IN 1978

9 AM

10 AM

11 AM

NOON

1 PM

2 PM

3 PM

4 PM

5 PM

6 PM

ON THIS DAY IN 1941: CHEERIE OATS (LATER RENAMED CHEERIOS) WERE INVENTED.

NOTES AND/OR DOODLES

20

YOUR WEEK AT A GLANCE

MONDAY	TUESDAY	WEDNESDAY	THURSDAY	FRIDAY	SATURDAY ☐
TODAY ☐	TODAY ☐	TODAY ☐	TODAY ☐	TODAY ☐	☐ SUNDAY

IT'S AMERICAN EAGLE DAY

IT'S ILLEGAL TO PICK UP A BALD EAGLE FEATHER WITHOUT A PERMIT.

LIONEL RICHIE WAS BORN IN 1949

NICOLE KIDMAN WAS BORN IN 1967

9 AM

10 AM

11 AM

NOON

1 PM

2 PM

3 PM

4 PM

5 PM

6 PM

ON THIS DAY IN 1975: THE MOVIE 'JAWS' OPENED IN THEATERS.

NOTES AND/OR DOODLES

LISTS, NOTES & MEMOIRS

MY PERSONAL PET PEEVES

OR SOME BORING TO-DO LIST

1
2
3
4
5
6
7
8
9
10
11
12

DISEASES I HAVE—ACCORDING TO WEBMD

OR A GROCERY LIST OR SOMETHING

1
2
3
4
5
6
7
8
9
10
11
12

A DRAWING OF AN ACID TRIP (YOU KNOW, IF I HAD TO GUESS)

(OR SOME SUPER BUSINESSY STUFF)

TV THEME SONGS (BEST TO WORST)

OR A MORE USEFUL (BUT STUPID) LIST

1
2
3
4
5
6
7
8
9
10
11
12

EVERYDAY TASKS THAT TERRIFY ME

OR A LIST OF LITERALLY ANYTHING ELSE

1
2
3
4
5
6
7
8
9
10
11
12

21

YOUR WEEK AT A GLANCE

MONDAY	TUESDAY	WEDNESDAY	THURSDAY	FRIDAY	SATURDAY ☐
TODAY ☐	TODAY ☐	TODAY ☐	TODAY ☐	TODAY ☐	☐ SUNDAY

IT'S NATIONAL DAY OF THE GONG

IN CHINA, CHAU GONGS WERE USED TO CLEAR THE WAY FOR OFFICIALS.

CHRIS PRATT WAS BORN IN 1979

PRINCE WILLIAM WAS BORN IN 1982

9 AM

10 AM

11 AM

NOON

1 PM

2 PM

3 PM

4 PM

5 PM

6 PM

ON THIS DAY IN 1939: LOU GEHRIG RETIRED FROM BASEBALL DUE TO ALS.

NOTES AND/OR DOODLES

22

YOUR WEEK AT A GLANCE

MONDAY	TUESDAY	WEDNESDAY	THURSDAY	FRIDAY	SATURDAY ☐
TODAY ☐	TODAY ☐	TODAY ☐	TODAY ☐	TODAY ☐	☐ SUNDAY

IT'S NATIONAL ONION RINGS DAY

EATING PARSLEY WILL HELP ELIMINATE ONION BREATH.

CYNDI LAUPER WAS BORN IN 1953

DONALD FAISON WAS BORN IN 1974

9 AM

10 AM

11 AM

NOON

1 PM

2 PM

3 PM

4 PM

5 PM

6 PM

ON THIS DAY IN 1990: ADAM SANDLER JOINED 'SATURDAY NIGHT LIVE.'

NOTES AND/OR DOODLES

YEAR: **JUNE**

YOUR WEEK AT A GLANCE

MONDAY	TUESDAY	WEDNESDAY	THURSDAY	FRIDAY	SATURDAY ☐
☐ TODAY	☐ TODAY	☐ TODAY	☐ TODAY	☐ TODAY	☐ SUNDAY

23

NOTES AND/OR DOODLES

IT'S NATIONAL HYDRATION DAY

WATER COVERS 70.9 PERCENT OF THE EARTH'S SURFACE.

CLARENCE THOMAS WAS BORN IN 1948

SELMA BLAIR WAS BORN IN 1972

9 AM

10 AM

11 AM

NOON

1 PM

2 PM

3 PM

4 PM

5 PM

6 PM

ON THIS DAY IN 2014: CLAUDE MONET'S 'WATER LILIES' SOLD FOR $54 MILLION.

YOUR WEEK AT A GLANCE

MONDAY	TUESDAY	WEDNESDAY	THURSDAY	FRIDAY	SATURDAY ☐
☐ TODAY	☐ TODAY	☐ TODAY	☐ TODAY	☐ TODAY	☐ SUNDAY

24

NOTES AND/OR DOODLES

IT'S WORLD UFO DAY

THERE ARE SIGHTINGS EVERY 3 MINUTES.

MINDY KALING WAS BORN IN 1979

SOLANGE WAS BORN IN 1986

9 AM

10 AM

11 AM

NOON

1 PM

2 PM

3 PM

4 PM

5 PM

6 PM

ON THIS DAY IN 1992: BILLY JOEL GOT AN HONORARY HIGH SCHOOL DIPLOMA.

LISTS, NOTES & MEMOIRS

FUTURE EXCUSES FOR CANCELING PLANS

OR A LIST OF LITERALLY ANYTHING ELSE

1
2
3
4
5
6
7
8
9
10
11
12

THINGS I NEED TO FINISH EVENTUALLY

OR A MORE USEFUL (BUT STUPID) LIST

1
2
3
4
5
6
7
8
9
10
11
12

A DRAWING OF CARPET MATCHING THE DRAPES

(OR SOME SUPER BUSINESSY STUFF)

THINGS THAT SMELL LIKE CHILDHOOD

OR SOME BORING TO-DO LIST

1
2
3
4
5
6
7
8
9
10
11
12

THINGS THAT TASTE LIKE ADULTHOOD

OR A GROCERY LIST OR SOMETHING

1
2
3
4
5
6
7
8
9
10
11
12

YEAR: **JUNE**

YOUR WEEK AT A GLANCE

MONDAY	TUESDAY	WEDNESDAY	THURSDAY	FRIDAY	SATURDAY ☐
☐ TODAY	☐ TODAY	☐ TODAY	☐ TODAY	☐ TODAY	☐ SUNDAY

25

NOTES AND/OR DOODLES

IT'S NATIONAL CATFISH DAY

THEIR ENTIRE BODIES ARE COVERED WITH OVER 27,000 TASTE BUDS.

RICKY GERVAIS WAS BORN IN 1961

GEORGE MICHAEL WAS BORN IN 1963

9 AM

10 AM

11 AM

NOON

1 PM

2 PM

3 PM

4 PM

5 PM

6 PM

ON THIS DAY IN 1993: THE LAST 'LATE NIGHT W/ DAVID LETTERMAN' AIRED.

YOUR WEEK AT A GLANCE

MONDAY	TUESDAY	WEDNESDAY	THURSDAY	FRIDAY	SATURDAY ☐
☐ TODAY	☐ TODAY	☐ TODAY	☐ TODAY	☐ TODAY	☐ SUNDAY

26

NOTES AND/OR DOODLES

IT'S TROPICAL COCKTAILS DAY

IN POLYNESIAN MYTHOLOGY, A TIKI REPRESENTS THE 1ST HUMAN ON EARTH.

AUBREY PLAZA WAS BORN IN 1984

NICK OFFERMAN WAS BORN IN 1970

9 AM

10 AM

11 AM

NOON

1 PM

2 PM

3 PM

4 PM

5 PM

6 PM

ON THIS DAY IN 2018: THE HELLO KITTY BULLET TRAIN WAS UNVEILED IN JAPAN.

27

YOUR WEEK AT A GLANCE

MONDAY	TUESDAY	WEDNESDAY	THURSDAY	FRIDAY	SATURDAY ☐
TODAY ☐	TODAY ☐	TODAY ☐	TODAY ☐	TODAY ☐	☐ SUNDAY

IT'S NATIONAL BINGO DAY

RUSSEL CROWE'S FIRST JOB WAS AS A BINGO CALLER.

HELEN KELLER WAS BORN IN 1880

VERA WANG WAS BORN IN 1949

9 AM

10 AM

11 AM

NOON

1 PM

2 PM

3 PM

4 PM

5 PM

6 PM

ON THIS DAY IN 1985: ROUTE 66 WAS REMOVED FROM THE U.S. HIGHWAY SYSTEM.

NOTES AND/OR DOODLES

28

YOUR WEEK AT A GLANCE

MONDAY	TUESDAY	WEDNESDAY	THURSDAY	FRIDAY	SATURDAY ☐
TODAY ☐	TODAY ☐	TODAY ☐	TODAY ☐	TODAY ☐	☐ SUNDAY

IT'S NATIONAL TAPIOCA DAY

IT'S PROCESSED FROM THE OTHERWISE POISONOUS CASSAVA ROOT.

(TAPIOCA—THE BADASS OF THE PUDDING WORLD)

ELON MUSK WAS BORN IN 1971

KATHY BATES WAS BORN IN 1948

9 AM

10 AM

11 AM

NOON

1 PM

2 PM

3 PM

4 PM

5 PM

6 PM

ON THIS DAY IN 1894: LABOR DAY BECAME AN OFFICIAL FEDERAL HOLIDAY.

NOTES AND/OR DOODLES

YOUR WEEK AT A GLANCE

MONDAY	TUESDAY	WEDNESDAY	THURSDAY	FRIDAY	SATURDAY ☐
☐ TODAY	☐ TODAY	☐ TODAY	☐ TODAY	☐ TODAY	☐ SUNDAY

29

NOTES AND/OR DOODLES

IT'S NATIONAL CAMERA DAY

THE MOST VIEWED PHOTO IS THE DEFAULT WALLPAPER OF WINDOWS XP.

COLIN JOST WAS BORN IN 1982

MELORA HARDIN WAS BORN IN 1967

9 AM

10 AM

11 AM

NOON

1 PM

2 PM

3 PM

4 PM

5 PM

6 PM

ON THIS DAY IN 1998: THE LIFETIME MOVIE NETWORK MADE ITS DEBUT.

YOUR WEEK AT A GLANCE

MONDAY	TUESDAY	WEDNESDAY	THURSDAY	FRIDAY	SATURDAY ☐
☐ TODAY	☐ TODAY	☐ TODAY	☐ TODAY	☐ TODAY	☐ SUNDAY

30

NOTES AND/OR DOODLES

IT'S INTERNATIONAL ASTEROID DAY

THERE ARE CURRENTLY OVER 822,000 KNOWN ASTEROIDS.

MIKE TYSON WAS BORN IN 1966

MICHAEL PHELPS WAS BORN IN 1985

9 AM

10 AM

11 AM

NOON

1 PM

2 PM

3 PM

4 PM

5 PM

6 PM

ON THIS DAY IN 1936: THE BOOK 'GONE WITH THE WIND' WAS 1ST PUBLISHED.

JUNE IN REVIEW

REASONS THAT JUNE WAS GREAT

'IT ENDED' IS A VALID ANSWER

1
2
3
4
5
6
7
8
9
10
11
12

MY JUNE ACCOMPLISHMENTS

- GOT SICK OF SUMMER BEFORE IT STARTED ☐
- PURCHASED CAMPING EQUIPMENT ☐
- GOT BUG SPRAY IN MY MOUTH ☐
- PERSPIRED AN ABOVE AVERAGE AMOUNT ☐
- REALIZED THAT CAMPING IS AWFUL ☐
- REMEMBERED FATHER'S DAY ☐
- TOOK HIM OUT TO A NICE DINNER ☐
- GOT INTO A FIGHT ABOUT POLITICS ☐
- FINALLY WENT TO A BASEBALL GAME ☐
- SPENT FIVE MINUTES IN DIRECT SUN ☐
- WENT BACK OUT TO THE PARKING LOT ☐
- CELEBRATED FLAGS EXISTING ☐
- WORE SANDALS IN PUBLIC ☐
- SPENT ALL DAY EVALUATING TOES ☐
- PUT SANDALS IN STORAGE ☐

IF JUNE WAS AN ANIMAL, DRAW ITS NATURAL HABITAT

CLICHÉS OVERHEARD THIS MONTH

- ☐ 'LOOKS LIKE SOMEBODY GOT SOME SUN'
- ☐ '10 DOLLARS FOR A HOT DOG?'
- ☐ 'THAT'S HIGHWAY ROBBERY'
- ☐ 'GLAMPING'
- ☐ 'UH NO THANKS, I'LL JUST HOLD IT'
- ☐ 'MAN CAVE'
- ☐ 'IT'S SUPPOSED TO BE A LITTLE BURNT'
- ☐ 'WE'LL JUST TAKE THE SCENIC ROUTE'
- ☐ 'OPE, THERE'S A WALL THERE'
- ☐ 'IT'S JUST AWKWARD TO CARRY'
- ☐ 'BEER? OKAY YA TALKED ME INTO IT'
- ☐ 'GUILTY AS CHARGED'
- ☐ 'I'M A SOCIAL MEDIA INFLUENCER'
- ☐ 'YOU'VE NEVER BEEN ON A FLOAT TRIP?'
- ☐ 'WHAT'S THE DAMAGE?'
- ☐ 'WE SURE COULD USE SOME RAIN'
- ☐ 'I'M LITERALLY OBSESSED'

REASONS THAT I'M GLAD JUNE IS OVER

USE ADDITIONAL PAPER IF NEEDED

1
2
3
4
5
6
7
8
9
10
11
12
13
14

JUNE IN REVIEW

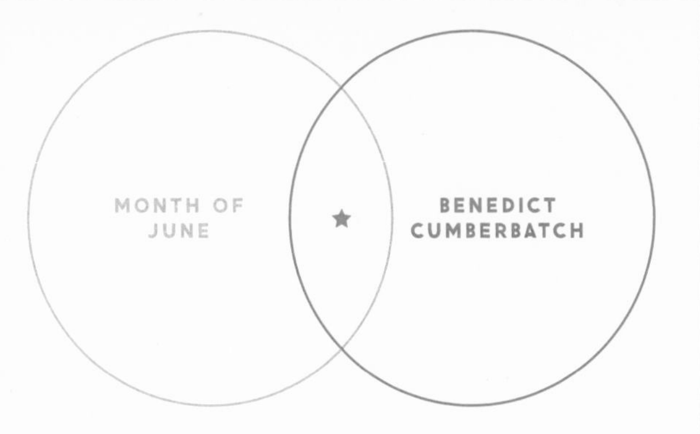

A JUNE VENN DIAGRAM

WHAT DID THEY HAVE IN COMMON?

1. UNEXPECTEDLY HOT
2.
3.
4.
5.
6.
7.
8.

AWKWARD THINGS THAT HAPPENED

(AND WILL KEEP ME UP AT NIGHT)

1.
2.
3.
4.
5.
6.
7.
8.
9.
10.
11.
12.
13.
14.
15.
16.
17.

ENJOYMENT OVER TIME

CHOOSE A COLOR KEY

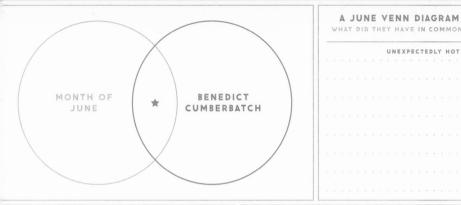

LINE	ITEM
——	THE CONCEPT OF SUMMER
— —	APPLYING SUNSCREEN
	IDEA OF CONVERTIBLES
	ACTUALLY BEING IN ONE
	WATCHING BASEBALL
	EATING NEAR BASEBALL
	SCHOOL BEING OUT
	PEOPLE YOUNGER THAN 12
	AIR CONDITIONING
	WEARING SWEATERS INSIDE

JUNE ENJOYMENT INDEX

ORIGINALLY KNOWN AS QUINTILIS (MEANING FIFTH MONTH).

WELCOME TO

OF WHATEVER YEAR
YOU SAY IT IS.

LET'S GO WITH:

. . . .

. . . .

. . . .

RENAMED TO HONOR THE ROMAN EMPEROR JULIUS CAESAR (AFTER HIS DEATH).

JULY AT A GLANCE

:YEAR

YOU MADE IT

TO JULY

×

CELEBRATE, IT'S:

NATIONAL HEMP MONTH

WORLD WATERCOLOR MONTH

NATIONAL HORSERADISH MONTH

INDEPENDENT RETAILER MONTH

NATIONAL ICE CREAM MONTH

×

OFFICIAL SYMBOLS:

BIRTHSTONE: RUBY

FLOWERS: LARKSPUR & WATER LILY

TREES: APPLE, FIR, & CYPRESS

CANCER (JUN 21 / JUL 22)

LEO (JUL 23 / AUG 22)

DATES TO KNOW*

LIKE, IMPORTANT ONES

×

CANADA DAY
JULY 1ST

INDEPENDENCE DAY
JULY 4TH

WORLD POPULATION DAY
JULY 11TH

BASTILLE DAY
JULY 14TH

NELSON MANDELA INTERNATIONAL DAY
JULY 18TH

ASALHA PUJA
(BUDDHISM)
ON THE FULL MOON DAY
OF THE 8TH LUNAR MONTH
(USUALLY IN JULY)

THE BIRTHDAY OF HAILE SELASSIE I
(RASTAFARIANISM)
JULY 23RD

PIONEER DAY
(MORMONISM)
JULY 24TH

THINGS TO ACCOMPLISH THIS MONTH

FOR EXAMPLE: FILL OUT A TO-DO LIST

1
2
3
4
5
6
7
8
9
10
11
12
13
14
15

THINGS THAT ARE NEVER GOING TO HAPPEN

THERE'S ALWAYS AUGUST (OR SEPTEMBER)

1
2
3
4
5
6
7
8
9
10
11
12
13
14
15

*A DISCLAIMER OF SORTS

HEY THERE. WE HERE AT BRASS MONKEY LIKE TO JOKE AROUND...BUT WE ALSO WANT TO TAKE A MINUTE TO RECOGNIZE JUST A FEW OF THE MANY HOLIDAYS & EVENTS THAT ARE IMPORTANT TO OUR FRIENDS AROUND THE GLOBE (AND AT HOME). YOU MAY BE DIFFERENT THAN US. WE MAY HAVE NEVER MET. BUT WE LOVE YOU ALL THE SAME.

SO IF YOU HAVEN'T HEARD OF A DAY, LOOK IT UP. LEARNING ABOUT & APPRECIATING CULTURES DIFFERENT THAN YOURS IS IMPORTANT...WAY MORE THAN POSTING A FEW 'STRAWBERRY JAM DAY' SELFIES.

JULY AT A GLANCE

YEAR:

IT'S JULY

START PLANNING

×

INDEPENDENCE DAY

JULY 4TH

CANADA DAY*

JULY 1ST (WAVING TO THE NORTH)

BASTILLE DAY*

JULY 14TH (WAVING TO THE EAST)

×

BIRTHDAYS

TO REMEMBER

*PSST: SINCE THIS HOLIDAY ISN'T EXACTLY FROM THE U.S. WE HAVEN'T ADDED IT INTO THIS CALENDAR YET—TO AVOID ANY CONFUSION. SO HELP US OUT AND ADD IT WHEN YOU GET A CHANCE.

YOU SHOULD TRY IT. IT'S FUN.

DAY OF WEEK S M T W T F S	DAY OF WEEK S M T W T F S	DAY OF WEEK S M T W T F S	DAY OF WEEK S M T W T F S	DAY OF WEEK S M T W T F S	DAY OF WEEK S M T W T F S	DAY OF WEEK S M T W T F S
01	02	03	INDEPENDENCE DAY 04	05	06	07
08	09	10	11	12	13	14
15	16	17	18	19	20	21
22	23	24	25	26	27	28
29	30	31	NOTES:			

JULY, AS EXPRESSED IN A DRAWING

JULY PREVIEW

A JULY VENN DIAGRAM

WHAT DO THEY HAVE IN COMMON?

1 A SIGN THINGS ARE HALF OVER
2
3
4
5
6
7
8

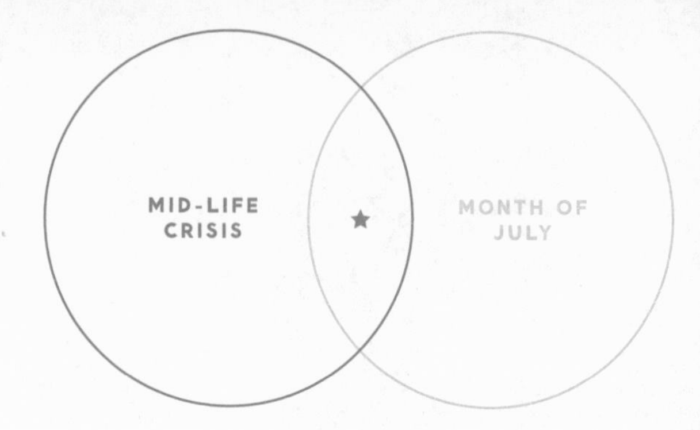

A DRAWING OF THE FIFTH OF JULY

SUPPLIES NEEDED FOR THE MONTH

ALCOHOL, AND OTHER NECESSITIES

1
2
3
4
5
6
7
8
9
10
11
12
13
14
15
16
17

JULY ENJOYMENT INDEX

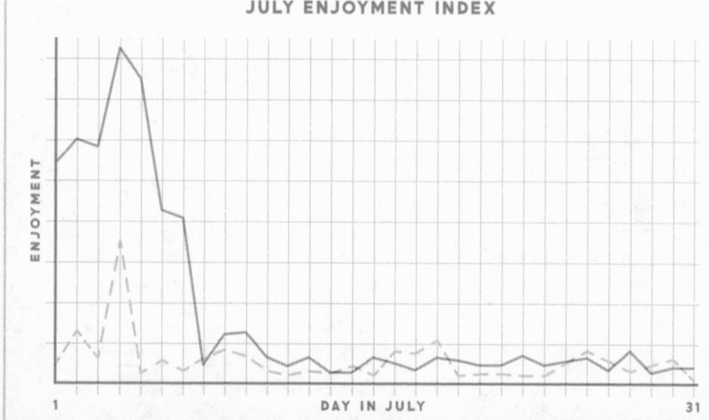

ENJOYMENT OVER TIME

CHOOSE A COLOR KEY

LINE	ITEM
——	EXPLOSIONS IN THE SKY
— —	GUNSHOT-LIKE SOUNDS
	BUYING MEAT IN BULK
	EATING OUTSIDE
	RED, WHITE & BLUE FOODS
	AMERICAN BEERS
	IMPORT BEERS
	'FREEDOM' AS A PREFIX
	100° TEMPERATURES
	SEVERE SUNBURNS

YEAR: **JULY**

YOUR WEEK AT A GLANCE

MONDAY	TUESDAY	WEDNESDAY	THURSDAY	FRIDAY	SATURDAY ☐
☐ TODAY	☐ TODAY	☐ TODAY	☐ TODAY	☐ TODAY	☐ SUNDAY

01

NOTES AND/OR DOODLES

IT'S EARLY BIRD DAY

SURE, THEY GET THE WORMS...BUT WORMS ARE KINDA GROSS ANYWAY.

DIANA SPENCER WAS BORN IN 1961

MISSY ELLIOTT WAS BORN IN 1971

9 AM

10 AM

11 AM

NOON

1 PM

2 PM

3 PM

4 PM

5 PM

6 PM

ON THIS DAY IN 1941: THE 1ST TV COMMERCIAL AIRED. IT WAS FOR WATCHES.

YOUR WEEK AT A GLANCE

MONDAY	TUESDAY	WEDNESDAY	THURSDAY	FRIDAY	SATURDAY ☐
☐ TODAY	☐ TODAY	☐ TODAY	☐ TODAY	☐ TODAY	☐ SUNDAY

02

NOTES AND/OR DOODLES

IT'S I FORGOT DAY

MOST CAN HOLD 7 ITEMS IN SHORT-TERM MEMORY FOR 20-30 SECONDS.

MARGOT ROBBIE WAS BORN IN 1990

MEDGAR EVERS WAS BORN IN 1925

9 AM

10 AM

11 AM

NOON

1 PM

2 PM

3 PM

4 PM

5 PM

6 PM

ON THIS DAY IN 1962: THE 1ST WAL-MART STORE OPENED IN ROGERS, ARKANSAS.

03

YOUR WEEK AT A GLANCE

MONDAY	TUESDAY	WEDNESDAY	THURSDAY	FRIDAY	SATURDAY ☐
TODAY ☐	TODAY ☐	TODAY ☐	TODAY ☐	TODAY ☐	☐ SUNDAY

IT'S DISOBEDIENCE DAY

BUT WE REFUSE TO PARTICIPATE.

TOM CRUISE WAS BORN IN 1962

CONNIE NIELSEN WAS BORN IN 1965

9 AM

10 AM

11 AM

NOON

1 PM

2 PM

3 PM

4 PM

5 PM

6 PM

ON THIS DAY IN 1985: 'BACK TO THE FUTURE' IS RELEASED.

NOTES AND/OR DOODLES

04

YOUR WEEK AT A GLANCE

MONDAY	TUESDAY	WEDNESDAY	THURSDAY	FRIDAY	SATURDAY ☐
TODAY ☐	TODAY ☐	TODAY ☐	TODAY ☐	TODAY ☐	☐ SUNDAY

IT'S INDEPENDENCE DAY

OH, AND IT'S ALSO NATIONAL BARBECUE DAY.

POST MALONE WAS BORN IN 1995

MALIA OBAMA WAS BORN IN 1998

9 AM

10 AM

11 AM

NOON

1 PM

2 PM

3 PM

4 PM

5 PM

6 PM

ON THIS DAY IN 1971: KOKO THE GORILLA WAS BORN AT THE SAN FRANCISCO ZOO.

NOTES AND/OR DOODLES

YEAR: **JULY**

YOUR WEEK AT A GLANCE

MONDAY	TUESDAY	WEDNESDAY	THURSDAY	FRIDAY	SATURDAY ☐
☐ TODAY	☐ TODAY	☐ TODAY	☐ TODAY	☐ TODAY	☐ SUNDAY

05

NOTES AND/OR DOODLES

IT'S NATIONAL WORKAHOLICS DAY

THIS ONE IS HITTING A LITTLE TOO CLOSE TO HOME RIGHT NOW.

(BUT...GREAT PLANNER RIGHT?)

MEGAN RAPINOE WAS BORN IN 1985 SUSAN WOJCICKI WAS BORN IN 1968

9 AM

10 AM

11 AM

NOON

1 PM

2 PM

3 PM

4 PM

5 PM

6 PM

ON THIS DAY IN 1996: DOLLY THE SHEEP (THE 1ST CLONED MAMMAL) WAS BORN.

YOUR WEEK AT A GLANCE

MONDAY	TUESDAY	WEDNESDAY	THURSDAY	FRIDAY	SATURDAY ☐
☐ TODAY	☐ TODAY	☐ TODAY	☐ TODAY	☐ TODAY	☐ SUNDAY

06

NOTES AND/OR DOODLES

IT'S INTERNATIONAL KISSING DAY

TWO-THIRDS OF PEOPLE TILT THEIR HEADS TO THE RIGHT TO KISS.

FRIDA KAHLO WAS BORN IN 1907 KEVIN HART WAS BORN IN 1979

9 AM

10 AM

11 AM

NOON

1 PM

2 PM

3 PM

4 PM

5 PM

6 PM

ON THIS DAY IN 1957: JOHN LENNON & PAUL MCCARTNEY MET FOR THE 1ST TIME.

07

YOUR WEEK AT A GLANCE

MONDAY	TUESDAY	WEDNESDAY	THURSDAY	FRIDAY	SATURDAY ☐
TODAY ☐	TODAY ☐	TODAY ☐	TODAY ☐	TODAY ☐	☐ SUNDAY

IT'S NATIONAL DIVE BAR DAY

THE GUTTER, IN BROOKLYN, NY, IS A FAVORITE OF OURS.

MICHELLE KWAN WAS BORN IN 1980

JACK WHITEHALL WAS BORN IN 1988

9 AM

10 AM

11 AM

NOON

1 PM

2 PM

3 PM

4 PM

5 PM

6 PM

ON THIS DAY IN 1947: POSSIBLE UFO DEBRIS WAS REPORTED IN ROSWELL, NM.

NOTES AND/OR DOODLES

08

YOUR WEEK AT A GLANCE

MONDAY	TUESDAY	WEDNESDAY	THURSDAY	FRIDAY	SATURDAY ☐
TODAY ☐	TODAY ☐	TODAY ☐	TODAY ☐	TODAY ☐	☐ SUNDAY

IT'S BE A KID AGAIN DAY

MAYBE PUT SOME PLAY-DOH IN THE CARPET—REALLY RUB IT IN THERE.

KEVIN BACON WAS BORN IN 1958

ANJELICA HUSTON WAS BORN IN 1951

9 AM

10 AM

11 AM

NOON

1 PM

2 PM

3 PM

4 PM

5 PM

6 PM

ON THIS DAY IN 1889: 'THE WALL STREET JOURNAL' WAS 1ST PUBLISHED.

NOTES AND/OR DOODLES

LISTS, NOTES & MEMOIRS

THINGS I LEARNED FROM MY PARENTS

OR SOME BORING TO-DO LIST

1
2
3
4
5
6
7
8
9
10
11
12

THINGS I LEARNED FROM TELEVISION

OR A GROCERY LIST OR SOMETHING

1
2
3
4
5
6
7
8
9
10
11
12

A DRAWING OF MY TOMBSTONE

(OR SOME SUPER BUSINESSY STUFF)

WORST COMPLIMENTS I'VE RECEIVED

OR A MORE USEFUL (BUT STUPID) LIST

1
2
3
4
5
6
7
8
9
10
11
12

RAD WORDS NO ONE USES ANYMORE

OR A LIST OF LITERALLY ANYTHING ELSE

1
2
3
4
5
6
7
8
9
10
11
12

09

YOUR WEEK AT A GLANCE

MONDAY	TUESDAY	WEDNESDAY	THURSDAY	FRIDAY	SATURDAY ☐
TODAY ☐	TODAY ☐	TODAY ☐	TODAY ☐	TODAY ☐	☐ SUNDAY

IT'S NATIONAL NO BRA DAY

ON MOST WOMEN, THE LEFT BREAST IS SLIGHTLY LARGER.

FRED SAVAGE WAS BORN IN 1976

TOM HANKS WAS BORN IN 1956

9 AM

10 AM

11 AM

NOON

1 PM

2 PM

3 PM

4 PM

5 PM

6 PM

ON THIS DAY IN 1981: DONKEY KONG WAS CREATED BY NINTENDO.

NOTES AND/OR DOODLES

10

YOUR WEEK AT A GLANCE

MONDAY	TUESDAY	WEDNESDAY	THURSDAY	FRIDAY	SATURDAY ☐
TODAY ☐	TODAY ☐	TODAY ☐	TODAY ☐	TODAY ☐	☐ SUNDAY

IT'S DON'T STEP ON A BEE DAY

HONESTLY THOUGH, WHO IS OUT THERE TRYING TO STEP ON BEES?

ARTHUR ASHE WAS BORN IN 1943

SOFÍA VERGARA WAS BORN IN 1972

9 AM

10 AM

11 AM

NOON

1 PM

2 PM

3 PM

4 PM

5 PM

6 PM

ON THIS DAY IN 1999: THE U.S. WOMEN'S SOCCER TEAM WON THE WORLD CUP.

NOTES AND/OR DOODLES

YEAR: JULY

YOUR WEEK AT A GLANCE

MONDAY	TUESDAY	WEDNESDAY	THURSDAY	FRIDAY	SATURDAY ☐ / ☐ SUNDAY
☐ TODAY	☐ TODAY	☐ TODAY	☐ TODAY	☐ TODAY	

11

NOTES AND/OR DOODLES

IT'S NATIONAL MOJITO DAY

A FAVORITE DRINK (AMONG MANY) OF ERNEST HEMINGWAY.

JUSTIN CHAMBERS WAS BORN IN 1970

LISA RINNA WAS BORN IN 1963

9 AM

10 AM

11 AM

NOON

1 PM

2 PM

3 PM

4 PM

5 PM

6 PM

ON THIS DAY IN 1960: 'TO KILL A MOCKINGBIRD' WAS FIRST PUBLISHED.

YOUR WEEK AT A GLANCE

MONDAY	TUESDAY	WEDNESDAY	THURSDAY	FRIDAY	SATURDAY ☐ / ☐ SUNDAY
☐ TODAY	☐ TODAY	☐ TODAY	☐ TODAY	☐ TODAY	

12

NOTES AND/OR DOODLES

IT'S ETCH A SKETCH DAY

THE FIRST PROTOTYPE HAD A JOYSTICK.

MALALA YOUSAFZAI WAS BORN IN 1997

RICHARD SIMMONS WAS BORN IN 1948

9 AM

10 AM

11 AM

NOON

1 PM

2 PM

3 PM

4 PM

5 PM

6 PM

ON THIS DAY IN 1962: THE ROLLING STONES PERFORMED THEIR FIRST CONCERT.

LISTS, NOTES & MEMOIRS

PERFECT SECOND JOBS FOR CELEBRITIES

OR A LIST OF LITERALLY ANYTHING ELSE

1
2
3
4
5
6
7
8
9
10
11
12

THINGS THAT SHOULDN'T BE TAXIDERMIED

OR A MORE USEFUL (BUT STUPID) LIST

1
2
3
4
5
6
7
8
9
10
11
12

A DRAWING OF THE ELEPHANT IN THE ROOM

(OR SOME SUPER BUSINESSY STUFF)

SONGS THAT I'M EMBARRASSED TO LIKE

OR SOME BORING TO-DO LIST

1
2
3
4
5
6
7
8
9
10
11
12

LIKELY FOOD ALLERGIES THAT I IGNORE

OR A GROCERY LIST OR SOMETHING

1
2
3
4
5
6
7
8
9
10
11
12

YEAR: **JULY**

YOUR WEEK AT A GLANCE

MONDAY	TUESDAY	WEDNESDAY	THURSDAY	FRIDAY	SATURDAY ☐
☐ TODAY	☐ TODAY	☐ TODAY	☐ TODAY	☐ TODAY	☐ SUNDAY

13

NOTES AND/OR DOODLES

IT'S NATIONAL FRENCH FRY DAY

THOMAS JEFFERSON INTRODUCED THEM TO AMERICA.

KEN JEONG WAS BORN IN 1969 LEON BRIDGES WAS BORN IN 1989

9 AM
10 AM
11 AM
NOON
1 PM
2 PM
3 PM
4 PM
5 PM
6 PM

ON THIS DAY IN 1977: A MASSIVE BLACKOUT ENGULFED NYC FOR 25 HRS.

YOUR WEEK AT A GLANCE

MONDAY	TUESDAY	WEDNESDAY	THURSDAY	FRIDAY	SATURDAY ☐
☐ TODAY	☐ TODAY	☐ TODAY	☐ TODAY	☐ TODAY	☐ SUNDAY

14

NOTES AND/OR DOODLES

IT'S NATIONAL MAC AND CHEESE DAY

PRO-TIP: IT PAIRS NICELY WITH CHARDONNAY.

CONOR MCGREGOR WAS BORN IN 1988 JANE LYNCH WAS BORN IN 1960

9 AM
10 AM
11 AM
NOON
1 PM
2 PM
3 PM
4 PM
5 PM
6 PM

ON THIS DAY IN 1938: HOWARD HUGHES COMPLETED A FLIGHT AROUND THE WORLD.

15

YOUR WEEK AT A GLANCE

MONDAY	TUESDAY	WEDNESDAY	THURSDAY	FRIDAY	SATURDAY ☐
TODAY ☐	TODAY ☐	TODAY ☐	TODAY ☐	TODAY ☐	☐ SUNDAY

IT'S NATIONAL BE A DORK DAY

PEDIG EDHELLEN? YEAH, YOU QUALIFY.

FOREST WHITAKER WAS BORN IN 1961 GABRIEL IGLESIAS WAS BORN IN 1976

9 AM

10 AM

11 AM

NOON

1 PM

2 PM

3 PM

4 PM

5 PM

6 PM

ON THIS DAY IN 1997: GIANNI VERSACE WAS MURDERED.

NOTES AND/OR DOODLES

16

YOUR WEEK AT A GLANCE

MONDAY	TUESDAY	WEDNESDAY	THURSDAY	FRIDAY	SATURDAY ☐
TODAY ☐	TODAY ☐	TODAY ☐	TODAY ☐	TODAY ☐	☐ SUNDAY

IT'S NATIONAL CORN FRITTER DAY

CORN COBS ALWAYS HAVE AN EVEN NUMBER OF ROWS.

IDA B. WELLS WAS BORN IN 1862 WILL FERRELL WAS BORN IN 1967

9 AM

10 AM

11 AM

NOON

1 PM

2 PM

3 PM

4 PM

5 PM

6 PM

ON THIS DAY IN 1969: APOLLO 11 LAUNCHED FROM CAPE KENNEDY.

NOTES AND/OR DOODLES

YEAR: JULY

YOUR WEEK AT A GLANCE

MONDAY	TUESDAY	WEDNESDAY	THURSDAY	FRIDAY	SATURDAY ☐
☐ TODAY	☐ TODAY	☐ TODAY	☐ TODAY	☐ TODAY	☐ SUNDAY

17

NOTES AND/OR DOODLES

IT'S NATIONAL TATTOO DAY

THE FIRST ELECTRIC TATTOO MACHINE WAS INVENTED IN 1891.

DAVID HASSELHOFF WAS BORN IN 1952

DIAHANN CARROLL WAS BORN IN 1935

9 AM

10 AM

11 AM

NOON

1 PM

2 PM

3 PM

4 PM

5 PM

6 PM

ON THIS DAY IN 1984: THE LEGAL U.S. DRINKING AGE WAS INCREASED TO 21.

YOUR WEEK AT A GLANCE

MONDAY	TUESDAY	WEDNESDAY	THURSDAY	FRIDAY	SATURDAY ☐
☐ TODAY	☐ TODAY	☐ TODAY	☐ TODAY	☐ TODAY	☐ SUNDAY

18

NOTES AND/OR DOODLES

IT'S NATIONAL SOUR CANDY DAY

'WORLD GONE SOUR' BY METHOD MAN WAS MADE FOR SOUR PATCH KIDS.

NELSON MANDELA WAS BORN IN 1918

KRISTIN BELL WAS BORN IN 1980

9 AM

10 AM

11 AM

NOON

1 PM

2 PM

3 PM

4 PM

5 PM

6 PM

ON THIS DAY IN 1992: THE FIRST PHOTO WAS POSTED TO THE WORLD WIDE WEB.

19

YOUR WEEK AT A GLANCE

MONDAY	TUESDAY	WEDNESDAY	THURSDAY	FRIDAY	SATURDAY ☐
TODAY ☐	TODAY ☐	TODAY ☐	TODAY ☐	TODAY ☐	☐ SUNDAY

IT'S STICK OUT YOUR TONGUE DAY

THE AVERAGE HUMAN TONGUE IS ABOUT 3 INCHES LONG.

BENEDICT CUMBERBATCH WAS BORN IN 1976 BRIAN MAY WAS BORN IN 1947

9 AM
10 AM
11 AM
NOON
1 PM
2 PM
3 PM
4 PM
5 PM
6 PM

ON THIS DAY IN 1995: 'THE ROAD RULES' MADE ITS DEBUT ON MTV.

NOTES AND/OR DOODLES

20

YOUR WEEK AT A GLANCE

MONDAY	TUESDAY	WEDNESDAY	THURSDAY	FRIDAY	SATURDAY ☐
TODAY ☐	TODAY ☐	TODAY ☐	TODAY ☐	TODAY ☐	☐ SUNDAY

IT'S NAP DAY

THERE'S AN ANNUAL NAPPING COMPETITION HELD IN MADRID.

CARLOS SANTANA WAS BORN IN 1947 SANDRA OH WAS BORN IN 1971

9 AM
10 AM
11 AM
NOON
1 PM
2 PM
3 PM
4 PM
5 PM
6 PM

ON THIS DAY IN 1969: NEIL ARMSTRONG 1ST WALKED ON THE MOON.

NOTES AND/OR DOODLES

LISTS, NOTES & MEMOIRS

ONE SENTENCE HORROR STORIES

OR SOME BORING TO-DO LIST

1
2
3
4
5
6
7
8
9
10
11
12

THE WORST MEALS I'VE EVER COOKED

OR A GROCERY LIST OR SOMETHING

1
2
3
4
5
6
7
8
9
10
11
12

A DRAWING OF A DESERT ISLAND (OR A DESSERT ISLAND)

(OR SOME SUPER BUSINESSY STUFF)

TORTURES BETTER THAN THE DENTIST

OR A MORE USEFUL (BUT STUPID) LIST

1
2
3
4
5
6
7
8
9
10
11
12

ORGANS THAT I PROBABLY DON'T NEED

OR A LIST OF LITERALLY ANYTHING ELSE

1
2
3
4
5
6
7
8
9
10
11
12

21

YOUR WEEK AT A GLANCE

MONDAY	TUESDAY	WEDNESDAY	THURSDAY	FRIDAY	SATURDAY ☐
TODAY ☐	TODAY ☐	TODAY ☐	TODAY ☐	TODAY ☐	☐ SUNDAY

IT'S NATIONAL JUNK FOOD DAY

AMERICANS EAT OVER 4 LBS OF POTATO CHIPS A YEAR.

ERNEST HEMINGWAY WAS BORN IN 1899

ROBIN WILLIAMS WAS BORN IN 1951

9 AM

10 AM

11 AM

NOON

1 PM

2 PM

3 PM

4 PM

5 PM

6 PM

ON THIS DAY IN 1925: JOHN SCOPES WAS FINED $100 FOR TEACHING EVOLUTION.

NOTES AND/OR DOODLES

22

YOUR WEEK AT A GLANCE

MONDAY	TUESDAY	WEDNESDAY	THURSDAY	FRIDAY	SATURDAY ☐
TODAY ☐	TODAY ☐	TODAY ☐	TODAY ☐	TODAY ☐	☐ SUNDAY

IT'S NATIONAL HOT DOG DAY

HOT DOGS WERE ONE OF THE FIRST FOODS EATEN ON THE MOON.

SELENA GOMEZ WAS BORN IN 1992

ALEX TREBEK WAS BORN IN 1940

9 AM

10 AM

11 AM

NOON

1 PM

2 PM

3 PM

4 PM

5 PM

6 PM

ON THIS DAY IN 1991: JEFFREY DAHMER WAS ARRESTED IN MILWAUKEE.

NOTES AND/OR DOODLES

YEAR: **JULY**

YOUR WEEK AT A GLANCE

MONDAY	TUESDAY	WEDNESDAY	THURSDAY	FRIDAY	SATURDAY ☐
☐ TODAY	☐ TODAY	☐ TODAY	☐ TODAY	☐ TODAY	☐ SUNDAY

23

NOTES AND/OR DOODLES

IT'S PEANUT BUTTER AND CHOCOLATE DAY

OVER 25,600 PEOPLE IN THE UNITED STATES ARE NAMED REECE.

MONICA LEWINSKY WAS BORN IN 1973

WOODY HARRELSON WAS BORN IN 1961

9 AM

10 AM

11 AM

NOON

1 PM

2 PM

3 PM

4 PM

5 PM

6 PM

ON THIS DAY IN 2011: AMY WINEHOUSE WAS FOUND DEAD IN HER APARTMENT.

YOUR WEEK AT A GLANCE

MONDAY	TUESDAY	WEDNESDAY	THURSDAY	FRIDAY	SATURDAY ☐
☐ TODAY	☐ TODAY	☐ TODAY	☐ TODAY	☐ TODAY	☐ SUNDAY

24

NOTES AND/OR DOODLES

IT'S NATIONAL TEQUILA DAY

A TRUE TEQUILA DOESN'T CONTAIN A WORM. IT'S ONLY IN MEZCAL.

AMELIA EARHART WAS BORN IN 1897

JENNIFER LOPEZ WAS BORN IN 1969

9 AM

10 AM

11 AM

NOON

1 PM

2 PM

3 PM

4 PM

5 PM

6 PM

ON THIS DAY IN 1969: APOLLO 11 SAFELY RETURNS TO EARTH.

LISTS, NOTES & MEMOIRS

TIMES THAT I ALMOST DIED

OR A LIST OF LITERALLY ANYTHING ELSE

1
2
3
4
5
6
7
8
9
10
11
12

POTENTIAL TITLES FOR MY MEMOIR

OR A MORE USEFUL (BUT STUPID) LIST

1
2
3
4
5
6
7
8
9
10
11
12

A DRAWING OF THE NEXT HIPSTER TREND

(OR SOME SUPER BUSINESSY STUFF)

WAYS TO LOOK BUSY IN MEETINGS

OR SOME BORING TO-DO LIST

1
2
3
4
5
6
7
8
9
10
11
12

ANIMALS THAT I MOST RELATE WITH

OR A GROCERY LIST OR SOMETHING

1
2
3
4
5
6
7
8
9
10
11
12

YEAR: **JULY**

YOUR WEEK AT A GLANCE

MONDAY	TUESDAY	WEDNESDAY	THURSDAY	FRIDAY	SATURDAY ☐ / ☐ SUNDAY
☐ TODAY	☐ TODAY	☐ TODAY	☐ TODAY	☐ TODAY	

25

NOTES AND/OR DOODLES

IT'S NATIONAL WINE AND CHEESE DAY

WE'VE ALREADY SCHEDULED OUR PTO.

IMAN WAS BORN IN 1955

WALTER PAYTON WAS BORN IN 1954

9 AM

10 AM

11 AM

NOON

1 PM

2 PM

3 PM

4 PM

5 PM

6 PM

ON THIS DAY IN 1978: LOUISE BROWN (THE WORLD'S 1ST IVF BABY) WAS BORN.

YOUR WEEK AT A GLANCE

MONDAY	TUESDAY	WEDNESDAY	THURSDAY	FRIDAY	SATURDAY ☐ / ☐ SUNDAY
☐ TODAY	☐ TODAY	☐ TODAY	☐ TODAY	☐ TODAY	

26

NOTES AND/OR DOODLES

IT'S COFFEE MILKSHAKE DAY

AND SUDDENLY, YOU HAVE AN EXCUSE TO BUY A COFFEE MILKSHAKE.

(YOU KNOW, POSTMATES IS A THING: 1107 HICKORY ST. KANSAS CITY, MO 64101)

HELEN MIRREN WAS BORN IN 1945

SANDRA BULLOCK WAS BORN IN 1964

9 AM

10 AM

11 AM

NOON

1 PM

2 PM

3 PM

4 PM

5 PM

6 PM

ON THIS DAY IN 1991: PAUL RUEBENS IS ARRESTED FOR EXPOSING HIMSELF.

27

YOUR WEEK AT A GLANCE

MONDAY	TUESDAY	WEDNESDAY	THURSDAY	FRIDAY	SATURDAY ☐
TODAY ☐	TODAY ☐	TODAY ☐	TODAY ☐	TODAY ☐	☐ SUNDAY

IT'S WALK ON STILTS DAY

BELGIUM HAS HELD STILT JOUSTING TOURNAMENTS FOR 600+ YEARS.

WINNIE HARLOW WAS BORN IN 1994

MAYA RUDOLPH WAS BORN IN 1972

9 AM

10 AM

11 AM

NOON

1 PM

2 PM

3 PM

4 PM

5 PM

6 PM

ON THIS DAY IN 2012: QUEEN ELIZABETH II OPENED THE LONDON OLYMPICS.

NOTES AND/OR DOODLES

28

YOUR WEEK AT A GLANCE

MONDAY	TUESDAY	WEDNESDAY	THURSDAY	FRIDAY	SATURDAY ☐
TODAY ☐	TODAY ☐	TODAY ☐	TODAY ☐	TODAY ☐	☐ SUNDAY

IT'S NATIONAL WATERPARK DAY

THERE'S AN ABANDONED WATER PARK HIDDEN INSIDE OF DISNEY WORLD.

SOULJA BOY WAS BORN IN 1990

SALLY STRUTHERS WAS BORN IN 1947

9 AM

10 AM

11 AM

NOON

1 PM

2 PM

3 PM

4 PM

5 PM

6 PM

ON THIS DAY IN 1933: THE FIRST SINGING TELEGRAM WAS DELIVERED.

NOTES AND/OR DOODLES

YEAR: **JULY**

YOUR WEEK AT A GLANCE

MONDAY	TUESDAY	WEDNESDAY	THURSDAY	FRIDAY	SATURDAY ☐
☐ TODAY	☐ TODAY	☐ TODAY	☐ TODAY	☐ TODAY	☐ SUNDAY

29

NOTES AND/OR DOODLES

IT'S NATIONAL LASAGNA DAY

TIME TO DUST OFF WEIRD AL'S PARODY OF 'LA BAMBA.'

GEDDY LEE WAS BORN IN 1953

PETER JENNINGS WAS BORN IN 1938

9 AM

10 AM

11 AM

NOON

1 PM

2 PM

3 PM

4 PM

5 PM

6 PM

ON THIS DAY IN 1981: PRINCE CHARLES MARRIED LADY DIANA.

YOUR WEEK AT A GLANCE

MONDAY	TUESDAY	WEDNESDAY	THURSDAY	FRIDAY	SATURDAY ☐
☐ TODAY	☐ TODAY	☐ TODAY	☐ TODAY	☐ TODAY	☐ SUNDAY

30

NOTES AND/OR DOODLES

IT'S NATIONAL CHILI DOG DAY

MICKEY MOUSE'S FIRST ON SCREEN WORDS WERE 'HOT DOGS.'

LISA KUDROW WAS BORN IN 1963

TERRY CREWS WAS BORN IN 1968

9 AM

10 AM

11 AM

NOON

1 PM

2 PM

3 PM

4 PM

5 PM

6 PM

ON THIS DAY IN 1975: JIMMY HOFFA DISAPPEARED.

JULY

:YEAR

31

YOUR WEEK AT A GLANCE

MONDAY	TUESDAY	WEDNESDAY	THURSDAY	FRIDAY	SATURDAY
TODAY	TODAY	TODAY	TODAY	TODAY	SUNDAY

IT'S NATIONAL AVOCADO DAY

TOM SELLECK AND JAMIE FOXX BOTH OWN AVOCADO FARMS.

RICO RODRIGUEZ WAS BORN IN 1998

B.J. NOVAK WAS BORN IN 1979

9 AM

10 AM

11 AM

NOON

1 PM

2 PM

3 PM

4 PM

5 PM

6 PM

ON THIS DAY IN 1989: THE NINTENDO GAME BOY WAS RELEASED IN THE U.S.

NOTES AND/OR DOODLES

A DRAWING OF MANHATTAN, NEW YORK

(OR MANHATTAN, KANSAS)

GREAT LITERATURE THAT I PRETEND TO HAVE READ

OR A GROCERY LIST OR SOMETHING

1
2
3
4
5
6
7
8
9
10
11
12
13
14
15
16
17
18

JULY IN REVIEW

MY JULY ACCOMPLISHMENTS

- [ ] BOUGHT DISCOUNT FIREWORKS
- [ ] MADE AREA ANIMALS LIVES A LIVING HELL
- [ ] KEPT ALL APPENDAGES INTACT
- [ ] VOWED TO COOK MORE ON THE GRILL
- [ ] ATTEMPTED TO CLEAN THE GRILL
- [ ] ORDERED TAKE-OUT
- [ ] TOOK 100S OF PHOTOS OF FIREWORKS
- [ ] NEVER LOOKED AT THE PHOTOS AGAIN
- [ ] ALMOST BOUGHT U.S. FLAG CLOTHING
- [ ] DECIDED THAT WAS TOO SUBTLE
- [ ] WORE RED, WHITE, & BLUE BODY PAINT
- [ ] CAR UPHOLSTERY NOW SMEARED PURPLE
- [ ] CONTEMPLATED BUYING A BOAT
- [ ] MADE A LIST OF POSSIBLE BOAT NAMES
- [ ] REALIZED THAT BOATS ARE EXPENSIVE

REASONS THAT JULY WAS GREAT

'IT ENDED' IS A VALID ANSWER

1
2
3
4
5
6
7
8
9
10
11
12

IF JULY WAS PERSONIFIED, DRAW ITS FAVORITE EMOJI

REASONS THAT I'M GLAD JULY IS OVER

USE ADDITIONAL PAPER IF NEEDED

1
2
3
4
5
6
7
8
9
10
11
12
13
14

CLICHÉS OVERHEARD THIS MONTH

- [ ] 'IT'S THE HUMIDITY THAT GETS YA'
- [ ] 'DO IT FOR 'MERICA!'
- [ ] 'BRR, IT'S FREEZING IN HERE'
- [ ] '10 HOTDOGS AND ONLY 8 BUNS?'
- [ ] 'BEER ME BRO'
- [ ] 'WHEN DO YOU THINK THEY'LL START?'
- [ ] 'HERE, HOLD MY BEER'
- [ ] 'DO YOU THINK WE NEED MORE ICE?'
- [ ] 'OOH, THAT'S A PRETTY ONE'
- [ ] 'WHICH ONE LOOKS BETTER FOR INSTA?'
- [ ] 'IT'S WHITE CLAW SUMMER BABY!'
- [ ] 'DOES MY FACE LOOK RED?'
- [ ] 'GEEZ, DID YOU GO KILL THE COW?'
- [ ] 'UH-OH, THIS IS MY SONG'
- [ ] 'CHRISTMAS IN JULY'
- [ ] 'OMG, HOW DID YOU GET SO TAN?'
- [ ] 'GO LONG'

ORIGINALLY KNOWN AS SEXTILIS (MEANING SIXTH MONTH).

WELCOME TO

× AUGUST ×

OF WHATEVER YEAR
YOU SAY IT IS.

LET'S GO WITH:

NAMED IN HONOR OF THE ROMAN EMPEROR (AT THE TIME) AUGUSTUS CAESAR.

AUGUST AT A GLANCE :YEAR

YOU MADE IT
TO AUGUST

×

CELEBRATE, IT'S:

BLACK BUSINESS MONTH

NATIONAL BACK TO SCHOOL MONTH

NATIONAL EYE EXAM MONTH

INTERNATIONAL PEACE MONTH

NATIONAL CATFISH MONTH

×

OFFICIAL SYMBOLS:

BIRTHSTONE: PERIDOT

FLOWERS: GLADIOLUS & POPPY

TREES: POPLAR, CEDAR, & PINE

LEO (JUL 23 / AUG 22)

VIRGO (AUG 23 / SEP 22)

DATES TO KNOW*
LIKE, IMPORTANT ONES

×

LAMMAS
(PAGAN)
AUGUST 1ST

RAKSHA BANDHAN
(HINDUISM)
THE LAST DAY OF THE HINDU LUNAR MONTH OF SHRAAVANA (OFTEN IN AUGUST)

OBON
(BUDDHISM)
COMMONLY HELD BETWEEN AUGUST 13TH AND 16TH

NATIONAL AVIATION DAY
AUGUST 19TH

ADMISSION DAY
(STATE OF HAWAII)
3RD FRIDAY OF AUGUST

WOMEN'S EQUALITY DAY
AUGUST 26TH

GANESH CHATURTHI
(HINDUISM)
STARTS ON THE FOURTH DAY OF THE HINDU LUNAR MONTH OF BHĀDRA (COULD FALL IN AUGUST OR SEPTEMBER)

THINGS TO ACCOMPLISH THIS MONTH
FOR EXAMPLE: FILL OUT A TO-DO LIST

1
2
3
4
5
6
7
8
9
10
11
12
13
14
15

THINGS THAT ARE NEVER GOING TO HAPPEN
THERE'S ALWAYS SEPTEMBER (OR OCTOBER)

1
2
3
4
5
6
7
8
9
10
11
12
13
14
15

*A DISCLAIMER OF SORTS

HEY THERE, WE HERE AT BRASS MONKEY LIKE TO JOKE AROUND...BUT WE ALSO WANT TO TAKE A MINUTE TO RECOGNIZE JUST A FEW OF THE MANY HOLIDAYS & EVENTS THAT ARE IMPORTANT TO OUR FRIENDS AROUND THE GLOBE (AND AT HOME). YOU MAY BE DIFFERENT THAN US. WE MAY HAVE NEVER MET. BUT WE LOVE YOU ALL THE SAME.

SO IF YOU HAVEN'T HEARD OF A DAY, LOOK IT UP. LEARNING ABOUT & APPRECIATING CULTURES DIFFERENT THAN YOURS IS IMPORTANT...WAY MORE THAN POSTING A FEW 'STRAWBERRY JAM DAY' SELFIES.

AUGUST AT A GLANCE

YEAR:

IT'S AUGUST
START PLANNING

×

NATIONAL AVIATION DAY
AUGUST 19TH

HAWAII ADMISSION DAY*
3RD FRIDAY OF AUGUST

WOMEN'S EQUALITY DAY
AUGUST 26TH

×

BIRTHDAYS
TO REMEMBER

*PSST: SINCE THIS HOLIDAY MOVES AROUND EACH YEAR (AND WE DON'T KNOW WHEN IN THE FUTURE YOU'RE USING THIS), HELP US OUT AND ADD IT TO THE CALENDAR.

ALSO, ARE THERE JET PACKS YET? OUR FINGERS ARE CROSSED.

S M T W T F S	S M T W T F S	S M T W T F S	S M T W T F S	S M T W T F S	S M T W T F S	S M T W T F S
01	02	03	04	05	06	07
08	09	10	11	12	13	14
15	16	17	18	N. AVIATION DAY 19	20	21
22	23	24	25	W. EQUALITY DAY 26	27	28
29	30	31	NOTES:			

AUGUST, AS EXPRESSED IN A DRAWING

AUGUST PREVIEW

AN AUGUST VENN DIAGRAM
WHAT DO THEY HAVE IN COMMON?

1 GREAT AT SMOTHERING PEOPLE
2
3
4
5
6
7
8

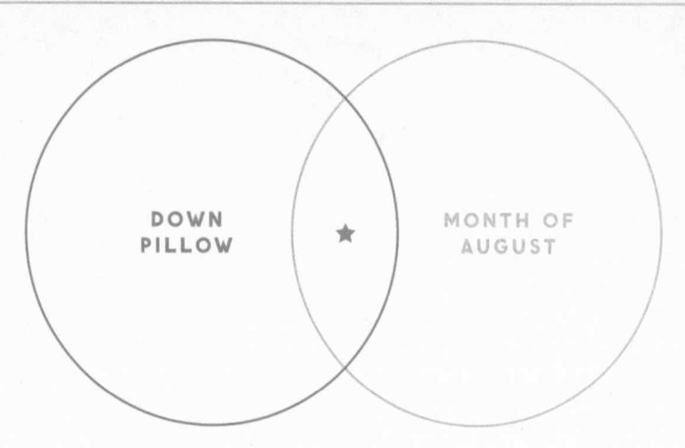

A DRAWING OF WHAT I DID TO DESERVE THIS

SUPPLIES NEEDED FOR THE MONTH
ALCOHOL, AND OTHER NECESSITIES

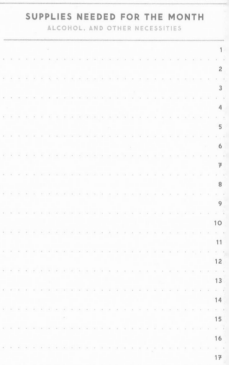

1
2
3
4
5
6
7
8
9
10
11
12
13
14
15
16
17

AUGUST ENJOYMENT INDEX

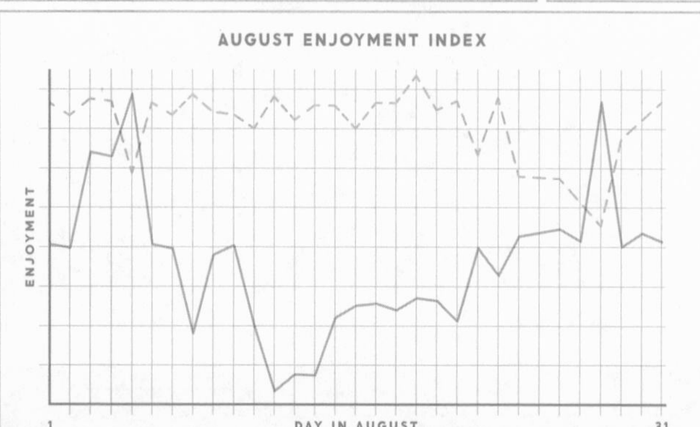

ENJOYMENT OVER TIME
CHOOSE A COLOR KEY

LINE	ITEM
——	BACK TO SCHOOL ADS
– –	BEING DONE WITH SCHOOL
	OUTDOOR CONCERTS
	INDOOR CONCERTS
	REALIZING I'M OLD
	100 PERCENT HUMIDITY
	NATURALLY CURLY HAIR
	DRINKING WATER
	SWEATING PROFUSELY
	THE IDEA OF SEPTEMBER

YEAR: **AUGUST**

YOUR WEEK AT A GLANCE

MONDAY	TUESDAY	WEDNESDAY	THURSDAY	FRIDAY	SATURDAY ☐
☐ TODAY	☐ TODAY	☐ TODAY	☐ TODAY	☐ TODAY	☐ SUNDAY

01

NOTES AND/OR DOODLES

IT'S NATIONAL PLANNER DAY

YOU SHOULD CELEBRATE BY POSTING YOUR FAVORITE ONE ONLINE.

(TAG US, AND WE'LL REWARD YOU FOR YOUR EFFORTS @BRASSMONKEYGOODS)

JASON MOMOA WAS BORN IN 1979 COOLIO WAS BORN IN 1963

9 AM

10 AM

11 AM

NOON

1 PM

2 PM

3 PM

4 PM

5 PM

6 PM

ON THIS DAY IN 1944: ANNE FRANK MADE THE LAST ENTRY IN HER DIARY.

YOUR WEEK AT A GLANCE

MONDAY	TUESDAY	WEDNESDAY	THURSDAY	FRIDAY	SATURDAY ☐
☐ TODAY	☐ TODAY	☐ TODAY	☐ TODAY	☐ TODAY	☐ SUNDAY

02

NOTES AND/OR DOODLES

IT'S NATIONAL ICE CREAM SANDWICH DAY

THE EARLIEST KNOWN RECIPE USED SPONGE CAKE INSTEAD OF COOKIES.

CHARLI XCX WAS BORN IN 1992 KEVIN SMITH WAS BORN IN 1970

9 AM

10 AM

11 AM

NOON

1 PM

2 PM

3 PM

4 PM

5 PM

6 PM

ON THIS DAY IN 1937: MARIJUANA WAS MADE ILLEGAL.

03

YOUR WEEK AT A GLANCE

MONDAY	TUESDAY	WEDNESDAY	THURSDAY	FRIDAY	SATURDAY ☐
TODAY ☐	TODAY ☐	TODAY ☐	TODAY ☐	TODAY ☐	☐ SUNDAY

IT'S GRAB SOME NUTS DAY

ANCIENT GREEKS BELIEVED THAT HAZELNUTS COULD TREAT BALDNESS.

TONY BENNETT WAS BORN IN 1926

MARTHA STEWART WAS BORN IN 1941

9 AM

10 AM

11 AM

NOON

1 PM

2 PM

3 PM

4 PM

5 PM

6 PM

ON THIS DAY IN 2012: MICHAEL PHELPS WON HIS 17TH GOLD MEDAL.

NOTES AND/OR DOODLES

04

YOUR WEEK AT A GLANCE

MONDAY	TUESDAY	WEDNESDAY	THURSDAY	FRIDAY	SATURDAY ☐
TODAY ☐	TODAY ☐	TODAY ☐	TODAY ☐	TODAY ☐	☐ SUNDAY

IT'S CHOCOLATE CHIP COOKIE DAY

13 PERCENT OF U.S. ADULTS ADMIT TO EATING 20 OR MORE AT A TIME.

LOUIS ARMSTRONG WAS BORN IN 1901

MEGHAN MARKLE WAS BORN IN 1981

9 AM

10 AM

11 AM

NOON

1 PM

2 PM

3 PM

4 PM

5 PM

6 PM

ON THIS DAY IN 1981: OLIVER NORTH WAS ASSIGNED TO WHITE HOUSE DUTY.

NOTES AND/OR DOODLES

YEAR: **AUGUST**

YOUR WEEK AT A GLANCE

MONDAY	TUESDAY	WEDNESDAY	THURSDAY	FRIDAY	SATURDAY ☐
☐ TODAY	☐ TODAY	☐ TODAY	☐ TODAY	☐ TODAY	☐ SUNDAY

05

NOTES AND/OR DOODLES

IT'S NATIONAL OYSTER DAY

A SINGLE OYSTER CAN FILTER 50 GALLONS OF WATER A DAY.

NEIL ARMSTRONG WAS BORN IN 1930

PATRICK EWING WAS BORN IN 1962

9 AM

10 AM

11 AM

NOON

1 PM

2 PM

3 PM

4 PM

5 PM

6 PM

ON THIS DAY IN 1914: THE 1ST ELECTRIC TRAFFIC LIGHT WAS INSTALLED.

YOUR WEEK AT A GLANCE

MONDAY	TUESDAY	WEDNESDAY	THURSDAY	FRIDAY	SATURDAY ☐
☐ TODAY	☐ TODAY	☐ TODAY	☐ TODAY	☐ TODAY	☐ SUNDAY

06

NOTES AND/OR DOODLES

IT'S NATIONAL ROOT BEER FLOAT DAY

ROOT BEER ACCOUNTS FOR 3 PERCENT OF THE U.S. SOFT DRINK MARKET.

ANDY WARHOL WAS BORN IN 1928

DAVID ROBINSON WAS BORN IN 1965

9 AM

10 AM

11 AM

NOON

1 PM

2 PM

3 PM

4 PM

5 PM

6 PM

ON THIS DAY IN 2012: NASA'S CURIOSITY ROVER LANDED ON MARS.

07

YOUR WEEK AT A GLANCE

MONDAY	TUESDAY	WEDNESDAY	THURSDAY	FRIDAY	SATURDAY ☐
TODAY ☐	TODAY ☐	TODAY ☐	TODAY ☐	TODAY ☐	☐ SUNDAY

IT'S PURPLE HEART DAY

JOHN F. KENNEDY IS THE ONLY U.S. PRESIDENT WITH A PURPLE HEART.

CHARLIZE THERON WAS BORN IN 1975

MICHAEL SHANNON WAS BORN IN 1974

9 AM

10 AM

11 AM

NOON

1 PM

2 PM

3 PM

4 PM

5 PM

6 PM

ON THIS DAY IN 1974: PHILIPPE PETIT WALKED AN ILLEGAL TIGHTROPE IN NYC.

NOTES AND/OR DOODLES

08

YOUR WEEK AT A GLANCE

MONDAY	TUESDAY	WEDNESDAY	THURSDAY	FRIDAY	SATURDAY ☐
TODAY ☐	TODAY ☐	TODAY ☐	TODAY ☐	TODAY ☐	☐ SUNDAY

IT'S INTERNATIONAL CAT DAY

A CAT WAS THE MAYOR OF TALKEETNA, ALASKA, FOR 20 YEARS.

ROGER FEDERER WAS BORN IN 1981

SHAWN MENDES WAS BORN IN 1998

9 AM

10 AM

11 AM

NOON

1 PM

2 PM

3 PM

4 PM

5 PM

6 PM

ON THIS DAY IN 1992: THE U.S. 'DREAM TEAM' WON GOLD AT THE OLYMPICS.

NOTES AND/OR DOODLES

LISTS, NOTES & MEMOIRS

THINGS NOT TO SAY AT A TOAST

OR SOME BORING TO-DO LIST

1
2
3
4
5
6
7
8
9
10
11
12

NON-FOOD ITEMS THAT SEEM DELICIOUS

OR A GROCERY LIST OR SOMETHING

1
2
3
4
5
6
7
8
9
10
11
12

A DRAWING OF AN EMOJI THAT SHOULD EXIST

(OR SOME SUPER BUSINESSY STUFF)

CHILDHOOD TOYS (BEST TO WORST)

OR A MORE USEFUL (BUT STUPID) LIST

1
2
3
4
5
6
7
8
9
10
11
12

INSULTS THAT ALSO RHYME

OR A LIST OF LITERALLY ANYTHING ELSE

1
2
3
4
5
6
7
8
9
10
11
12

09

YOUR WEEK AT A GLANCE

MONDAY	TUESDAY	WEDNESDAY	THURSDAY	FRIDAY	SATURDAY ☐
TODAY ☐	TODAY ☐	TODAY ☐	TODAY ☐	TODAY ☐	☐ SUNDAY

IT'S BOOK LOVERS DAY

THERE IS A WORD FOR LOVING THE SMELL OF OLD BOOKS—BIBLIOSMIA.

WHITNEY HOUSTON WAS BORN IN 1963 ANNA KENDRICK WAS BORN IN 1985

9 AM

10 AM

11 AM

NOON

1 PM

2 PM

3 PM

4 PM

5 PM

6 PM

ON THIS DAY IN 1930: BETTY BOOP MADE HER CARTOON DEBUT.

NOTES AND/OR DOODLES

10

YOUR WEEK AT A GLANCE

MONDAY	TUESDAY	WEDNESDAY	THURSDAY	FRIDAY	SATURDAY ☐
TODAY ☐	TODAY ☐	TODAY ☐	TODAY ☐	TODAY ☐	☐ SUNDAY

IT'S NATIONAL LAZY DAY

THE FIRST LA-Z-BOY RECLINER WAS A FOLDING WOOD-SLAT CHAIR.

ANTONIO BANDERAS WAS BORN IN 1960 JUSTIN THEROUX WAS BORN IN 1971

9 AM

10 AM

11 AM

NOON

1 PM

2 PM

3 PM

4 PM

5 PM

6 PM

ON THIS DAY IN 1993: RUTH BADER GINSBURG JOINED THE U.S. SUPREME COURT.

NOTES AND/OR DOODLES

YEAR: **AUGUST**

YOUR WEEK AT A GLANCE

MONDAY	TUESDAY	WEDNESDAY	THURSDAY	FRIDAY	SATURDAY ☐ / ☐ SUNDAY
☐ TODAY	☐ TODAY	☐ TODAY	☐ TODAY	☐ TODAY	

11

NOTES AND/OR DOODLES

IT'S PLAY IN THE SAND DAY

DUE TO IT'S DEMAND, THERE'S AN ILLEGAL BLACK MARKET FOR SAND.

STEVE WOZNIAK WAS BORN IN 1950

CHRIS HEMSWORTH WAS BORN IN 1983

9 AM

10 AM

11 AM

NOON

1 PM

2 PM

3 PM

4 PM

5 PM

6 PM

ON THIS DAY IN 1951: THE FIRST MLB GAME WAS TELEVISED IN COLOR.

YOUR WEEK AT A GLANCE

MONDAY	TUESDAY	WEDNESDAY	THURSDAY	FRIDAY	SATURDAY ☐ / ☐ SUNDAY
☐ TODAY	☐ TODAY	☐ TODAY	☐ TODAY	☐ TODAY	

12

NOTES AND/OR DOODLES

IT'S VINYL RECORD DAY

A BRAZILIAN BILLIONAIRE OWNS OVER 6 MILLION ALBUMS.

CARA DELEVINGNE WAS BORN IN 1992

PETE SAMPRAS WAS BORN IN 1971

9 AM

10 AM

11 AM

NOON

1 PM

2 PM

3 PM

4 PM

5 PM

6 PM

ON THIS DAY IN 1981: THE IBM PERSONAL COMPUTER WAS RELEASED.

LISTS, NOTES & MEMOIRS

BEST HUMAN NAMES TO GIVE TO DOGS

OR A LIST OF LITERALLY ANYTHING ELSE

1
2
3
4
5
6
7
8
9
10
11
12

BEST FOOD NAMES TO GIVE TO CATS

OR A MORE USEFUL (BUT STUPID) LIST

1
2
3
4
5
6
7
8
9
10
11
12

A DRAWING OF CLOWN COLLEGE

(OR SOME SUPER BUSINESSY STUFF)

USELESS TRIVIA FACTS THAT I KNOW

OR SOME BORING TO-DO LIST

1
2
3
4
5
6
7
8
9
10
11
12

REALITY SHOWS THAT SHOULD EXIST

OR A GROCERY LIST OR SOMETHING

1
2
3
4
5
6
7
8
9
10
11
12

YEAR: **AUGUST**

YOUR WEEK AT A GLANCE

MONDAY	TUESDAY	WEDNESDAY	THURSDAY	FRIDAY	SATURDAY ☐
☐ TODAY	☐ TODAY	☐ TODAY	☐ TODAY	☐ TODAY	☐ SUNDAY

13

NOTES AND/OR DOODLES

IT'S BLACK WOMEN'S EQUAL PAY DAY

BLACK WOMEN EARN 62 CENTS FOR EVERY DOLLAR THAT WHITE MEN DO.

SRIDEVI KAPOOR WAS BORN IN 1963

ALFRED HITCHCOCK WAS BORN IN 1899

9 AM

10 AM

11 AM

NOON

1 PM

2 PM

3 PM

4 PM

5 PM

6 PM

ON THIS DAY IN 1997: THE FIRST EPISODE OF 'SOUTH PARK' AIRED.

YOUR WEEK AT A GLANCE

MONDAY	TUESDAY	WEDNESDAY	THURSDAY	FRIDAY	SATURDAY ☐
☐ TODAY	☐ TODAY	☐ TODAY	☐ TODAY	☐ TODAY	☐ SUNDAY

14

NOTES AND/OR DOODLES

IT'S NATIONAL WIFFLE BALL DAY

EACH BALL HAS 8 HOLES, DESIGNED TO HELP IT CURVE.

HALLE BERRY WAS BORN IN 1966

STEVE MARTIN WAS BORN IN 1945

9 AM

10 AM

11 AM

NOON

1 PM

2 PM

3 PM

4 PM

5 PM

6 PM

ON THIS DAY IN 2000: 'DORA THE EXPLORER' PREMIERED ON NICK JR.

AUGUST

:YEAR

15

YOUR WEEK AT A GLANCE

MONDAY	TUESDAY	WEDNESDAY	THURSDAY	FRIDAY	SATURDAY ☐
TODAY ☐	TODAY ☐	TODAY ☐	TODAY ☐	TODAY ☐	☐ SUNDAY

IT'S NATIONAL FAILURES DAY

* CRYSTAL PEPSI HAS ENTERED THE CHAT *

JENNIFER LAWRENCE WAS BORN IN 1990

JULIA CHILD WAS BORN IN 1912

9 AM

10 AM

11 AM

NOON

1 PM

2 PM

3 PM

4 PM

5 PM

6 PM

ON THIS DAY IN 1969: THE WOODSTOCK MUSIC FESTIVAL OPENED IN UPSTATE NY.

NOTES AND/OR DOODLES

16

YOUR WEEK AT A GLANCE

MONDAY	TUESDAY	WEDNESDAY	THURSDAY	FRIDAY	SATURDAY ☐
TODAY ☐	TODAY ☐	TODAY ☐	TODAY ☐	TODAY ☐	☐ SUNDAY

IT'S NATIONAL ROLLER COASTER DAY

CEDAR POINT IN SANDUSKY, OHIO, IS THEIR CAPITAL OF THE WORLD.

MADONNA WAS BORN IN 1958

STEVE CARELL WAS BORN IN 1962

9 AM

10 AM

11 AM

NOON

1 PM

2 PM

3 PM

4 PM

5 PM

6 PM

ON THIS DAY IN 1954: THE 1ST ISSUE OF 'SPORTS ILLUSTRATED' WAS PUBLISHED.

NOTES AND/OR DOODLES

YEAR: **AUGUST**

YOUR WEEK AT A GLANCE

MONDAY	TUESDAY	WEDNESDAY	THURSDAY	FRIDAY	SATURDAY ☐
☐ TODAY	☐ TODAY	☐ TODAY	☐ TODAY	☐ TODAY	☐ SUNDAY

17

NOTES AND/OR DOODLES

IT'S NATIONAL NUMBER 2 PENCIL DAY

BREAD CRUMBS WERE USED BEFORE ERASERS WERE INVENTED.

ROBERT DE NIRO WAS BORN IN 1943 — HELEN MCCRORY WAS BORN IN 1968

9 AM

10 AM

11 AM

NOON

1 PM

2 PM

3 PM

4 PM

5 PM

6 PM

ON THIS DAY IN 1907: THE PIKE PLACE MARKET OPENED IN SEATTLE.

YOUR WEEK AT A GLANCE

MONDAY	TUESDAY	WEDNESDAY	THURSDAY	FRIDAY	SATURDAY ☐
☐ TODAY	☐ TODAY	☐ TODAY	☐ TODAY	☐ TODAY	☐ SUNDAY

18

NOTES AND/OR DOODLES

IT'S PINOT NOIR DAY

THE 2004 MOVIE 'SIDEWAYS' MADE IT TRENDY AGAIN.

PATRICK SWAYZE WAS BORN IN 1952 — ANDY SAMBERG WAS BORN IN 1978

9 AM

10 AM

11 AM

NOON

1 PM

2 PM

3 PM

4 PM

5 PM

6 PM

ON THIS DAY IN 1962: RINGO STARR JOINED THE BEATLES (REPLACING PETE BEST).

19

YOUR WEEK AT A GLANCE

MONDAY	TUESDAY	WEDNESDAY	THURSDAY	FRIDAY	SATURDAY ☐
TODAY ☐	TODAY ☐	TODAY ☐	TODAY ☐	TODAY ☐	☐ SUNDAY

IT'S INTERNATIONAL ORANGUTAN DAY

HUMANS SHARE NEARLY 97 PERCENT OF THE SAME DNA.

COCO CHANEL WAS BORN IN 1883

JOHN STAMOS WAS BORN IN 1963

9 AM

10 AM

11 AM

NOON

1 PM

2 PM

3 PM

4 PM

5 PM

6 PM

ON THIS DAY IN 1934: THE FIRST SOAP BOX DERBY WAS HELD IN DAYTON, OHIO.

NOTES AND/OR DOODLES

20

YOUR WEEK AT A GLANCE

MONDAY	TUESDAY	WEDNESDAY	THURSDAY	FRIDAY	SATURDAY ☐
TODAY ☐	TODAY ☐	TODAY ☐	TODAY ☐	TODAY ☐	☐ SUNDAY

IT'S NATIONAL BACON LOVER'S DAY

THE UNITED CHURCH OF BACON HAS OVER 25,000 MEMBERS.

DEMI LAVATO WAS BORN IN 1992

AMY ADAMS WAS BORN IN 1974

9 AM

10 AM

11 AM

NOON

1 PM

2 PM

3 PM

4 PM

5 PM

6 PM

ON THIS DAY IN 2016: SOUTH KOREAN GOLFER INBEE PARK WON A GOLD MEDAL.

NOTES AND/OR DOODLES

LISTS, NOTES & MEMOIRS

MY JAMS (SONGS AND/OR PRESERVES)

OR SOME BORING TO-DO LIST

1
2
3
4
5
6
7
8
9
10
11
12

REASONS WHY I CAN'T HAVE NICE THINGS

OR A GROCERY LIST OR SOMETHING

1
2
3
4
5
6
7
8
9
10
11
12

A DRAWING OF THE HOTEL LOST & FOUND

(OR SOME SUPER BUSINESSY STUFF)

THINGS TO SAVE FROM A FIRE

OR A MORE USEFUL (BUT STUPID) LIST

1
2
3
4
5
6
7
8
9
10
11
12

THINGS TO THROW INTO A FIRE

OR A LIST OF LITERALLY ANYTHING ELSE

1
2
3
4
5
6
7
8
9
10
11
12

21

YOUR WEEK AT A GLANCE

MONDAY	TUESDAY	WEDNESDAY	THURSDAY	FRIDAY	SATURDAY ☐
TODAY ☐	TODAY ☐	TODAY ☐	TODAY ☐	TODAY ☐	☐ SUNDAY

IT'S NATIONAL SPUMONI DAY

A FROZEN ITALIAN DESSERT THAT YOU SHOULD PROBABLY JUST LOOK UP.

USAIN BOLT WAS BORN IN 1986

KACEY MUSGRAVES WAS BORN IN 1988

9 AM

10 AM

11 AM

NOON

1 PM

2 PM

3 PM

4 PM

5 PM

6 PM

ON THIS DAY IN 1911: THE MONA LISA WAS STOLEN BY A LOUVRE EMPLOYEE.

NOTES AND/OR DOODLES

22

YOUR WEEK AT A GLANCE

MONDAY	TUESDAY	WEDNESDAY	THURSDAY	FRIDAY	SATURDAY ☐
TODAY ☐	TODAY ☐	TODAY ☐	TODAY ☐	TODAY ☐	☐ SUNDAY

IT'S NATIONAL EAT A PEACH DAY

PRETTY MUCH EVERY STREET IN ATLANTA IS NAMED AFTER ONE.

(WE'RE EXAGGERATING...BUT BARELY)

KRISTEN WIIG WAS BORN IN 1973

JAMES CORDEN WAS BORN IN 1978

9 AM

10 AM

11 AM

NOON

1 PM

2 PM

3 PM

4 PM

5 PM

6 PM

ON THIS DAY IN 1902: THE CADILLAC MOTOR COMPANY WAS FOUNDED.

NOTES AND/OR DOODLES

YOUR WEEK AT A GLANCE

MONDAY	TUESDAY	WEDNESDAY	THURSDAY	FRIDAY	SATURDAY ☐
☐ TODAY	☐ TODAY	☐ TODAY	☐ TODAY	☐ TODAY	☐ SUNDAY

23

NOTES AND/OR DOODLES

IT'S CUBAN SANDWICH DAY

THE SANDWICH ORIGINATED IN THE YBOR CITY NEIGHBORHOOD OF TAMPA.

KOBE BRYANT WAS BORN IN 1978

RIVER PHOENIX WAS BORN IN 1970

9 AM

10 AM

11 AM

NOON

1 PM

2 PM

3 PM

4 PM

5 PM

6 PM

ON THIS DAY IN 2007: THE HASHTAG WAS FIRST USED ON TWITTER.

YOUR WEEK AT A GLANCE

MONDAY	TUESDAY	WEDNESDAY	THURSDAY	FRIDAY	SATURDAY ☐
☐ TODAY	☐ TODAY	☐ TODAY	☐ TODAY	☐ TODAY	☐ SUNDAY

24

NOTES AND/OR DOODLES

IT'S PLUTO DEMOTED DAY

IT WAS NAMED BY VENETIA BURNEY, AN 11-YEAR-OLD FROM ENGLAND.

MARSHA P. JOHNSON WAS BORN IN 1945

RUPERT GRINT WAS BORN IN 1988

9 AM

10 AM

11 AM

NOON

1 PM

2 PM

3 PM

4 PM

5 PM

6 PM

ON THIS DAY IN 1989: PETE ROSE WAS BANNED FROM BASEBALL FOR LIFE.

LISTS, NOTES & MEMOIRS

GREAT MOVIES I HATE FOR NO REASON

OR A LIST OF LITERALLY ANYTHING ELSE

1
2
3
4
5
6
7
8
9
10
11
12

POSSIBILITIES FOR LAST WORDS

OR A MORE USEFUL (BUT STUPID) LIST

1
2
3
4
5
6
7
8
9
10
11
12

A DRAWING OF A NEW YORK MINUTE (OR A NEBRASKA HOUR)

(OR SOME SUPER BUSINESSY STUFF)

TOPICS THAT I KNOW NOTHING ABOUT

OR SOME BORING TO-DO LIST

1
2
3
4
5
6
7
8
9
10
11
12

THE FEW TIMES THAT I'VE BEEN WRONG

OR A GROCERY LIST OR SOMETHING

1
2
3
4
5
6
7
8
9
10
11
12

YEAR: **AUGUST**

YOUR WEEK AT A GLANCE

MONDAY	TUESDAY	WEDNESDAY	THURSDAY	FRIDAY	SATURDAY ☐
☐ TODAY	☐ TODAY	☐ TODAY	☐ TODAY	☐ TODAY	☐ SUNDAY

25

NOTES AND/OR DOODLES

IT'S KISS AND MAKE UP DAY

GENE SIMMONS' TONGUE IS 7 INCHES LONG.

(WRONG KISS AND MAKEUP, SORRY)

SEAN CONNERY WAS BORN IN 1930

BLAKE LIVELY WAS BORN IN 1987

9 AM

10 AM

11 AM

NOON

1 PM

2 PM

3 PM

4 PM

5 PM

6 PM

ON THIS DAY IN 1916: THE NATIONAL PARK SERVICE WAS CREATED.

YOUR WEEK AT A GLANCE

MONDAY	TUESDAY	WEDNESDAY	THURSDAY	FRIDAY	SATURDAY ☐
☐ TODAY	☐ TODAY	☐ TODAY	☐ TODAY	☐ TODAY	☐ SUNDAY

26

NOTES AND/OR DOODLES

IT'S WOMEN'S EQUALITY DAY

NEW ZEALAND WAS THE 1ST COUNTRY TO GIVE WOMEN VOTING RIGHTS.

MOTHER TERESA WAS BORN IN 1910

MELISSA MCCARTHY WAS BORN IN 1970

9 AM

10 AM

11 AM

NOON

1 PM

2 PM

3 PM

4 PM

5 PM

6 PM

ON THIS DAY IN 1990: BO JACKSON HIT HIS 4TH CONSECUTIVE HOME RUN.

27

YOUR WEEK AT A GLANCE

MONDAY	TUESDAY	WEDNESDAY	THURSDAY	FRIDAY	SATURDAY ☐
TODAY ☐	TODAY ☐	TODAY ☐	TODAY ☐	TODAY ☐	☐ SUNDAY

IT'S WORLD ROCK PAPER SCISSORS DAY

MEN MOST COMMONLY CHOOSE ROCK ON THEIR FIRST THROW.

AARON PAUL WAS BORN IN 1979 — CÉSAR MILLAN WAS BORN IN 1969

9 AM
10 AM
11 AM
NOON
1 PM
2 PM
3 PM
4 PM
5 PM
6 PM

ON THIS DAY IN 1955: THE 1ST 'GUINNESS BOOK OF RECORDS' WAS RELEASED.

NOTES AND/OR DOODLES

28

YOUR WEEK AT A GLANCE

MONDAY	TUESDAY	WEDNESDAY	THURSDAY	FRIDAY	SATURDAY ☐
TODAY ☐	TODAY ☐	TODAY ☐	TODAY ☐	TODAY ☐	☐ SUNDAY

IT'S NATIONAL BOW TIE DAY

A PERSON WHO COLLECTS TIES IS CALLED A GRABATOLOGIST.

SHANIA TWAIN WAS BORN IN 1965 — JACK BLACK WAS BORN IN 1969

9 AM
10 AM
11 AM
NOON
1 PM
2 PM
3 PM
4 PM
5 PM
6 PM

ON THIS DAY IN 1996: PRINCE CHARLES AND PRINCESS DIANA DIVORCED.

NOTES AND/OR DOODLES

YEAR: **AUGUST**

YOUR WEEK AT A GLANCE

MONDAY · TUESDAY · WEDNESDAY · THURSDAY · FRIDAY · SATURDAY · SUNDAY
TODAY · TODAY · TODAY · TODAY · TODAY

29

NOTES AND/OR DOODLES

IT'S RECORD STORE DAY

VINYL ALBUM SALES HAVE INCREASED EVERY YEAR SINCE 2005.

LIAM PAYNE WAS BORN IN 1993

CARLA GUGINO WAS BORN IN 1971

9 AM
10 AM
11 AM
NOON
1 PM
2 PM
3 PM
4 PM
5 PM
6 PM

ON THIS DAY IN 1898: THE GOODYEAR TIRE COMPANY WAS FOUNDED.

YOUR WEEK AT A GLANCE

MONDAY · TUESDAY · WEDNESDAY · THURSDAY · FRIDAY · SATURDAY · SUNDAY
TODAY · TODAY · TODAY · TODAY · TODAY

30

NOTES AND/OR DOODLES

IT'S NATIONAL BEACH DAY

OVER 22 STATES IN THE U.S. OFFER NUDE BEACHES.

(ACCORDING TO THE AMERICAN ASSOCIATION FOR NUDE RECREATION—SERIOUSLY)

LISA LING WAS BORN IN 1973

CAMERON DIAZ WAS BORN IN 1972

9 AM
10 AM
11 AM
NOON
1 PM
2 PM
3 PM
4 PM
5 PM
6 PM

ON THIS DAY IN 1993: 'THE LATE SHOW WITH DAVID LETTERMAN' DEBUTED ON CBS.

AUGUST :YEAR

31

YOUR WEEK AT A GLANCE

MONDAY	TUESDAY	WEDNESDAY	THURSDAY	FRIDAY	SATURDAY ☐
TODAY ☐	TODAY ☐	TODAY ☐	TODAY ☐	TODAY ☐	☐ SUNDAY

IT'S EAT OUTSIDE DAY

IN 2020, WE CELEBRATED ALL YEAR LONG.

SARA RAMÍREZ WAS BORN IN 1975

RICHARD GERE WAS BORN IN 1949

9 AM

10 AM

11 AM

NOON

1 PM

2 PM

3 PM

4 PM

5 PM

6 PM

ON THIS DAY IN 1803: LEWIS & CLARK BEGAN THEIR EXPEDITION TO THE WEST.

NOTES AND/OR DOODLES

A DRAWING OF THE BROOKLYN BRIDGE

(OR PLAYING BRIDGE IN BROOKLYN)

CELEBRITIES THAT I SHOULD BE MORE FAMOUS THAN

OR A GROCERY LIST OR SOMETHING

1
2
3
4
5
6
7
8
9
10
11
12
13
14
15
16
17
18

AUGUST IN REVIEW

MY AUGUST ACCOMPLISHMENTS

- [ ] SERIOUSLY WORRIED ABOUT MELTING
- [ ] WAS CONSTANTLY WET (IN A BAD WAY)
- [ ] MADE PLANS FOR OTHER, BETTER MONTHS
- [ ] ACTUALLY GOT TIRED OF DRINKING
- [ ] WENT TO AN OUTDOOR CONCERT
- [ ] CAN STILL SMELL THE B.O. AND WEED
- [ ] TOOK AN OBLIGATORY VACATION
- [ ] THOUGHT ABOUT HAVING A GARAGE SALE
- [ ] REALIZED PEOPLE DON'T WANT GARBAGE
- [ ] LOST ALL HOPE
- [ ] SAW BACK TO SCHOOL ADVERTISEMENTS
- [ ] HAD HOPE ONCE AGAIN
- [ ] REMEMBERED THAT 'BURNING MAN' EXISTS
- [ ] LAUGHED AT THAT FOR AWHILE
- [ ] CRIED SOFTLY UNTIL SEPTEMBER

REASONS THAT AUGUST WAS GREAT

'IT ENDED' IS A VALID ANSWER

1
2
3
4
5
6
7
8
9
10
11
12

IF AUGUST WAS PERSONIFIED, SHOW US WHERE IT HURT YOU

REASONS THAT I'M GLAD AUGUST IS OVER

USE ADDITIONAL PAPER IF NEEDED

1
2
3
4
5
6
7
8
9
10
11
12
13
14

CLICHÉS OVERHEARD THIS MONTH

- 'I CAN'T BELIEVE IT'S ALREADY AUGUST' [ ]
- 'IT WAS MORE OF A STAYCATION' [ ]
- 'WORKIN' HARD? OR HARDLY WORKIN'?' [ ]
- 'SHEESH, IT'S LIKE A SAUNA OUT HERE' [ ]
- 'THIS IS WHERE WE SAT LAST TIME!' [ ]
- 'BEEN STAYIN' OUT OF TROUBLE?' [ ]
- 'I CAN'T WAIT FOR SWEATER WEATHER' [ ]
- 'YOU'VE GOT TO SEE WHERE WE STAYED' [ ]
- 'GEEZ, I WAS WORRIED YOU FELL IN' [ ]
- 'SUMMER IS ALMOST OVER' [ ]
- 'WOW, THAT'S GOT A LITTLE KICK TO IT' [ ]
- 'IT'S ALWAYS THE LAST PLACE I LOOK' [ ]
- 'CAN YOU BELIEVE THIS HUMIDITY?' [ ]
- 'YOU COULD FRY AN EGG OUT THERE' [ ]
- 'HOW WAS YOUR VACAY?' [ ]
- 'I'M LITERALLY SCREAMING' [ ]
- 'EVERYTHING HAPPENS FOR A REASON' [ ]

ORIGINALLY THE SEVENTH MONTH OF THE YEAR (IN THE ROMAN CALENDAR).

WELCOME TO

× SEPTEMBER ×

OF WHATEVER YEAR
YOU SAY IT IS.

LET'S GO WITH:

ITS NAME COMES FROM THE LATIN WORD 'SEPTEM' (MEANING SEVEN).

SEPTEMBER AT A GLANCE :YEAR

YOU MADE IT
TO SEPTEMBER

×

CELEBRATE, IT'S:

NATIONAL MUSHROOM MONTH

CLASSICAL MUSIC MONTH

NATIONAL SQUARE DANCE MONTH

SELF IMPROVEMENT MONTH

NATIONAL COURTESY MONTH

×

OFFICIAL SYMBOLS:

BIRTHSTONE: SAPPHIRE

FLOWERS: ASTER & MORNING GLORY

TREES: LIME, OLIVE, & HAZELNUT

VIRGO (AUG 23 / SEP 22)

LIBRA (SEP 23 / OCT 22)

DATES TO KNOW*
LIKE, IMPORTANT ONES

×

LABOR DAY
FIRST MONDAY IN SEPTEMBER

PATRIOT DAY
SEPTEMBER 11TH

ENKUTATASH
(ETHIOPIA)
SEPTEMBER 11TH

ROSH HASHANAH
(JUDAISM)
163 DAYS AFTER THE FIRST DAY OF PASSOVER (USUALLY SEPTEMBER)

YOM KIPPUR
(JUDAISM)
9 DAYS AFTER THE FIRST DAY OF ROSH HASHANAH

NATIVE AMERICAN DAY
FOURTH FRIDAY OF SEPTEMBER
(CALIFORNIA & NEVADA)

MESKEL
(ETHIOPIAN ORTHODOX)
SEPTEMBER 27TH (OR 28TH)

START OF FALL
(AUTUMNAL EQUINOX)
SEPTEMBER 22ND (OR 23RD)

THINGS TO ACCOMPLISH THIS MONTH
FOR EXAMPLE: FILL OUT A TO-DO LIST

1
2
3
4
5
6
7
8
9
10
11
12
13
14
15

THINGS THAT ARE NEVER GOING TO HAPPEN
THERE'S ALWAYS OCTOBER (OR NOVEMBER)

1
2
3
4
5
6
7
8
9
10
11
12
13
14
15

*A DISCLAIMER OF SORTS

HEY THERE. WE HERE AT BRASS MONKEY LIKE TO JOKE AROUND...BUT WE ALSO WANT TO TAKE A MINUTE TO RECOGNIZE JUST A FEW OF THE MANY HOLIDAYS & EVENTS THAT ARE IMPORTANT TO OUR FRIENDS AROUND THE GLOBE (AND AT HOME). YOU MAY BE DIFFERENT THAN US. WE MAY HAVE NEVER MET. BUT WE LOVE YOU ALL THE SAME.

SO IF YOU HAVEN'T HEARD OF A DAY, LOOK IT UP. LEARNING ABOUT & APPRECIATING CULTURES DIFFERENT THAN YOURS IS IMPORTANT...WAY MORE THAN POSTING A FEW 'STRAWBERRY JAM DAY' SELFIES.

SEPTEMBER AT A GLANCE

YEAR:

IT'S SEPTEMBER

START PLANNING

×

LABOR DAY*
FIRST MONDAY IN SEPTEMBER

PATRIOT DAY
SEPTEMBER 11TH

START OF FALL*
SEPTEMBER 22ND (OR 23RD)

×

BIRTHDAYS

TO REMEMBER

*PSST: SINCE THIS HOLIDAY MOVES AROUND EACH YEAR (AND WE DON'T KNOW WHEN IN THE FUTURE YOU'RE USING THIS), HELP US OUT AND ADD IT TO THE CALENDAR.

ALSO, ARE THERE JET PACKS YET? OUR FINGERS ARE CROSSED.

S M T W T F S	S M T W T F S	S M T W T F S	S M T W T F S	S M T W T F S	S M T W T F S	S M T W T F S
01	02	03	04	05	06	07
08	09	10	PATRIOT DAY 11	12	13	14
15	16	17	18	19	20	21
22	23	24	25	26	27	28
29	30					

NOTES:

SEPTEMBER, AS EXPRESSED IN A DRAWING

LISTS, NOTES & MEMOIRS

EVENTS TO OVERDRESS FOR

OR A LIST OF LITERALLY ANYTHING ELSE

1
2
3
4
5
6
7
8
9
10
11
12

EVENTS TO BARELY DRESS FOR

OR A MORE USEFUL (BUT STUPID) LIST

1
2
3
4
5
6
7
8
9
10
11
12

A DRAWING OF MY GREAT WHITE BUFFALO

(OR SOME SUPER BUSINESSY STUFF)

WORDS THAT I, LIKE, SAY TOO MUCH

OR SOME BORING TO-DO LIST

1
2
3
4
5
6
7
8
9
10
11
12

BEST IDEAS FOR A BREAKFAST CEREAL

OR A GROCERY LIST OR SOMETHING

1
2
3
4
5
6
7
8
9
10
11
12

YEAR:

SEPTEMBER

YOUR WEEK AT A GLANCE

MONDAY	TUESDAY	WEDNESDAY	THURSDAY	FRIDAY	SATURDAY ☐
☐ TODAY	☐ TODAY	☐ TODAY	☐ TODAY	☐ TODAY	☐ SUNDAY

01

NOTES AND/OR DOODLES

IT'S NATIONAL CHERRY POPOVER DAY

THE WORLD RECORD FOR SPITTING A CHERRY PIT IS 93 FT 6.5 IN.

PADMA LAKSHMI WAS BORN IN 1970

ZENDAYA WAS BORN IN 1996

9 AM

10 AM

11 AM

NOON

1 PM

2 PM

3 PM

4 PM

5 PM

6 PM

ON THIS DAY IN 1878: EMMA NUT BECAME THE 1ST FEMALE TELEPHONE OPERATOR.

YOUR WEEK AT A GLANCE

MONDAY	TUESDAY	WEDNESDAY	THURSDAY	FRIDAY	SATURDAY ☐
☐ TODAY	☐ TODAY	☐ TODAY	☐ TODAY	☐ TODAY	☐ SUNDAY

02

NOTES AND/OR DOODLES

IT'S WORLD COCONUT DAY

FALLING COCONUTS KILL ABOUT 150 PEOPLE EACH YEAR.

KEANU REEVES WAS BORN IN 1964

SALMA HAYEK WAS BORN IN 1966

9 AM

10 AM

11 AM

NOON

1 PM

2 PM

3 PM

4 PM

5 PM

6 PM

ON THIS DAY IN 1982: 'CHEERS' PREMIERED ON NBC.

03

YOUR WEEK AT A GLANCE

MONDAY	TUESDAY	WEDNESDAY	THURSDAY	FRIDAY	SATURDAY ☐
TODAY ☐	TODAY ☐	TODAY ☐	TODAY ☐	TODAY ☐	☐ SUNDAY

IT'S SKYSCRAPER DAY

THE BURJ KHALIFA IN DUBAI IS THE WORLD'S TALLEST AT 2,717 FEET.

SHAUN WHITE WAS BORN IN 1986

STEVE JONES WAS BORN IN 1955

9 AM

10 AM

11 AM

NOON

1 PM

2 PM

3 PM

4 PM

5 PM

6 PM

ON THIS DAY IN 1995: EBAY (THEN CALLED AUCTIONWEB) WAS FOUNDED.

NOTES AND/OR DOODLES

04

YOUR WEEK AT A GLANCE

MONDAY	TUESDAY	WEDNESDAY	THURSDAY	FRIDAY	SATURDAY ☐
TODAY ☐	TODAY ☐	TODAY ☐	TODAY ☐	TODAY ☐	☐ SUNDAY

IT'S NATIONAL MACADAMIA NUT DAY

IT TAKES 300 LBS. OF PRESSURE PER SQUARE INCH TO BREAK ITS SHELL.

BEYONCE KNOWLES WAS BORN IN 1981

DREW PINSKY WAS BORN IN 1958

9 AM

10 AM

11 AM

NOON

1 PM

2 PM

3 PM

4 PM

5 PM

6 PM

ON THIS DAY IN 2002: KELLY CLARKSON WON THE 1ST SEASON OF AMERICAN IDOL.

NOTES AND/OR DOODLES

YEAR: SEPTEMBER

YOUR WEEK AT A GLANCE

MONDAY	TUESDAY	WEDNESDAY	THURSDAY	FRIDAY	SATURDAY ☐
☐ TODAY	☐ TODAY	☐ TODAY	☐ TODAY	☐ TODAY	☐ SUNDAY

05

NOTES AND/OR DOODLES

IT'S KENTUCKY DERBY DAY

OVER 120,000 MINT JULEPS ARE CONSUMED AT THE RACE EVERY YEAR.

FREDDI MERCURY WAS BORN IN 1946

BOB NEWHART WAS BORN IN 1929

9 AM

10 AM

11 AM

NOON

1 PM

2 PM

3 PM

4 PM

5 PM

6 PM

ON THIS DAY IN 1882: THE 1ST LABOR DAY PARADE WAS HELD IN NYC.

YOUR WEEK AT A GLANCE

MONDAY	TUESDAY	WEDNESDAY	THURSDAY	FRIDAY	SATURDAY ☐
☐ TODAY	☐ TODAY	☐ TODAY	☐ TODAY	☐ TODAY	☐ SUNDAY

06

NOTES AND/OR DOODLES

IT'S FIGHT PROCRASTINATION DAY

FROM THE LATIN 'PROCRASTINARE'—MEANING 'FORWARD UNTIL NEXT DAY.'

IDRIS ELBA WAS BORN IN 1972

FOXY BROWN WAS BORN IN 1978

9 AM

10 AM

11 AM

NOON

1 PM

2 PM

3 PM

4 PM

5 PM

6 PM

ON THIS DAY IN 1995: CAL RIPKEN JR. PLAYED IN HIS 2,131ST CONSECUTIVE GAME.

07

YOUR WEEK AT A GLANCE

MONDAY	TUESDAY	WEDNESDAY	THURSDAY	FRIDAY	SATURDAY ☐
TODAY ☐	TODAY ☐	TODAY ☐	TODAY ☐	TODAY ☐	☐ SUNDAY

IT'S NATIONAL BEER LOVER'S DAY

WEIHENSTEPHAN BREWERY, THE WORLD'S OLDEST, OPENED IN 1040.

EASY-E WAS BORN IN 1964

BUDDY HOLLY WAS BORN IN 1936

9 AM

10 AM

11 AM

NOON

1 PM

2 PM

3 PM

4 PM

5 PM

6 PM

ON THIS DAY IN 1993: 'THE CHEVY CHASE SHOW' DEBUTED. IT LASTED 6 WEEKS.

NOTES AND/OR DOODLES

08

YOUR WEEK AT A GLANCE

MONDAY	TUESDAY	WEDNESDAY	THURSDAY	FRIDAY	SATURDAY ☐
TODAY ☐	TODAY ☐	TODAY ☐	TODAY ☐	TODAY ☐	☐ SUNDAY

IT'S INTERNATIONAL LITERACY DAY

1 IN 4 CHILDREN IN THE U.S. GROW UP WITHOUT LEARNING TO READ.

(VISIT RIF.ORG TO HELP)

PINK WAS BORN IN 1979

AVICII WAS BORN IN 1989

9 AM

10 AM

11 AM

NOON

1 PM

2 PM

3 PM

4 PM

5 PM

6 PM

ON THIS DAY IN 1504: MICHELANGELO'S STATUE OF DAVID WAS UNVEILED.

NOTES AND/OR DOODLES

LISTS, NOTES & MEMOIRS

PERSONAL PET PEEVES

OR SOME BORING TO-DO LIST

1
2
3
4
5
6
7
8
9
10
11
12

ADDITIONAL ALLURING ALLITERATIONS

OR A GROCERY LIST OR SOMETHING

1
2
3
4
5
6
7
8
9
10
11
12

A DRAWING OF THE WRONG SIDE OF THE BED

(OR SOME SUPER BUSINESSY STUFF)

CANDY HEARTS THAT SHOULD EXIST

OR A MORE USEFUL (BUT STUPID) LIST

1
2
3
4
5
6
7
8
9
10
11
12

THINGS THAT I'M THE SAME AGE AS

OR A LIST OF LITERALLY ANYTHING ELSE

1
2
3
4
5
6
7
8
9
10
11
12

SEPTEMBER

:YEAR

09

YOUR WEEK AT A GLANCE

MONDAY	TUESDAY	WEDNESDAY	THURSDAY	FRIDAY	SATURDAY ☐
TODAY ☐	TODAY ☐	TODAY ☐	TODAY ☐	TODAY ☐	☐ SUNDAY

IT'S INTERNATIONAL SUDOKU DAY

THERE ARE 5,472,730,538 POSSIBLE SOLUTIONS TO A 9X9 GRID.

OTIS REDDING WAS BORN IN 1941

MICHELLE WILLIAMS WAS BORN IN 1980

9 AM

10 AM

11 AM

NOON

1 PM

2 PM

3 PM

4 PM

5 PM

6 PM

ON THIS DAY IN 1956: ELVIS PRESLEY 1ST APPEARED ON 'THE ED SULLIVAN SHOW.'

NOTES AND/OR DOODLES

10

YOUR WEEK AT A GLANCE

MONDAY	TUESDAY	WEDNESDAY	THURSDAY	FRIDAY	SATURDAY ☐
TODAY ☐	TODAY ☐	TODAY ☐	TODAY ☐	TODAY ☐	☐ SUNDAY

IT'S WORLD SUICIDE PREVENTION DAY

IF YOU'RE WORRIED ABOUT SOMEONE YOU KNOW, REACH OUT TO THEM.

(GET 24/7, FREE, & CONFIDENTIAL SUPPORT: 1-800-273-8255)

MISTY COPELAND WAS BORN IN 1982

COLIN FIRTH WAS BORN IN 1960

9 AM

10 AM

11 AM

NOON

1 PM

2 PM

3 PM

4 PM

5 PM

6 PM

ON THIS DAY IN 1991: NIRVANA RELEASED 'SMELLS LIKE TEEN SPIRIT.'

NOTES AND/OR DOODLES

YOUR WEEK AT A GLANCE

MONDAY	TUESDAY	WEDNESDAY	THURSDAY	FRIDAY	SATURDAY ☐
☐ TODAY	☐ TODAY	☐ TODAY	☐ TODAY	☐ TODAY	☐ SUNDAY

11

NOTES AND/OR DOODLES

IT'S PATRIOT DAY

THE FIRST PLANE STRUCK THE NORTH WTC TOWER AT 8:45 A.M.

TARAJI P. HENSON WAS BORN IN 1970

HARRY CONNICK JR. WAS BORN IN 1967

9 AM

10 AM

11 AM

NOON

1 PM

2 PM

3 PM

4 PM

5 PM

6 PM

ON THIS DAY IN 2001: THINGS WOULD NEVER BE THE SAME AGAIN.

YOUR WEEK AT A GLANCE

MONDAY	TUESDAY	WEDNESDAY	THURSDAY	FRIDAY	SATURDAY ☐
☐ TODAY	☐ TODAY	☐ TODAY	☐ TODAY	☐ TODAY	☐ SUNDAY

12

NOTES AND/OR DOODLES

IT'S VIDEO GAME DAY

THE PLAYSTATION 2 IS THE BEST SELLING CONSOLE OF ALL TIME.

PAUL F. TOMPKINS WAS BORN IN 1968

JENNIFER HUDSON WAS BORN IN 1981

9 AM

10 AM

11 AM

NOON

1 PM

2 PM

3 PM

4 PM

5 PM

6 PM

ON THIS DAY IN 1978: 'TAXI' PREMIERED ON ABC.

LISTS, NOTES & MEMOIRS

USELESS THINGS I'M GREAT AT

OR A LIST OF LITERALLY ANYTHING ELSE

1
2
3
4
5
6
7
8
9
10
11
12

IMPORTANT THINGS I'M TERRIBLE AT

OR A MORE USEFUL (BUT STUPID) LIST

1
2
3
4
5
6
7
8
9
10
11
12

A DRAWING OF A POETIC LICENSE

(OR SOME SUPER BUSINESSY STUFF)

CHAPTERS IN THE BOOK ABOUT MY LIFE

OR SOME BORING TO-DO LIST

1
2
3
4
5
6
7
8
9
10
11
12

EMBARRASSING ARGUMENTS I'VE HAD

OR A GROCERY LIST OR SOMETHING

1
2
3
4
5
6
7
8
9
10
11
12

YEAR: **SEPTEMBER**

YOUR WEEK AT A GLANCE

MONDAY	TUESDAY	WEDNESDAY	THURSDAY	FRIDAY	SATURDAY ☐
☐ TODAY	☐ TODAY	☐ TODAY	☐ TODAY	☐ TODAY	☐ SUNDAY

13

NOTES AND/OR DOODLES

IT'S FORTUNE COOKIE DAY

'NOW IS THE TIME TO TRY SOMETHING NEW.'

(IN BED)

TYLER PERRY WAS BORN IN 1969

NIALL HORAN WAS BORN IN 1993

9 AM

10 AM

11 AM

NOON

1 PM

2 PM

3 PM

4 PM

5 PM

6 PM

ON THIS DAY IN 1997: 'CANDLE IN THE WIND' BY ELTON JOHN WAS RELEASED.

YOUR WEEK AT A GLANCE

MONDAY	TUESDAY	WEDNESDAY	THURSDAY	FRIDAY	SATURDAY ☐
☐ TODAY	☐ TODAY	☐ TODAY	☐ TODAY	☐ TODAY	☐ SUNDAY

14

NOTES AND/OR DOODLES

IT'S NATIONAL COLORING DAY

COLORING UTILIZES BOTH HEMISPHERES OF THE BRAIN.

AMY WINEHOUSE WAS BORN IN 1983

NAS WAS BORN IN 1973

9 AM

10 AM

11 AM

NOON

1 PM

2 PM

3 PM

4 PM

5 PM

6 PM

ON THIS DAY IN 1901: THE 1ST BODYBUILDING CONTEST WAS HELD IN LONDON.

15

YOUR WEEK AT A GLANCE

MONDAY	TUESDAY	WEDNESDAY	THURSDAY	FRIDAY	SATURDAY ☐
TODAY ☐	TODAY ☐	TODAY ☐	TODAY ☐	TODAY ☐	☐ SUNDAY

IT'S INTERNATIONAL DOT DAY

POINTILLISM IS PAINTING WITH DOTS INSTEAD OF BRUSH STROKES.

PRINCE HARRY WAS BORN IN 1984

TOM HARDY WAS BORN IN 1977

9 AM

10 AM

11 AM

NOON

1 PM

2 PM

3 PM

4 PM

5 PM

6 PM

ON THIS DAY IN 1997: THE GOOGLE.COM DOMAIN NAME WAS REGISTERED.

NOTES AND/OR DOODLES

16

YOUR WEEK AT A GLANCE

MONDAY	TUESDAY	WEDNESDAY	THURSDAY	FRIDAY	SATURDAY ☐
TODAY ☐	TODAY ☐	TODAY ☐	TODAY ☐	TODAY ☐	☐ SUNDAY

IT'S NATIONAL GUACAMOLE DAY

GUACAMOLE LITERALLY TRANSLATES TO 'AVOCADO SAUCE.'

B.B. KING WAS BORN IN 1925

AMY POEHLER WAS BORN IN 1971

9 AM

10 AM

11 AM

NOON

1 PM

2 PM

3 PM

4 PM

5 PM

6 PM

ON THIS DAY IN 1908: WILLIAM C. CURANT FOUNDED GENERAL MOTORS.

NOTES AND/OR DOODLES

YEAR: **SEPTEMBER**

YOUR WEEK AT A GLANCE

MONDAY	TUESDAY	WEDNESDAY	THURSDAY	FRIDAY	SATURDAY ☐
☐ TODAY	☐ TODAY	☐ TODAY	☐ TODAY	☐ TODAY	☐ SUNDAY

17

NOTES AND/OR DOODLES

IT'S NATIONAL APPLE DUMPLING DAY

THE CRABAPPLE IS THE ONLY VARIETY NATIVE TO NORTH AMERICA.

PATRICK MAHOMES WAS BORN IN 1995

PHIL JACKSON WAS BORN IN 1945

9 AM

10 AM

11 AM

NOON

1 PM

2 PM

3 PM

4 PM

5 PM

6 PM

ON THIS DAY IN 1849: HARRIET TUBMAN ESCAPED FROM SLAVERY.

YOUR WEEK AT A GLANCE

MONDAY	TUESDAY	WEDNESDAY	THURSDAY	FRIDAY	SATURDAY ☐
☐ TODAY	☐ TODAY	☐ TODAY	☐ TODAY	☐ TODAY	☐ SUNDAY

18

NOTES AND/OR DOODLES

IT'S WORLD BAMBOO DAY

CERTAIN TYPES CAN GROW 35 INCHES TALLER IN A SINGLE DAY.

JASON SUDEIKIS WAS BORN IN 1975

JAMES GANDOLFINI WAS BORN IN 1961

9 AM

10 AM

11 AM

NOON

1 PM

2 PM

3 PM

4 PM

5 PM

6 PM

ON THIS DAY IN 1970: JIMI HENDRIX DIED IN LONDON (AT THE AGE OF 27).

19

YOUR WEEK AT A GLANCE

MONDAY	TUESDAY	WEDNESDAY	THURSDAY	FRIDAY	SATURDAY ☐
TODAY ☐	TODAY ☐	TODAY ☐	TODAY ☐	TODAY ☐	☐ SUNDAY

IT'S INTERNATIONAL TALK LIKE A PIRATE DAY

WHICH WAS LIKELY THE SAME AS HOW EVERYONE ELSE SPOKE.

(YOU'RE OFF TO A GREAT START)

JIMMY FALLON WAS BORN IN 1974 JEREMY IRONS WAS BORN IN 1948

9 AM
10 AM
11 AM
NOON
1 PM
2 PM
3 PM
4 PM
5 PM
6 PM

ON THIS DAY IN 1876: MELVILL BISSELL PATENTED THE 1ST CARPET-SWEEPER.

NOTES AND/OR DOODLES

20

YOUR WEEK AT A GLANCE

MONDAY	TUESDAY	WEDNESDAY	THURSDAY	FRIDAY	SATURDAY ☐
TODAY ☐	TODAY ☐	TODAY ☐	TODAY ☐	TODAY ☐	☐ SUNDAY

IT'S NATIONAL PEPPERONI PIZZA DAY

OVER 251,770,000 LBS. OF PEPPERONI ARE CONSUMED EVERY YEAR.

GEORGE R.R. MARTIN WAS BORN IN 1948 SOPHIA LOREN WAS BORN IN 1934

9 AM
10 AM
11 AM
NOON
1 PM
2 PM
3 PM
4 PM
5 PM
6 PM

ON THIS DAY IN 1973: BILLIE JEAN DEFEATED BOBBY RIGGS (TENNIS).

NOTES AND/OR DOODLES

LISTS, NOTES & MEMOIRS

COMFORT FOODS

OR SOME BORING TO-DO LIST

1
2
3
4
5
6
7
8
9
10
11
12

UNCOMFORTABLE FOODS

OR A GROCERY LIST OR SOMETHING

1
2
3
4
5
6
7
8
9
10
11
12

A DRAWING OF CASINO CARPET AT 2 A.M.

(OR SOME SUPER BUSINESSY STUFF)

OPPOSITES THAT ACTUALLY ATTRACT

OR A MORE USEFUL (BUT STUPID) LIST

1
2
3
4
5
6
7
8
9
10
11
12

PEOPLE THAT I PLAN TO HAUNT

OR A LIST OF LITERALLY ANYTHING ELSE

1
2
3
4
5
6
7
8
9
10
11
12

21

YOUR WEEK AT A GLANCE

MONDAY	TUESDAY	WEDNESDAY	THURSDAY	FRIDAY	SATURDAY ☐
TODAY ☐	TODAY ☐	TODAY ☐	TODAY ☐	TODAY ☐	☐ SUNDAY

IT'S MINIATURE GOLF DAY

IN THE 1920s, THERE WERE OVER 150 ROOFTOP COURSES IN NYC.

JASON DERULO WAS BORN IN 1989

BILL MURRAY WAS BORN IN 1950

9 AM

10 AM

11 AM

NOON

1 PM

2 PM

3 PM

4 PM

5 PM

6 PM

ON THIS DAY IN 1996: JOHN F. KENNEDY JR. MARRIED CAROLYN BESSETTE.

NOTES AND/OR DOODLES

22

YOUR WEEK AT A GLANCE

MONDAY	TUESDAY	WEDNESDAY	THURSDAY	FRIDAY	SATURDAY ☐
TODAY ☐	TODAY ☐	TODAY ☐	TODAY ☐	TODAY ☐	☐ SUNDAY

IT'S NATIONAL ELEPHANT APPRECIATION DAY

THEY ARE AFRAID OF BEES...BUT THEN AGAIN, SO ARE WE.

SCOTT BAIO WAS BORN IN 1960

JOAN JETT WAS BORN IN 1958

9 AM

10 AM

11 AM

NOON

1 PM

2 PM

3 PM

4 PM

5 PM

6 PM

ON THIS DAY IN 1994: 'FRIENDS' PREMIERED ON NBC.

NOTES AND/OR DOODLES

YEAR: **SEPTEMBER**

YOUR WEEK AT A GLANCE

MONDAY	TUESDAY	WEDNESDAY	THURSDAY	FRIDAY	SATURDAY ☐
☐ TODAY	☐ TODAY	☐ TODAY	☐ TODAY	☐ TODAY	☐ SUNDAY

23

NOTES AND/OR DOODLES

IT'S NATIONAL GREAT AMERICAN POT PIE DAY

GEEZ, CALM DOWN GUYS. JUST 'POT PIE DAY' WOULD HAVE BEEN FINE.

JOHN COLTRANE WAS BORN IN 1926

MELANIE BRIDGES WAS BORN IN 1977

9 AM

10 AM

11 AM

NOON

1 PM

2 PM

3 PM

4 PM

5 PM

6 PM

ON THIS DAY IN 1986: THE ROSE WAS SELECTED AS THE U.S. NATIONAL FLOWER.

YOUR WEEK AT A GLANCE

MONDAY	TUESDAY	WEDNESDAY	THURSDAY	FRIDAY	SATURDAY ☐
☐ TODAY	☐ TODAY	☐ TODAY	☐ TODAY	☐ TODAY	☐ SUNDAY

24

NOTES AND/OR DOODLES

IT'S NATIONAL PUNCTUATION DAY

THE ACTUAL TERM FOR THE # SYMBOL IS OCTOTHORPE.

JIM HENSON WAS BORN IN 1936

NIA VARDALOS WAS BORN IN 1962

9 AM

10 AM

11 AM

NOON

1 PM

2 PM

3 PM

4 PM

5 PM

6 PM

ON THIS DAY IN 1961: 'I LOVE LUCY' AIRED ITS FINAL EPISODE.

LISTS, NOTES & MEMOIRS

SONGS CURRENTLY STUCK IN MY HEAD
OR A LIST OF LITERALLY ANYTHING ELSE

1
2
3
4
5
6
7
8
9
10
11
12

THINGS I ACCIDENTALLY COLLECT
OR A MORE USEFUL (BUT STUPID) LIST

1
2
3
4
5
6
7
8
9
10
11
12

A DRAWING OF A TERRIBLE IDEA

(OR SOME SUPER BUSINESSY STUFF)

PERSONAL HUMBLEBRAGS*
OR SOME BORING TO-DO LIST

1
2
3
4
5
6
7
8
9
10
11
12

WAYS THAT MY NAME IS MISSPELLED
OR A GROCERY LIST OR SOMETHING

1
2
3
4
5
6
7
8
9
10
11
12

*WE MISS YOU HARRIS

YEAR: **SEPTEMBER**

YOUR WEEK AT A GLANCE

MONDAY	TUESDAY	WEDNESDAY	THURSDAY	FRIDAY	SATURDAY ☐
☐ TODAY	☐ TODAY	☐ TODAY	☐ TODAY	☐ TODAY	☐ SUNDAY

25

NOTES AND/OR DOODLES

IT'S NATIONAL COOKING DAY

PUFFERFISH IS THE MOST DANGEROUS DISH TO PREPARE (OR EAT).

CHRISTOPHER REEVE WAS BORN IN 1952

DONALD GLOVER WAS BORN IN 1983

9 AM

10 AM

11 AM

NOON

1 PM

2 PM

3 PM

4 PM

5 PM

6 PM

ON THIS DAY IN 1911: GROUND WAS BROKEN FOR FENWAY PARK IN BOSTON.

YOUR WEEK AT A GLANCE

MONDAY	TUESDAY	WEDNESDAY	THURSDAY	FRIDAY	SATURDAY ☐
☐ TODAY	☐ TODAY	☐ TODAY	☐ TODAY	☐ TODAY	☐ SUNDAY

26

NOTES AND/OR DOODLES

IT'S LUMBERJACK DAY

IT CONSISTENTLY RANKS AS THE WORST POSSIBLE JOB.

T.S. ELIOT WAS BORN IN 1888

SERENA WILLIAMS WAS BORN IN 1981

9 AM

10 AM

11 AM

NOON

1 PM

2 PM

3 PM

4 PM

5 PM

6 PM

ON THIS DAY IN 1969: 'THE BRADY BUNCH' DEBUTED ON NBC.

27

YOUR WEEK AT A GLANCE

MONDAY	TUESDAY	WEDNESDAY	THURSDAY	FRIDAY	SATURDAY ☐
TODAY ☐	TODAY ☐	TODAY ☐	TODAY ☐	TODAY ☐	☐ SUNDAY

IT'S NATIONAL CORNED BEEF HASH DAY

ABRAHAM LINCOLN'S INAUGURAL DINNER WAS CORNED BEEF & CABBAGE.

GWYNETH PALTROW WAS BORN IN 1972

LIL WAYNE WAS BORN IN 1982

9 AM

10 AM

11 AM

NOON

1 PM

2 PM

3 PM

4 PM

5 PM

6 PM

ON THIS DAY IN 1937: THE 1ST SANTA CLAUS TRAINING SCHOOL OPENED IN NYC.

NOTES AND/OR DOODLES

28

YOUR WEEK AT A GLANCE

MONDAY	TUESDAY	WEDNESDAY	THURSDAY	FRIDAY	SATURDAY ☐
TODAY ☐	TODAY ☐	TODAY ☐	TODAY ☐	TODAY ☐	☐ SUNDAY

IT'S NATIONAL GOOD NEIGHBOR DAY

MR. ROGERS WAS RED-GREEN COLORBLIND.

BRIGITTE BARDOT WAS BORN IN 1934

NAOMI WATTS WAS BORN IN 1968

9 AM

10 AM

11 AM

NOON

1 PM

2 PM

3 PM

4 PM

5 PM

6 PM

ON THIS DAY IN 2020: THE COVID-19 GLOBAL DEATH TOLL PASSED 1 MILLION.

NOTES AND/OR DOODLES

YOUR WEEK AT A GLANCE

MONDAY	TUESDAY	WEDNESDAY	THURSDAY	FRIDAY	SATURDAY ☐
☐ TODAY	☐ TODAY	☐ TODAY	☐ TODAY	☐ TODAY	☐ SUNDAY

29

NOTES AND/OR DOODLES

IT'S NATIONAL COFFEE DAY

THE WORLD'S FIRST WEBCAM WATCHED A COFFEE POT.

HALSEY WAS BORN IN 1994

JERRY LEE LEWIS WAS BORN IN 1935

9 AM

10 AM

11 AM

NOON

1 PM

2 PM

3 PM

4 PM

5 PM

6 PM

ON THIS DAY IN 1976: BOY GEORGE WAS EXPELLED FROM SCHOOL.

YOUR WEEK AT A GLANCE

MONDAY	TUESDAY	WEDNESDAY	THURSDAY	FRIDAY	SATURDAY ☐
☐ TODAY	☐ TODAY	☐ TODAY	☐ TODAY	☐ TODAY	☐ SUNDAY

30

NOTES AND/OR DOODLES

IT'S EXTRA VIRGIN OLIVE OIL DAY

RIPENESS IS THE ONLY DIFFERENCE BETWEEN GREEN & BLACK OLIVES.

TRUMAN CAPOTE WAS BORN IN 1924

MARION COTILLARD WAS BORN IN 1975

9 AM

10 AM

11 AM

NOON

1 PM

2 PM

3 PM

4 PM

5 PM

6 PM

ON THIS DAY IN 1946: 22 NAZI LEADERS WERE FOUND GUILTY OF WAR CRIMES.

SEPTEMBER IN REVIEW

REASONS THAT SEPTEMBER WAS GREAT

'IT ENDED' IS A VALID ANSWER

1
2
3
4
5
6
7
8
9
10
11
12

MY SEPTEMBER ACCOMPLISHMENTS

- WORE WHITE AFTER LABOR DAY ☐
- WATCHED TEACHERS GET DEPRESSED ☐
- ENJOYED GOING OUTSIDE FOR ONCE ☐
- SAW A SINGLE LEAF FALL ☐
- GAVE UP ON MOWING FOR THE YEAR ☐
- FOUGHT OFF PUMPKIN FLAVORED FOODS ☐
- DECIDED TO HAVE A BONFIRE ☐
- REALIZED IT'S WAY TOO WARM FOR THAT ☐
- DIDN'T FORGET SEPTEMBER 11TH ☐
- DID A CHILD'S HOMEWORK FOR THEM ☐
- GOT A BAD GRADE ON SAID HOMEWORK ☐
- TOOK LABOR DAY OFF ON PRINCIPLE ☐
- WASTED A VACATION DAY ☐
- FEIGNED EXCITEMENT ABOUT FOOTBALL ☐
- PREMATURELY BOUGHT A WINTER HAT ☐

IF SEPTEMBER WAS PERSONIFIED, DRAW ITS RESUME

CLICHÉS OVERHEARD THIS MONTH

- ☐ 'I LOVE ANYTHING PUMPKIN-SPICED'
- ☐ 'IT'LL BE SNOWING BEFORE YOU KNOW IT'
- ☐ 'WE CAN'T WORK, IT'S LABOR DAY'
- ☐ 'OH, I LOVE YOUR INFINITY SCARF'
- ☐ 'WE HAVE FUN, DON'T WE?'
- ☐ 'THIS CALLS FOR PSLs'
- ☐ 'ENJOY THE ONE WEEK OF FALL'
- ☐ 'I LOVE SWEATER WEATHER!'
- ☐ 'DO YOU THINK I'LL NEED A JACKET?'
- ☐ 'THIS YEAR WENT BY SO FAST'
- ☐ 'WHY CAN'T IT BE LIKE THIS ALL YEAR?'
- ☐ 'YAAAS GIRL'
- ☐ 'IT'S SUNDAY, FUN DAY!'
- ☐ 'OMG, I HAVE THOSE SAME BOOTS'
- ☐ 'WELL, LOOK WHO THE CAT DRAGGED IN'
- ☐ 'I'M SO OVER TODAY'
- ☐ 'I MISS SUMMER ALREADY'

REASONS THAT I'M GLAD SEPTEMBER IS OVER

USE ADDITIONAL PAPER IF NEEDED

1
2
3
4
5
6
7
8
9
10
11
12
13
14

SEPTEMBER IN REVIEW

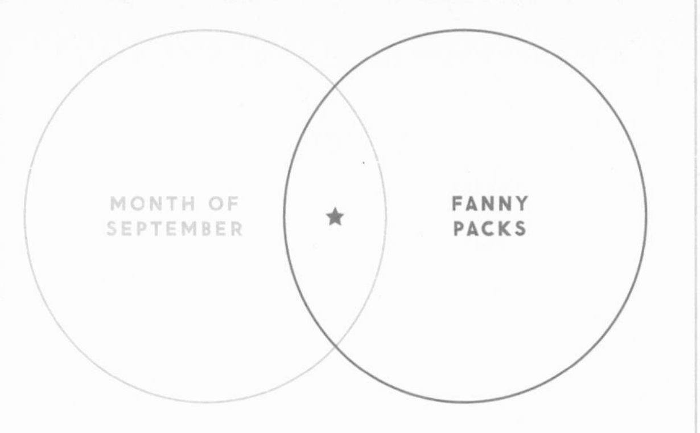

SEPTEMBER VENN DIAGRAM

WHAT DID THEY HAVE IN COMMON?

SLOWLY BECOMING COOL AGAIN 1
2
3
4
5
6
7
8

AWKWARD THINGS THAT HAPPENED

(AND WILL KEEP ME UP AT NIGHT)

1
2
3
4
5
6
7
8
9
10
11
12
13
14
15
16
17

A DRAWING OF THE NEXT THEMED LATTE TREND

ENJOYMENT OVER TIME

CHOOSE A COLOR KEY

LINE	ITEM
——	WEARING SWEATERS
— —	WEARING SHORTS
	PUMPKIN FLAVORING
	ANY OTHER FLAVOR AT ALL
	BEING OUTDOORS
	SETTING WOOD ON FIRE
	DRINKING (BEER)
	DRINKING (LIQUOR)
	LUMBERJACK FANTASIES
	FLAPJACK FANTASIES

SEPTEMBER ENJOYMENT INDEX

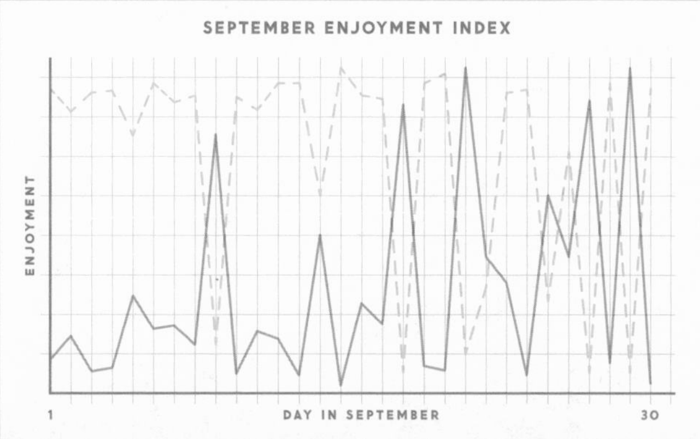

ORIGINALLY THE EIGHTH MONTH OF THE YEAR (IN THE ROMAN CALENDAR).

WELCOME TO

× OCTOBER ×

OF WHATEVER YEAR
YOU SAY IT IS.

LET'S GO WITH:

☐☐☐☐

. . . .

. . . .

. . . .

ITS NAME COMES FROM THE LATIN WORD 'OCTO' (MEANING EIGHT).

OCTOBER AT A GLANCE :YEAR

YOU MADE IT
TO OCTOBER

×

CELEBRATE, IT'S:

NATIONAL CRIME PREVENTION MONTH

BAT APPRECIATION MONTH

NATIONAL DENTAL HYGIENE MONTH

NATIONAL PIZZA MONTH

SQUIRREL AWARENESS MONTH

×

OFFICIAL SYMBOLS:

BIRTHSTONE: OPAL

FLOWERS: MARIGOLD & COSMO

TREES: ROWAN, MAPLE, & WALNUT

LIBRA (SEP 23 / OCT 22)

SCORPIO (OCT 23 / NOV 21)

DATES TO KNOW*
LIKE, IMPORTANT ONES

×

SUKKOT
(JUDAISM)
15TH DAY OF THE HEBREW MONTH OF TISHREI (COULD BE SEPTEMBER OR OCTOBER)

INDIGENOUS PEOPLES' DAY
SECOND MONDAY OF OCTOBER

COLUMBUS DAY
SECOND MONDAY OF OCTOBER

CANADIAN THANKSGIVING
SECOND MONDAY IN OCTOBER

DUSSEHRA
(HINDUISM)
10TH DAY OF THE MONTH OF ASHWIN IN THE HINDU CALENDAR (SEPTEMBER OR OCTOBER)

NATIONAL COMING OUT DAY
OCTOBER 11TH

MILVIAN BRIDGE DAY
(CHRISTIAN)
OCTOBER 28TH

HALLOWEEN
OCTOBER 31ST

THINGS TO ACCOMPLISH THIS MONTH
FOR EXAMPLE: FILL OUT A TO-DO LIST

1
2
3
4
5
6
7
8
9
10
11
12
13
14
15

THINGS THAT ARE NEVER GOING TO HAPPEN
THERE'S ALWAYS NOVEMBER (OR DECEMBER)

1
2
3
4
5
6
7
8
9
10
11
12
13
14
15

*A DISCLAIMER OF SORTS

HEY THERE. WE HERE AT BRASS MONKEY LIKE TO JOKE AROUND...BUT WE ALSO WANT TO TAKE A MINUTE TO RECOGNIZE JUST A FEW OF THE MANY HOLIDAYS & EVENTS THAT ARE IMPORTANT TO OUR FRIENDS AROUND THE GLOBE (AND AT HOME). YOU MAY BE DIFFERENT THAN US. WE MAY HAVE NEVER MET. BUT WE LOVE YOU ALL THE SAME.

SO IF YOU HAVEN'T HEARD OF A DAY, LOOK IT UP. LEARNING ABOUT & APPRECIATING CULTURES DIFFERENT THAN YOURS IS IMPORTANT...WAY MORE THAN POSTING A FEW 'STRAWBERRY JAM DAY' SELFIES.

OCTOBER AT A GLANCE

YEAR:

IT'S OCTOBER

START PLANNING

×

INDIGENOUS PEOPLES' DAY*
SECOND MONDAY OF OCTOBER

COLUMBUS DAY*
SECOND MONDAY OF OCTOBER

HALLOWEEN
OCTOBER 31ST

×

BIRTHDAYS

TO REMEMBER

*PSST: SINCE THIS HOLIDAY MOVES AROUND EACH YEAR (AND WE DON'T KNOW WHEN IN THE FUTURE YOU'RE USING THIS), HELP US OUT AND ADD IT TO THE CALENDAR.

ALSO, ARE THERE JET PACKS YET? OUR FINGERS ARE CROSSED.

DAY OF WEEK S M T W T F S	DAY OF WEEK S M T W T F S	DAY OF WEEK S M T W T F S	DAY OF WEEK S M T W T F S	DAY OF WEEK S M T W T F S	DAY OF WEEK S M T W T F S	DAY OF WEEK S M T W T F S
01	02	03	04	05	06	07
08	09	10	11	12	13	14
15	16	17	18	19	20	21
22	23	24	25	26	27	28
29	30	HALLOWEEN 31	NOTES:			

OCTOBER, AS EXPRESSED IN A DRAWING

OCTOBER PREVIEW

OCTOBER VENN DIAGRAM

WHAT DO THEY HAVE IN COMMON?

1 WHITE GIRLS DIE FOR IT

2

3

4

5

6

7

8

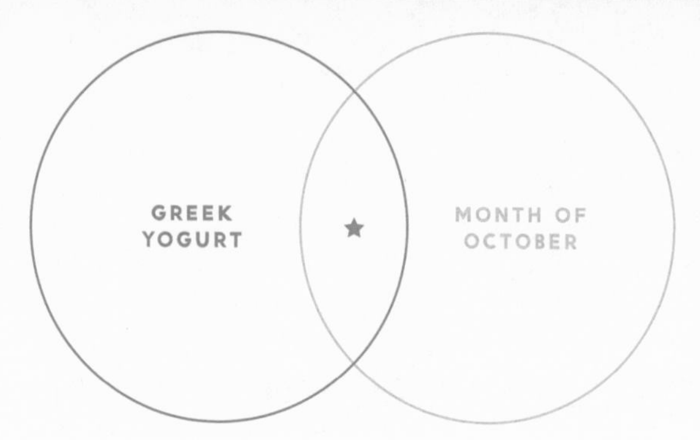

DRAW THE PERFECT JACK O' LANTERN

SUPPLIES NEEDED FOR THE MONTH

ALCOHOL, AND OTHER NECESSITIES

1

2

3

4

5

6

7

8

9

10

11

12

13

14

15

16

17

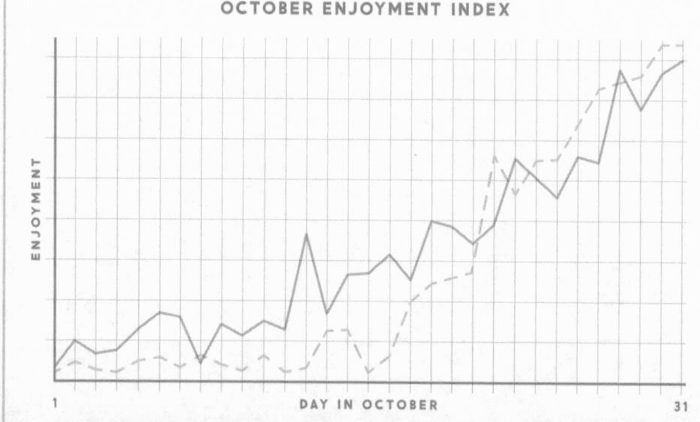

ENJOYMENT OVER TIME

CHOOSE A COLOR KEY

LINE	ITEM
——	CUTTING HOLES IN GOURDS
– –	ILLUMINATING VEGETABLES
	FULL-SIZE CANDY BARS
	MINIATURE CANDY BARS
	PAYING TO BE SCARED
	BEING SCARED FOR FREE
	TRICK-OR-TREATING
	BUYING YOUR OWN CANDY
	LOOKING AT TREES
	STOMPING ON TREE PARTS

YOUR WEEK AT A GLANCE

MONDAY	TUESDAY	WEDNESDAY	THURSDAY	FRIDAY	SATURDAY ☐
☐ TODAY	☐ TODAY	☐ TODAY	☐ TODAY	☐ TODAY	☐ SUNDAY

01

NOTES AND/OR DOODLES

IT'S INTERNATIONAL MUSIC DAY

IN 2016, MOZART SOLD MORE CDs THAN BEYONCÉ.

JULIE ANDREWS WAS BORN IN 1935

BRIE LARSON WAS BORN IN 1989

9 AM

10 AM

11 AM

NOON

1 PM

2 PM

3 PM

4 PM

5 PM

6 PM

ON THIS DAY IN 1971: WALT DISNEY WORLD OPENED IN ORLANDO, FLORIDA.

YOUR WEEK AT A GLANCE

MONDAY	TUESDAY	WEDNESDAY	THURSDAY	FRIDAY	SATURDAY ☐
☐ TODAY	☐ TODAY	☐ TODAY	☐ TODAY	☐ TODAY	☐ SUNDAY

02

NOTES AND/OR DOODLES

IT'S NATIONAL DENIM DAY

THE AVERAGE AMERICAN OWNS 7 PAIRS OF JEANS.

ANNIE LEIBOVITZ WAS BORN IN 1949

STING WAS BORN IN 1951

9 AM

10 AM

11 AM

NOON

1 PM

2 PM

3 PM

4 PM

5 PM

6 PM

ON THIS DAY IN 1967: THURGOOD MARSHALL JOINED THE U.S. SUPREME COURT.

OCTOBER

:YEAR

03

YOUR WEEK AT A GLANCE

MONDAY	TUESDAY	WEDNESDAY	THURSDAY	FRIDAY	SATURDAY ☐
TODAY ☐	TODAY ☐	TODAY ☐	TODAY ☐	TODAY ☐	☐ SUNDAY

IT'S NATIONAL CARAMEL CUSTARD DAY

CARAMELIZATION OCCURS WHEN SUGAR IS HEATED TO AT LEAST 300° F.

CHUBBY CHECKER WAS BORN IN 1941

GWEN STEFANI WAS BORN IN 1969

9 AM

10 AM

11 AM

NOON

1 PM

2 PM

3 PM

4 PM

5 PM

6 PM

ON THIS DAY IN 2018: A SINGLE BOTTLE OF WHISKEY SOLD FOR $1.1 MILLION.

NOTES AND/OR DOODLES

04

YOUR WEEK AT A GLANCE

MONDAY	TUESDAY	WEDNESDAY	THURSDAY	FRIDAY	SATURDAY ☐
TODAY ☐	TODAY ☐	TODAY ☐	TODAY ☐	TODAY ☐	☐ SUNDAY

IT'S NATIONAL TOOT YOUR FLUTE DAY

IT NEEDS MORE AIR THAN ANY OTHER INSTRUMENT, INCLUDING THE TUBA.

DAKOTA JOHNSON WAS BORN IN 1994

CHRISTOPH WALTZ WAS BORN IN 1956

9 AM

10 AM

11 AM

NOON

1 PM

2 PM

3 PM

4 PM

5 PM

6 PM

ON THIS DAY IN 2006: WIKILEAKS WAS LAUNCHED BY JULIAN ASSANGE.

NOTES AND/OR DOODLES

YEAR: **OCTOBER**

YOUR WEEK AT A GLANCE

MONDAY	TUESDAY	WEDNESDAY	THURSDAY	FRIDAY	SATURDAY ☐
☐ TODAY	☐ TODAY	☐ TODAY	☐ TODAY	☐ TODAY	☐ SUNDAY

05

NOTES AND/OR DOODLES

IT'S NATIONAL KISS A WRESTLER DAY

LIKELY FOUNDED BY A LONELY WRESTLER SOMEWHERE.

KATE WINSLET WAS BORN IN 1975

NEIL DEGRASSE WAS BORN IN 1958

9 AM

10 AM

11 AM

NOON

1 PM

2 PM

3 PM

4 PM

5 PM

6 PM

ON THIS DAY IN 1962: 'DR. NO,' THE 1ST JAMES BOND FILM, WAS RELEASED.

YOUR WEEK AT A GLANCE

MONDAY	TUESDAY	WEDNESDAY	THURSDAY	FRIDAY	SATURDAY ☐
☐ TODAY	☐ TODAY	☐ TODAY	☐ TODAY	☐ TODAY	☐ SUNDAY

06

NOTES AND/OR DOODLES

IT'S GARLIC LOVERS DAY

THE STICKY JUICE IN THE CLOVES CAN BE USED AS AN ADHESIVE.

ELISABETH SHUE WAS BORN IN 1963

LOAN GRUFFUDD WAS BORN IN 1973

9 AM

10 AM

11 AM

NOON

1 PM

2 PM

3 PM

4 PM

5 PM

6 PM

ON THIS DAY IN 1993: MICHAEL JORDAN RETIRED FROM THE NBA (THE 1ST TIME).

OCTOBER

:YEAR

07

YOUR WEEK AT A GLANCE

MONDAY	TUESDAY	WEDNESDAY	THURSDAY	FRIDAY	SATURDAY ☐
TODAY ☐	TODAY ☐	TODAY ☐	TODAY ☐	TODAY ☐	☐ SUNDAY

IT'S NATIONAL BATHTUB DAY

ARCHIMEDES DISCOVERED THE PHYSICS OF DISPLACEMENT WHILE BATHING.

SIMON COWELL WAS BORN IN 1959

TONI BRAXTON WAS BORN IN 1967

9 AM

10 AM

11 AM

NOON

1 PM

2 PM

3 PM

4 PM

5 PM

6 PM

ON THIS DAY IN 1950: MOTHER TERESA FOUNDED THE MISSIONARIES OF CHARITY.

NOTES AND/OR DOODLES

08

YOUR WEEK AT A GLANCE

MONDAY	TUESDAY	WEDNESDAY	THURSDAY	FRIDAY	SATURDAY ☐
TODAY ☐	TODAY ☐	TODAY ☐	TODAY ☐	TODAY ☐	☐ SUNDAY

IT'S NATIONAL PIEROGI DAY

THE WORD PIEROGI IS ALREADY PLURAL. THE SINGULAR FORM IS 'PIEROG.'

JOHNNY RAMONE WAS BORN IN 1948

BRUNO MARS WAS BORN IN 1985

9 AM

10 AM

11 AM

NOON

1 PM

2 PM

3 PM

4 PM

5 PM

6 PM

ON THIS DAY IN 1945: THE MICROWAVE OVEN WAS PATENTED.

NOTES AND/OR DOODLES

LISTS, NOTES & MEMOIRS

SOUNDS THAT I CAN'T STAND

OR SOME BORING TO-DO LIST

1
2
3
4
5
6
7
8
9
10
11
12

THINGS I COULD COUNT TO FALL ASLEEP

OR A GROCERY LIST OR SOMETHING

1
2
3
4
5
6
7
8
9
10
11
12

A DRAWING OF OBSOLETE TECHNOLOGY

(OR SOME SUPER BUSINESSY STUFF)

IMAGINARY START-UPS TO INVEST IN

OR A MORE USEFUL (BUT STUPID) LIST

1
2
3
4
5
6
7
8
9
10
11
12

MORE ACCURATE TITLES FOR MOVIES

OR A LIST OF LITERALLY ANYTHING ELSE

1
2
3
4
5
6
7
8
9
10
11
12

09

YOUR WEEK AT A GLANCE

MONDAY	TUESDAY	WEDNESDAY	THURSDAY	FRIDAY	SATURDAY ☐
TODAY ☐	TODAY ☐	TODAY ☐	TODAY ☐	TODAY ☐	☐ SUNDAY

IT'S MOLDY CHEESE DAY

CHESSES LIKE CAMEMBERT & BRIE ARE CREATED THANKS TO MOLD.

JOHN LENNON WAS BORN IN 1940

BELLA HADID WAS BORN IN 1996

9 AM

10 AM

11 AM

NOON

1 PM

2 PM

3 PM

4 PM

5 PM

6 PM

ON THIS DAY IN 2012: MALALA YOUSAFZAI IS SHOT 3 TIMES BY A TALIBAN GUNMAN.

NOTES AND/OR DOODLES

10

YOUR WEEK AT A GLANCE

MONDAY	TUESDAY	WEDNESDAY	THURSDAY	FRIDAY	SATURDAY ☐
TODAY ☐	TODAY ☐	TODAY ☐	TODAY ☐	TODAY ☐	☐ SUNDAY

IT'S NATIONAL LOVE YOUR HAIR DAY

THE AVERAGE HEAD HAS OVER 100,000 STRANDS OF HAIR ON IT.

MARIO LOPEZ WAS BORN IN 1973

MÝA WAS BORN IN 1979

9 AM

10 AM

11 AM

NOON

1 PM

2 PM

3 PM

4 PM

5 PM

6 PM

ON THIS DAY IN 1987: 'HERE I GO AGAIN' BY WHITESNAKE HIT NUMBER 1.

NOTES AND/OR DOODLES

YEAR: **OCTOBER**

YOUR WEEK AT A GLANCE

MONDAY	TUESDAY	WEDNESDAY	THURSDAY	FRIDAY	SATURDAY ☐
☐ TODAY	☐ TODAY	☐ TODAY	☐ TODAY	☐ TODAY	☐ SUNDAY

11

NOTES AND/OR DOODLES

IT'S NATIONAL COMING OUT DAY

WE SUPPORT YOU.

CARDI B WAS BORN IN 1992

LUKE PERRY WAS BORN IN 1966

9 AM

10 AM

11 AM

NOON

1 PM

2 PM

3 PM

4 PM

5 PM

6 PM

ON THIS DAY IN 1975: 'SATURDAY NIGHT LIVE' PREMIERED ON NBC.

YOUR WEEK AT A GLANCE

MONDAY	TUESDAY	WEDNESDAY	THURSDAY	FRIDAY	SATURDAY ☐
☐ TODAY	☐ TODAY	☐ TODAY	☐ TODAY	☐ TODAY	☐ SUNDAY

12

NOTES AND/OR DOODLES

IT'S PULLED PORK DAY

A PIG COULD RUN A 7 MINUTE MILE. IF IT WANTED TO.

LUCIANO PAVAROTTI WAS BORN IN 1935

KIRK CAMERON WAS BORN IN 1970

9 AM

10 AM

11 AM

NOON

1 PM

2 PM

3 PM

4 PM

5 PM

6 PM

ON THIS DAY IN 1810: THE 1ST OKTOBERFEST WAS CELEBRATED IN GERMANY.

LISTS, NOTES & MEMOIRS

FOODS THAT I CAN'T PRONOUNCE

OR A LIST OF LITERALLY ANYTHING ELSE

1
2
3
4
5
6
7
8
9
10
11
12

BEST ARTIFICIAL FRUIT FLAVORS

OR A MORE USEFUL (BUT STUPID) LIST

1
2
3
4
5
6
7
8
9
10
11
12

A DRAWING OF NEVER ENDING BREADSTICKS

(OR SOME SUPER BUSINESSY STUFF)

PURCHASES, POST WINNING THE LOTTERY

OR SOME BORING TO-DO LIST

1
2
3
4
5
6
7
8
9
10
11
12

APOLOGIES I SHOULD MAKE IN ADVANCE

OR A GROCERY LIST OR SOMETHING

1
2
3
4
5
6
7
8
9
10
11
12

YEAR: OCTOBER

YOUR WEEK AT A GLANCE

MONDAY	TUESDAY	WEDNESDAY	THURSDAY	FRIDAY	SATURDAY ☐
☐ TODAY	☐ TODAY	☐ TODAY	☐ TODAY	☐ TODAY	☐ SUNDAY

13

NOTES AND/OR DOODLES

IT'S TREAT YO' SELF DAY

PARKS AND REC WAS ORIGINALLY TITLED 'PUBLIC SERVICE.'

PAUL SIMON WAS BORN IN 1941 ASHANTI WAS BORN IN 1980

9 AM

10 AM

11 AM

NOON

1 PM

2 PM

3 PM

4 PM

5 PM

6 PM

ON THIS DAY IN 2016: BOB DYLAN WON THE NOBEL PRIZE FOR LITERATURE.

YOUR WEEK AT A GLANCE

MONDAY	TUESDAY	WEDNESDAY	THURSDAY	FRIDAY	SATURDAY ☐
☐ TODAY	☐ TODAY	☐ TODAY	☐ TODAY	☐ TODAY	☐ SUNDAY

14

NOTES AND/OR DOODLES

it's national lowercase day

BENJAMIN FRANKLIN REPORTEDLY WANTED TO BANISH THE LETTER C.

USHER WAS BORN IN 1978 RALPH LAUREN WAS BORN IN 1939

9 AM

10 AM

11 AM

NOON

1 PM

2 PM

3 PM

4 PM

5 PM

6 PM

ON THIS DAY IN 1982: PRESIDENT REAGAN DECLARED A 'WAR ON DRUGS'.

15

YOUR WEEK AT A GLANCE

MONDAY	TUESDAY	WEDNESDAY	THURSDAY	FRIDAY	SATURDAY ☐
TODAY ☐	TODAY ☐	TODAY ☐	TODAY ☐	TODAY ☐	☐ SUNDAY

IT'S NATIONAL CHEESE CURD DAY

A LADY IN AN AIRPORT ONCE OFFERED US SOME OUT OF A SWEATY TRASH BAG.

(THAT REALLY HAPPENED. IT WAS GROSS. AND WE'LL NEVER FORGET IT)

EMERIL LAGASSE WAS BORN IN 1959

DOMINIC WEST WAS BORN IN 1969

9 AM

10 AM

11 AM

NOON

1 PM

2 PM

3 PM

4 PM

5 PM

6 PM

ON THIS DAY IN 1987: BOB BARKER STOPPED DYING HIS HAIR.

NOTES AND/OR DOODLES

16

YOUR WEEK AT A GLANCE

MONDAY	TUESDAY	WEDNESDAY	THURSDAY	FRIDAY	SATURDAY ☐
TODAY ☐	TODAY ☐	TODAY ☐	TODAY ☐	TODAY ☐	☐ SUNDAY

IT'S NATIONAL LEARN A WORD DAY

THE LONGEST ENGLISH WORD IS NEARLY 190,000 LETTERS LONG.

(SO MAYBE START WITH AN EASIER ONE)

ANGELA LANSBURY WAS BORN IN 1925

NAOMI OSAKA WAS BORN IN 1997

9 AM

10 AM

11 AM

NOON

1 PM

2 PM

3 PM

4 PM

5 PM

6 PM

ON THIS DAY IN 1995: THE MILLION MAN MARCH TOOK PLACE IN WASHINGTON D.C.

NOTES AND/OR DOODLES

YEAR: **OCTOBER**

YOUR WEEK AT A GLANCE

MONDAY	TUESDAY	WEDNESDAY	THURSDAY	FRIDAY	SATURDAY ☐
☐ TODAY	☐ TODAY	☐ TODAY	☐ TODAY	☐ TODAY	☐ SUNDAY

17

NOTES AND/OR DOODLES

IT'S BLACK POETRY DAY

JUPITER HAMMON WAS THE 1ST AFRICAN AMERICAN POET TO BE PUBLISHED.

EVEL KNIEVEL WAS BORN IN 1938

MAE JEMISON WAS BORN IN 1956

9 AM

10 AM

11 AM

NOON

1 PM

2 PM

3 PM

4 PM

5 PM

6 PM

ON THIS DAY IN 1979: MOTHER TERESA WON THE NOBEL PEACE PRIZE.

YOUR WEEK AT A GLANCE

MONDAY	TUESDAY	WEDNESDAY	THURSDAY	FRIDAY	SATURDAY ☐
☐ TODAY	☐ TODAY	☐ TODAY	☐ TODAY	☐ TODAY	☐ SUNDAY

18

NOTES AND/OR DOODLES

IT'S NATIONAL NO BEARD DAY

SYMPTOMS OF POGONOPHOBIA (BEARD FEAR) ARE NAUSEA & SWEATING.

ZAC EFRON WAS BORN IN 1987

NE-YO WAS BORN IN 1979

9 AM

10 AM

11 AM

NOON

1 PM

2 PM

3 PM

4 PM

5 PM

6 PM

ONE THIS DAY IN 1898: THE U.S. TOOK POSSESSION OF PUERTO RICO.

19

YOUR WEEK AT A GLANCE

MONDAY	TUESDAY	WEDNESDAY	THURSDAY	FRIDAY	SATURDAY ☐
TODAY ☐	TODAY ☐	TODAY ☐	TODAY ☐	TODAY ☐	☐ SUNDAY

IT'S NATIONAL SEAFOOD BISQUE DAY

IT'S EITHER DELICIOUS OR DEADLY, DEPENDING ON YOUR ALLERGIES.

REBECCA FERGUSON WAS BORN IN 1983 JON FAVREAU WAS BORN IN 1966

9 AM

10 AM

11 AM

NOON

1 PM

2 PM

3 PM

4 PM

5 PM

6 PM

ON THIS DAY IN 1960: MARTIN LUTHER KING JR. WAS ARRESTED IN ATLANTA.

NOTES AND/OR DOODLES

20

YOUR WEEK AT A GLANCE

MONDAY	TUESDAY	WEDNESDAY	THURSDAY	FRIDAY	SATURDAY ☐
TODAY ☐	TODAY ☐	TODAY ☐	TODAY ☐	TODAY ☐	☐ SUNDAY

IT'S NATIONAL SUSPENDERS DAY

SAMUEL CLEMENS HAS A PATENT FOR AN ALTERNATIVE DESIGN.

SNOOP DOGG WAS BORN IN 1971 JOHN KRASINSKI WAS BORN IN 1979

9 AM

10 AM

11 AM

NOON

1 PM

2 PM

3 PM

4 PM

5 PM

6 PM

ON THIS DAY IN 1951: CBS STARTED USING THE 'EYEBALL' LOGO.

NOTES AND/OR DOODLES

LISTS, NOTES & MEMOIRS

BEST WAYS TO START A BREAKUP LETTER

OR SOME BORING TO-DO LIST

1
2
3
4
5
6
7
8
9
10
11
12

WORST WAYS TO START A LOVE LETTER

OR A GROCERY LIST OR SOMETHING

1
2
3
4
5
6
7
8
9
10
11
12

A DRAWING OF THE GARDEN OF EDEN (OR THE GARDEN STATE)

(OR SOME SUPER BUSINESSY STUFF)

FOODS WITH MISLEADING NAMES

OR A MORE USEFUL (BUT STUPID) LIST

1
2
3
4
5
6
7
8
9
10
11
12

THINGS THAT ROBOTS SHOULD BE DOING

OR A LIST OF LITERALLY ANYTHING ELSE

1
2
3
4
5
6
7
8
9
10
11
12

21

YOUR WEEK AT A GLANCE

MONDAY	TUESDAY	WEDNESDAY	THURSDAY	FRIDAY	SATURDAY ☐
TODAY ☐	TODAY ☐	TODAY ☐	TODAY ☐	TODAY ☐	☐ SUNDAY

IT'S INTERNATIONAL DAY OF THE NACHO

THE DISH WAS 1ST CREATED BY A MAN IN MEXICO NAMED, WELL, NACHO.

CARRIE FISHER WAS BORN IN 1956

ANDREW SCOTT WAS BORN IN 1976

9 AM

10 AM

11 AM

NOON

1 PM

2 PM

3 PM

4 PM

5 PM

6 PM

ON THIS DAY IN 1959: THE GUGGENHEIM MUSEUM OPENED IN NEW YORK CITY.

NOTES AND/OR DOODLES

22

YOUR WEEK AT A GLANCE

MONDAY	TUESDAY	WEDNESDAY	THURSDAY	FRIDAY	SATURDAY ☐
TODAY ☐	TODAY ☐	TODAY ☐	TODAY ☐	TODAY ☐	☐ SUNDAY

IT'S NATIONAL COLOR DAY

THE COLOR SEEN BY THE EYE IN PERFECT DARKNESS IS CALLED EIGENGRAU.

SHAGGY WAS BORN IN 1968

JEFF GOLDBLUM WAS BORN IN 1952

9 AM

10 AM

11 AM

NOON

1 PM

2 PM

3 PM

4 PM

5 PM

6 PM

ON THIS DAY IN 1969: PAUL MCCARTNEY DENIED RUMORS OF HIS OWN DEATH.

NOTES AND/OR DOODLES

YEAR: **OCTOBER**

YOUR WEEK AT A GLANCE

MONDAY	TUESDAY	WEDNESDAY	THURSDAY	FRIDAY	SATURDAY ☐
☐ TODAY	☐ TODAY	☐ TODAY	☐ TODAY	☐ TODAY	☐ SUNDAY

23

NOTES AND/OR DOODLES

IT'S NATIONAL BOSTON CREAM PIE DAY

TECHNICALLY, BOSTON CREAM PIE IS A CAKE & CHEESECAKE IS A PIE.

PELÉ WAS BORN IN 1940

EMILIA CLARKE WAS BORN IN 1986

9 AM

10 AM

11 AM

NOON

1 PM

2 PM

3 PM

4 PM

5 PM

6 PM

ON THIS DAY IN 2001: THE 1ST APPLE IPOD WAS RELEASED.

YOUR WEEK AT A GLANCE

MONDAY	TUESDAY	WEDNESDAY	THURSDAY	FRIDAY	SATURDAY ☐
☐ TODAY	☐ TODAY	☐ TODAY	☐ TODAY	☐ TODAY	☐ SUNDAY

24

NOTES AND/OR DOODLES

IT'S NATIONAL BOLOGNA DAY

AROUND 1,632 PEOPLE IN THE U.S. HAVE THE LAST NAME 'BOLOGNA.'

DRAKE WAS BORN IN 1986

BD WONG WAS BORN IN 1960

9 AM

10 AM

11 AM

NOON

1 PM

2 PM

3 PM

4 PM

5 PM

6 PM

ON THIS DAY IN 1926: HARRY HOUDINI PERFORMED FOR THE LAST TIME.

LISTS, NOTES & MEMOIRS

HALLOWEEN CANDIES (BEST TO WORST)

OR A LIST OF LITERALLY ANYTHING ELSE

1
2
3
4
5
6
7
8
9
10
11
12

REASONS I'M NOT READY FOR WINTER

OR A MORE USEFUL (BUT STUPID) LIST

1
2
3
4
5
6
7
8
9
10
11
12

A DRAWING OF SNAIL MAIL

(OR SOME SUPER BUSINESSY STUFF)

DISHES BEST SERVED HOT

OR SOME BORING TO-DO LIST

1
2
3
4
5
6
7
8
9
10
11
12

REVENGES BEST SERVED COLD

OR A GROCERY LIST OR SOMETHING

1
2
3
4
5
6
7
8
9
10
11
12

YEAR: **OCTOBER**

YOUR WEEK AT A GLANCE

MONDAY	TUESDAY	WEDNESDAY	THURSDAY	FRIDAY	SATURDAY / SUNDAY
TODAY	TODAY	TODAY	TODAY	TODAY	

25

NOTES AND/OR DOODLES

IT'S WORLD PASTA DAY

BEFORE MACHINERY, PASTA WAS KNEADED BY FOOT.

PABLO PICASSO WAS BORN IN 1881

KATY PERRY WAS BORN IN 1984

9 AM

10 AM

11 AM

NOON

1 PM

2 PM

3 PM

4 PM

5 PM

6 PM

ON THIS DAY IN 1962: NELSON MANDELA WAS SENTENCED TO 5 YEARS IN PRISON.

YOUR WEEK AT A GLANCE

MONDAY	TUESDAY	WEDNESDAY	THURSDAY	FRIDAY	SATURDAY / SUNDAY
TODAY	TODAY	TODAY	TODAY	TODAY	

26

NOTES AND/OR DOODLES

IT'S NATIONAL PUMPKIN DAY

THE FIRST JACK O' LANTERNS WERE MADE WITH LARGE TURNIPS.

SETH MACFARLANE WAS BORN IN 1973

RITA WILSON WAS BORN IN 1956

9 AM

10 AM

11 AM

NOON

1 PM

2 PM

3 PM

4 PM

5 PM

6 PM

ON THIS DAY IN 1949: THE U.S. MINIMUM WAGE INCREASED TO 75 CENTS.

27

YOUR WEEK AT A GLANCE

MONDAY	TUESDAY	WEDNESDAY	THURSDAY	FRIDAY	SATURDAY ☐
TODAY ☐	TODAY ☐	TODAY ☐	TODAY ☐	TODAY ☐	☐ SUNDAY

IT'S BOXER SHORTS DAY

10 PERCENT OF MEN REPORT HAVING A LUCKY PAIR OF UNDERWEAR.

KELLY OSBOURNE WAS BORN IN 1984

JOHN CLEESE WAS BORN IN 1939

9 AM

10 AM

11 AM

NOON

1 PM

2 PM

3 PM

4 PM

5 PM

6 PM

ON THIS DAY IN 1985: THE KANSAS CITY ROYALS WON THE WORLD SERIES.

NOTES AND/OR DOODLES

28

YOUR WEEK AT A GLANCE

MONDAY	TUESDAY	WEDNESDAY	THURSDAY	FRIDAY	SATURDAY ☐
TODAY ☐	TODAY ☐	TODAY ☐	TODAY ☐	TODAY ☐	☐ SUNDAY

IT'S INTERNATIONAL ANIMATION DAY

THE PIXAR LAMP IS NAMED 'LUXO JUNIOR.'

FRANK OCEAN WAS BORN IN 1987

JULIA ROBERTS WAS BORN IN 1967

9 AM

10 AM

11 AM

NOON

1 PM

2 PM

3 PM

4 PM

5 PM

6 PM

ON THIS DAY IN 1965: CONSTRUCTION ON THE ST. LOUIS ARCH WAS COMPLETED.

NOTES AND/OR DOODLES

YEAR: **OCTOBER**

YOUR WEEK AT A GLANCE

MONDAY	TUESDAY	WEDNESDAY	THURSDAY	FRIDAY	SATURDAY ☐
☐ TODAY	☐ TODAY	☐ TODAY	☐ TODAY	☐ TODAY	☐ SUNDAY

29

NOTES AND/OR DOODLES

IT'S NATIONAL OATMEAL DAY

QUAKER OATS WAS THE 1ST COMPANY TO PUT RECIPES ON PACKAGING.

BOB ROSS WAS BORN IN 1942

GABRIELLE UNION WAS BORN IN 1972

9 AM

10 AM

11 AM

NOON

1 PM

2 PM

3 PM

4 PM

5 PM

6 PM

ON THIS DAY IN 1998: JOHN GLENN BECAME THE OLDEST PERSON TO GO TO SPACE.

YOUR WEEK AT A GLANCE

MONDAY	TUESDAY	WEDNESDAY	THURSDAY	FRIDAY	SATURDAY ☐
☐ TODAY	☐ TODAY	☐ TODAY	☐ TODAY	☐ TODAY	☐ SUNDAY

30

NOTES AND/OR DOODLES

IT'S BUY A DOUGHNUT DAY

BOSTON HAS THE MOST DOUGHNUT SHOPS PER CAPITA.

NIA LONG WAS BORN IN 1970

HENRY WINKLER WAS BORN IN 1945

9 AM

10 AM

11 AM

NOON

1 PM

2 PM

3 PM

4 PM

5 PM

6 PM

ON THIS DAY IN 2003: 'WICKED' FIRST PREMIERED ON BROADWAY.

OCTOBER

:YEAR

31

YOUR WEEK AT A GLANCE

MONDAY	TUESDAY	WEDNESDAY	THURSDAY	FRIDAY	SATURDAY
TODAY	TODAY	TODAY	TODAY	TODAY	SUNDAY

IT'S HALLOWEEN

OH, AND IT'S ALSO NATIONAL DOORBELL DAY.

PIPER PERABO WAS BORN IN 1976

ROB SCHNEIDER WAS BORN IN 1963

9 AM

10 AM

11 AM

NOON

1 PM

2 PM

3 PM

4 PM

5 PM

6 PM

ON THIS DAY IN 1994: VENUS WILLIAMS MADE HER PROFESSIONAL DEBUT AT 14.

NOTES AND/OR DOODLES

A DRAWING OF THE GOLD RUSH

(OR GEOFFREY RUSH, IN GOLD)

WORST IDEAS FOR SEXY HALLOWEEN COSTUMES

OR A GROCERY LIST OR SOMETHING

1
2
3
4
5
6
7
8
9
10
11
12
13
14
15
16
17
18

OCTOBER IN REVIEW

MY OCTOBER ACCOMPLISHMENTS

- [ ] BOUGHT BAGS OF CANDY TO HAND OUT
- [ ] DIDN'T TURN THE PORCH LIGHT ON
- [ ] ATE ALL THE CANDY ALONE IN THE DARK
- [ ] WATCHED THE LEAVES CHANGE COLOR
- [ ] WATCHED THE LEAVES FALL
- [ ] WATCHED THE LEAVES JUST LAY THERE
- [ ] MADE A COSTUME FOR A PARTY
- [ ] DISCOVERED IT WAS A RETIREMENT PARTY
- [ ] INVITED TO GO TO A HAUNTED HOUSE
- [ ] ENDED THAT FRIENDSHIP
- [ ] WAS FORCED TO GO TO A PUMPKIN PATCH
- [ ] WATCHED PEOPLE POSE WITH PUMPKINS
- [ ] RUINED SOMEONE'S INSTAGRAM POST
- [ ] WAS KICKED OUT OF A PUMPKIN PATCH
- [ ] COUNTED UGG BOOTS TO FALL ASLEEP

REASONS THAT OCTOBER WAS GREAT

'IT ENDED' IS A VALID ANSWER

1
2
3
4
5
6
7
8
9
10
11
12

IF OCTOBER WAS PERSONIFIED, DRAW ITS HAIRSTYLE

REASONS THAT I'M GLAD OCTOBER IS OVER

USE ADDITIONAL PAPER IF NEEDED

1
2
3
4
5
6
7
8
9
10
11
12
13
14

CLICHES OVERHEARD THIS MONTH

- [ ] 'CHRISTMAS COMMERCIALS ALREADY!?'
- [ ] 'DON'T THE TREES LOOK GORGEOUS?'
- [ ] 'WHAT ARE YOU SUPPOSED TO BE?'
- [ ] 'I AM IN LOVE WITH CIDERS'
- [ ] 'THROW THE LEAVES AGAIN FOR MY SNAP'
- [ ] 'HOW ABOUT TRICK-OR-DRINK INSTEAD?'
- [ ] 'OOOOOH, SPOOOOOKY'
- [ ] 'OH, SOUP SOUNDS GOOD DOESN'T IT?'
- [ ] 'LET'S GO SEE THE LEAVES'
- [ ] 'IT'S HOODIE SEASON!'
- [ ] 'THAT CANDLE SMELLS AMAAAZING'
- [ ] 'LET'S HAVE A PUMPKIN CARVING PARTY'
- [ ] 'WHO'S WINNING?'
- [ ] 'OMG, SHOULD I GET A WHITE PUMPKIN?'
- [ ] 'LUMBERSEXUAL'
- [ ] 'HOW ABOUT COORDINATING COSTUMES!?'
- [ ] 'GET THIS CANDY AWAY FROM ME'

ORIGINALLY THE NINTH MONTH OF THE YEAR (IN THE ROMAN CALENDAR).

WELCOME TO

× NOVEMBER ×

OF WHATEVER YEAR
YOU SAY IT IS.

LET'S GO WITH:

ITS NAME COMES FROM THE LATIN WORD 'NOVEM' (MEANING NINE).

NOVEMBER AT A GLANCE :YEAR

YOU MADE IT
TO NOVEMBER

✖

CELEBRATE, IT'S:

NATIONAL NOVEL WRITING MONTH

ADOPT A SENIOR PET MONTH

NATIONAL GRATITUDE MONTH

BANANA PUDDING LOVERS MONTH

SPINACH AND SQUASH MONTH

✖

OFFICIAL SYMBOLS:

BIRTHSTONE: TOPAZ

FLOWER: CHRYSANTHEMUM

TREES: WALNUT, CHESTNUT, & ASH

SCORPIO (OCT 23 / NOV 21)

SAGITTARIUS (NOV 22 / DEC 21)

DATES TO KNOW*
LIKE, IMPORTANT ONES

✖

DAY OF THE DEAD
(MEXICAN)
NOVEMBER 1ST & 2ND

DAYLIGHT SAVING TIME ENDS
FIRST SUNDAY OF NOVEMBER

ELECTION DAY
FIRST TUESDAY OF NOVEMBER

DIWALI
(HINDUISM)
STARTS ON THE 15TH DAY OF THE HINDU MONTH OF KARTIK (OCTOBER OR NOVEMBER)

VETERANS DAY
NOVEMBER 11TH

TRANSGENDER DAY OF REMEMBRANCE
NOVEMBER 20TH

THANKSGIVING
FOURTH THURSDAY OF NOVEMBER

NATIVE AMERICAN HERITAGE DAY
FRIDAY AFTER THANKSGIVING

THINGS TO ACCOMPLISH THIS MONTH
FOR EXAMPLE: FILL OUT A TO-DO LIST

1
2
3
4
5
6
7
8
9
10
11
12
13
14
15

THINGS THAT ARE NEVER GOING TO HAPPEN
THERE'S ALWAYS DECEMBER (OR NEXT YEAR)

1
2
3
4
5
6
7
8
9
10
11
12
13
14
15

*A DISCLAIMER OF SORTS

HEY THERE. WE HERE AT BRASS MONKEY LIKE TO JOKE AROUND...BUT WE ALSO WANT TO TAKE A MINUTE TO RECOGNIZE JUST A FEW OF THE MANY HOLIDAYS & EVENTS THAT ARE IMPORTANT TO OUR FRIENDS AROUND THE GLOBE (AND AT HOME). YOU MAY BE DIFFERENT THAN US, WE MAY HAVE NEVER MET, BUT WE LOVE YOU ALL THE SAME.

SO IF YOU HAVEN'T HEARD OF A DAY, LOOK IT UP. LEARNING ABOUT & APPRECIATING CULTURES DIFFERENT THAN YOURS IS IMPORTANT...WAY MORE THAN POSTING A FEW 'STRAWBERRY JAM DAY' SELFIES.

YEAR:

NOVEMBER AT A GLANCE

S M T W T F S	S M T W T F S	S M T W T F S	S M T W T F S	S M T W T F S	S M T W T F S	S M T W T F S
01	02	03	04	05	06	07
08	09	10	VETERANS DAY 11	12	13	14
15	16	17	18	19	20	21
22	23	24	25	26	27	28
29	30					

NOTES:

NOVEMBER, AS EXPRESSED IN A DRAWING

IT'S NOVEMBER

START PLANNING

×

DAYLIGHT SAVING TIME*
ENDS FIRST SUNDAY OF NOVEMBER

VETERANS DAY
NOVEMBER 11TH

THANKSGIVING*
FOURTH THURSDAY OF NOVEMBER

×

BIRTHDAYS

TO REMEMBER

*PSST: SINCE THIS HOLIDAY MOVES AROUND EACH YEAR (AND WE DON'T KNOW WHEN IN THE FUTURE YOU'RE USING THIS), HELP US OUT AND ADD IT TO THE CALENDAR.

ALSO, ARE THERE JET PACKS YET? OUR FINGERS ARE CROSSED.

LISTS, NOTES & MEMOIRS

CURRENTLY EXPIRED ITEMS IN MY FRIDGE

OR A LIST OF LITERALLY ANYTHING ELSE

1
2
3
4
5
6
7
8
9
10
11
12

THINGS THAT I CAN'T BE TRUSTED WITH

OR A MORE USEFUL (BUT STUPID) LIST

1
2
3
4
5
6
7
8
9
10
11
12

A DRAWING OF 'HIGHLIGHTS FOR ADULTS'

(OR SOME SUPER BUSINESSY STUFF)

ACTIVITIES THAT ARE OVERRATED

OR SOME BORING TO-DO LIST

1
2
3
4
5
6
7
8
9
10
11
12

PEOPLE THAT I'VE TRIED TO HIDE FROM

OR A GROCERY LIST OR SOMETHING

1
2
3
4
5
6
7
8
9
10
11
12

YEAR: **NOVEMBER**

YOUR WEEK AT A GLANCE

MONDAY	TUESDAY	WEDNESDAY	THURSDAY	FRIDAY	SATURDAY ☐
☐ TODAY	☐ TODAY	☐ TODAY	☐ TODAY	☐ TODAY	☐ SUNDAY

01

NOTES AND/OR DOODLES

IT'S INTERNATIONAL SCENTED CANDLE DAY

WE'RE GETTING A HEADACHE JUST THINKING ABOUT IT.

PENN BADGLEY WAS BORN IN 1986

ANTHONY KIEDIS WAS BORN IN 1962

9 AM

10 AM

11 AM

NOON

1 PM

2 PM

3 PM

4 PM

5 PM

6 PM

ON THIS DAY IN 2015: THE KANSAS CITY ROYALS WON THE WORLD SERIES.

YOUR WEEK AT A GLANCE

MONDAY	TUESDAY	WEDNESDAY	THURSDAY	FRIDAY	SATURDAY ☐
☐ TODAY	☐ TODAY	☐ TODAY	☐ TODAY	☐ TODAY	☐ SUNDAY

02

NOTES AND/OR DOODLES

IT'S COOKIE MONSTER DAY

HE ORIGINALLY HAD (TERRIFYINGLY) POINTY TEETH.

NELLY WAS BORN IN 1974

DAVID SCHWIMMER WAS BORN IN 1966

9 AM

10 AM

11 AM

NOON

1 PM

2 PM

3 PM

4 PM

5 PM

6 PM

ON THIS DAY IN 2003: 'ARRESTED DEVELOPMENT' DEBUTED ON FOX.

03

YOUR WEEK AT A GLANCE

MONDAY	TUESDAY	WEDNESDAY	THURSDAY	FRIDAY	SATURDAY ☐
TODAY ☐	TODAY ☐	TODAY ☐	TODAY ☐	TODAY ☐	☐ SUNDAY

IT'S CLICHÉ DAY

GET OUT THERE AND GIVE IT A HUNDRED AND TEN PERCENT.

CHARLES BRONSON WAS BORN IN 1921 DOLPH LUNDGREN WAS BORN IN 1957

9 AM

10 AM

11 AM

NOON

1 PM

2 PM

3 PM

4 PM

5 PM

6 PM

ON THIS DAY IN 1988: GERALDO RIVERA'S NOSE WAS BROKEN ON SET.

NOTES AND/OR DOODLES

04

YOUR WEEK AT A GLANCE

MONDAY	TUESDAY	WEDNESDAY	THURSDAY	FRIDAY	SATURDAY ☐
TODAY ☐	TODAY ☐	TODAY ☐	TODAY ☐	TODAY ☐	☐ SUNDAY

IT'S NATIONAL CANDY DAY

SNICKERS WAS NAMED AFTER ONE OF FRANK MARS' FAVORITE HORSES.

SEAN COMBS WAS BORN IN 1969 KATHY GRIFFIN WAS BORN IN 1960

9 AM

10 AM

11 AM

NOON

1 PM

2 PM

3 PM

4 PM

5 PM

6 PM

ON THIS DAY IN 1922: THE ENTRANCE TO KING TUTANKHAMEN'S TOMB WAS FOUND.

NOTES AND/OR DOODLES

YEAR: **NOVEMBER**

YOUR WEEK AT A GLANCE

MONDAY	TUESDAY	WEDNESDAY	THURSDAY	FRIDAY	SATURDAY ☐
☐ TODAY	☐ TODAY	☐ TODAY	☐ TODAY	☐ TODAY	☐ SUNDAY

05

NOTES AND/OR DOODLES

IT'S NATIONAL LOVE YOUR RED HAIR DAY

THE ODDS OF HAVING BLUE EYES WITH RED HAIR IS 0.17 PERCENT.

TILDA SWINTON WAS BORN IN 1960

FAMKE JANSSEN WAS BORN IN 1964

9 AM

10 AM

11 AM

NOON

1 PM

2 PM

3 PM

4 PM

5 PM

6 PM

ON THIS DAY IN 1935: PARKER BROTHERS RELEASED THE GAME 'MONOPOLY.'

YOUR WEEK AT A GLANCE

MONDAY	TUESDAY	WEDNESDAY	THURSDAY	FRIDAY	SATURDAY ☐
☐ TODAY	☐ TODAY	☐ TODAY	☐ TODAY	☐ TODAY	☐ SUNDAY

06

NOTES AND/OR DOODLES

IT'S SAXOPHONE DAY

ALTHOUGH MADE OF BRASS, IT'S A WOODWIND INSTRUMENT.

EMMA STONE WAS BORN IN 1988

SALLY FIELD WAS BORN IN 1946

9 AM

10 AM

11 AM

NOON

1 PM

2 PM

3 PM

4 PM

5 PM

6 PM

ON THIS DAY IN 1975: 'GOOD MORNING AMERICA' PREMIERED ON ABC.

NOVEMBER

:YEAR

07

YOUR WEEK AT A GLANCE

MONDAY	TUESDAY	WEDNESDAY	THURSDAY	FRIDAY	SATURDAY ☐
TODAY ☐	TODAY ☐	TODAY ☐	TODAY ☐	TODAY ☐	☐ SUNDAY

IT'S BITTERSWEET CHOCOLATE WITH ALMONDS DAY

BITTERSWEET CHOCOLATE WITHOUT ALMONDS CAN GO TO HELL.

LORDE WAS BORN IN 1996

JONI MITCHELL WAS BORN IN 1943

9 AM

10 AM

11 AM

NOON

1 PM

2 PM

3 PM

4 PM

5 PM

6 PM

ON THIS DAY IN 1991: MAGIC JOHNSON ANNOUNCED THAT HE IS HIV-POSITIVE.

NOTES AND/OR DOODLES

08

YOUR WEEK AT A GLANCE

MONDAY	TUESDAY	WEDNESDAY	THURSDAY	FRIDAY	SATURDAY ☐
TODAY ☐	TODAY ☐	TODAY ☐	TODAY ☐	TODAY ☐	☐ SUNDAY

IT'S NATIONAL HARVEY WALLBANGER DAY

NAMED AFTER A REGULAR AT THE 'BLACKWATCH BAR' IN HOLLYWOOD, CA.

GORDON RAMSAY WAS BORN IN 1966

TECH N9NE WAS BORN IN 1971

9 AM

10 AM

11 AM

NOON

1 PM

2 PM

3 PM

4 PM

5 PM

6 PM

ON THIS DAY IN 1966: RONALD REAGAN WAS ELECTED GOVERNOR OF CALIFORNIA.

NOTES AND/OR DOODLES

LISTS, NOTES & MEMOIRS

ICE CREAM FLAVORS (BEST TO WORST)

OR SOME BORING TO-DO LIST

1
2
3
4
5
6
7
8
9
10
11
12

FOODS I HAVE TO POINT TO ON MENUS

OR A GROCERY LIST OR SOMETHING

1
2
3
4
5
6
7
8
9
10
11
12

A DRAWING OF THE DARK WEB

(OR SOME SUPER BUSINESSY STUFF)

NICKNAMES THAT I SHOULD BE GIVEN

OR A MORE USEFUL (BUT STUPID) LIST

1
2
3
4
5
6
7
8
9
10
11
12

A PERFECT DINNER PARTY GUEST LIST

OR A LIST OF LITERALLY ANYTHING ELSE

1
2
3
4
5
6
7
8
9
10
11
12

NOVEMBER :YEAR

09

YOUR WEEK AT A GLANCE

MONDAY	TUESDAY	WEDNESDAY	THURSDAY	FRIDAY	SATURDAY ☐
TODAY ☐	TODAY ☐	TODAY ☐	TODAY ☐	TODAY ☐	☐ SUNDAY

IT'S CARL SAGAN DAY

WEAR A TURTLENECK SWEATER WITH A BROWN JACKET IN HIS HONOR.

VANESSA MINNILLO WAS BORN IN 1980

ERIC DANE WAS BORN IN 1972

9 AM

10 AM

11 AM

NOON

1 PM

2 PM

3 PM

4 PM

5 PM

6 PM

ON THIS DAY IN 1967: THE 1ST ISSUE OF 'ROLLING STONE' WAS PUBLISHED.

NOTES AND/OR DOODLES

10

YOUR WEEK AT A GLANCE

MONDAY	TUESDAY	WEDNESDAY	THURSDAY	FRIDAY	SATURDAY ☐
TODAY ☐	TODAY ☐	TODAY ☐	TODAY ☐	TODAY ☐	☐ SUNDAY

IT'S SESAME STREET DAY

OSCAR THE GROUCH WAS ORIGINALLY ORANGE.

TRACY MORGAN WAS BORN IN 1968

SINBAD WAS BORN IN 1956

9 AM

10 AM

11 AM

NOON

1 PM

2 PM

3 PM

4 PM

5 PM

6 PM

ON THIS DAY IN 1989: THE BERLIN WALL BEGAN TO COME DOWN.

NOTES AND/OR DOODLES

YEAR: **NOVEMBER**

YOUR WEEK AT A GLANCE

MONDAY	TUESDAY	WEDNESDAY	THURSDAY	FRIDAY	SATURDAY ☐
☐ TODAY	☐ TODAY	☐ TODAY	☐ TODAY	☐ TODAY	☐ SUNDAY

11

NOTES AND/OR DOODLES

IT'S VETERANS DAY

OH, AND IT'S ALSO SINGLES' DAY.

LEONARDO DICAPRIO WAS BORN IN 1974

DEMI MOORE WAS BORN IN 1962

9 AM

10 AM

11 AM

NOON

1 PM

2 PM

3 PM

4 PM

5 PM

6 PM

ON THIS DAY IN 1994: BILL GATES BOUGHT DA VINCI'S 'CODEX' FOR $30M.

YOUR WEEK AT A GLANCE

MONDAY	TUESDAY	WEDNESDAY	THURSDAY	FRIDAY	SATURDAY ☐
☐ TODAY	☐ TODAY	☐ TODAY	☐ TODAY	☐ TODAY	☐ SUNDAY

12

NOTES AND/OR DOODLES

IT'S HAPPY HOUR DAY

HAPPY HOUR DRINKING 1ST BECAME WIDESPREAD DURING PROHIBITION.

(ALANIS MORISSETTE WOULD LIKELY CALL THAT IRONIC)

RYAN GOSLING WAS BORN IN 1980

GRACE KELLY WAS BORN IN 1929

9 AM

10 AM

11 AM

NOON

1 PM

2 PM

3 PM

4 PM

5 PM

6 PM

ON THIS DAY IN 1954: THE ELLIS ISLAND IMMIGRATION CENTER WAS CLOSED.

LISTS, NOTES & MEMOIRS

FASHION TRENDS THAT I CAN'T PULL OFF

OR A LIST OF LITERALLY ANYTHING ELSE

1
2
3
4
5
6
7
8
9
10
11
12

MY FAVORITE FICTIONAL LAWYERS

OR A MORE USEFUL (BUT STUPID) LIST

1
2
3
4
5
6
7
8
9
10
11
12

A DRAWING OF GOING COLD TURKEY (OR GOING TO TURKEY, WITH A COLD)

(OR SOME SUPER BUSINESSY STUFF)

TATTOOS THAT I'VE ALMOST GOTTEN

OR SOME BORING TO-DO LIST

1
2
3
4
5
6
7
8
9
10
11
12

NON-IDEAL TIMES TO FALL ASLEEP

OR A GROCERY LIST OR SOMETHING

1
2
3
4
5
6
7
8
9
10
11
12

YEAR: NOVEMBER

YOUR WEEK AT A GLANCE

MONDAY	TUESDAY	WEDNESDAY	THURSDAY	FRIDAY	SATURDAY ☐ / ☐ SUNDAY
☐ TODAY	☐ TODAY	☐ TODAY	☐ TODAY	☐ TODAY	

13

NOTES AND/OR DOODLES

IT'S START A RUMOR DAY

DEMI MOORE GAVE BIRTH TO RUMER WILLIS IN KENTUCKY.

(THAT'S WHAT WE HEARD ANYWAY)

JOE MANTEGNA WAS BORN IN 1947 GERARD BUTLER WAS BORN IN 1969

9 AM

10 AM

11 AM

NOON

1 PM

2 PM

3 PM

4 PM

5 PM

6 PM

ON THIS DAY IN 1940: WALT DISNEY RELEASED 'FANTASIA.'

YOUR WEEK AT A GLANCE

MONDAY	TUESDAY	WEDNESDAY	THURSDAY	FRIDAY	SATURDAY ☐ / ☐ SUNDAY
☐ TODAY	☐ TODAY	☐ TODAY	☐ TODAY	☐ TODAY	

14

NOTES AND/OR DOODLES

IT'S NATIONAL PICKLE DAY

CLEOPATRA CLAIMED THAT PICKLES MADE HER BEAUTIFUL.

CONDOLEEZZA RICE WAS BORN IN 1954 CLAUDE MONET WAS BORN IN 1840

9 AM

10 AM

11 AM

NOON

1 PM

2 PM

3 PM

4 PM

5 PM

6 PM

ON THIS DAY IN 1851: 'MOBY-DICK' BY HERMAN MELVILLE WAS 1ST PUBLISHED.

15

YOUR WEEK AT A GLANCE

MONDAY	TUESDAY	WEDNESDAY	THURSDAY	FRIDAY	SATURDAY ☐
TODAY ☐	TODAY ☐	TODAY ☐	TODAY ☐	TODAY ☐	☐ SUNDAY

IT'S NATIONAL RAISIN BRAN CEREAL DAY

THE TERM 'RAISIN BRAN' CAN'T BE TRADEMARKED, SO 3 BRANDS SELL IT.

GEORGIA O'KEEFFE WAS BORN IN 1887

RANDY SAVAGE WAS BORN IN 1952

9 AM

10 AM

11 AM

NOON

1 PM

2 PM

3 PM

4 PM

5 PM

6 PM

ON THIS DAY IN 1969: THE 1ST WENDY'S HAMBURGERS OPENED IN COLUMBUS, OH.

NOTES AND/OR DOODLES

16

YOUR WEEK AT A GLANCE

MONDAY	TUESDAY	WEDNESDAY	THURSDAY	FRIDAY	SATURDAY ☐
TODAY ☐	TODAY ☐	TODAY ☐	TODAY ☐	TODAY ☐	☐ SUNDAY

IT'S NATIONAL FAST FOOD DAY

CHIPOTLE BUYS SOME OF THEIR AVOCADOS FROM JASON MRAZ.

PETE DAVIDSON WAS BORN IN 1993

LISA BONET WAS BORN IN 1967

9 AM

10 AM

11 AM

NOON

1 PM

2 PM

3 PM

4 PM

5 PM

6 PM

ON THIS DAY IN 1907: OKLAHOMA BECAME THE 46TH STATE OF THE U.S.

NOTES AND/OR DOODLES

YEAR: **NOVEMBER**

YOUR WEEK AT A GLANCE

MONDAY	TUESDAY	WEDNESDAY	THURSDAY	FRIDAY	SATURDAY ☐
☐ TODAY	☐ TODAY	☐ TODAY	☐ TODAY	☐ TODAY	☐ SUNDAY

17

NOTES AND/OR DOODLES

IT'S INTERNATIONAL HAPPY GOSE DAY

THIS TART BEER, WITH GERMAN ORIGINS, IS PRONOUNCED GOZE-UH.

RUPAUL WAS BORN IN 1960

DANNY DEVITO WAS BORN IN 1944

9 AM

10 AM

11 AM

NOON

1 PM

2 PM

3 PM

4 PM

5 PM

6 PM

ON THIS DAY IN 1978: THE 'STAR WARS HOLIDAY SPECIAL' AIRED (THE ONLY TIME).

YOUR WEEK AT A GLANCE

MONDAY	TUESDAY	WEDNESDAY	THURSDAY	FRIDAY	SATURDAY ☐
☐ TODAY	☐ TODAY	☐ TODAY	☐ TODAY	☐ TODAY	☐ SUNDAY

18

NOTES AND/OR DOODLES

IT'S PUSH-BUTTON PHONE DAY

WHEN WE WERE KIDS, WE HAD TO MEMORIZE THINGS. IT WAS HELL.

SOJOURNER TRUTH WAS BORN IN 1797

OWEN WILSON WAS BORN IN 1968

9 AM

10 AM

11 AM

NOON

1 PM

2 PM

3 PM

4 PM

5 PM

6 PM

ON THIS DAY IN 1993: VINCE MCMAHON WAS CHARGED W/ STEROID DISTRIBUTION.

19

YOUR WEEK AT A GLANCE

MONDAY	TUESDAY	WEDNESDAY	THURSDAY	FRIDAY	SATURDAY ☐
TODAY ☐	TODAY ☐	TODAY ☐	TODAY ☐	TODAY ☐	☐ SUNDAY

IT'S PLAY MONOPOLY DAY

MARVIN GARDENS WAS MISSPELLED—IT SHOULD'VE BEEN MARVEN GARDENS.

(AN ACTUAL NEIGHBORHOOD IN ATLANTIC CITY)

ADAM DRIVER WAS BORN IN 1983

TYGA WAS BORN IN 1989

9 AM

10 AM

11 AM

NOON

1 PM

2 PM

3 PM

4 PM

5 PM

6 PM

ON THIS DAY IN 1991: TROJAN AIRED THE 1ST CONDOM AD ON NETWORK TV.

NOTES AND/OR DOODLES

20

YOUR WEEK AT A GLANCE

MONDAY	TUESDAY	WEDNESDAY	THURSDAY	FRIDAY	SATURDAY ☐
TODAY ☐	TODAY ☐	TODAY ☐	TODAY ☐	TODAY ☐	☐ SUNDAY

IT'S NATIONAL ABSURDITY DAY

MICHAEL BAY DIRECTED THE 1ST 'GOT MILK?' AD.

(AND THERE'S NOT A SINGLE EXPLOSION)

JOEL MCHALE WAS BORN IN 1971

BO DEREK WAS BORN IN 1956

9 AM

10 AM

11 AM

NOON

1 PM

2 PM

3 PM

4 PM

5 PM

6 PM

ON THIS DAY IN 1973: 'A CHARLIE BROWN THANKSGIVING' AIRED ON CBS.

NOTES AND/OR DOODLES

LISTS, NOTES & MEMOIRS

THINGS THAT I'M THANKFUL FOR

OR SOME BORING TO-DO LIST

1
2
3
4
5
6
7
8
9
10
11
12

FAMILY MEMBERS I CAN'T BE RELATED TO

OR A GROCERY LIST OR SOMETHING

1
2
3
4
5
6
7
8
9
10
11
12

A DRAWING OF MY UNCLE'S LATEST FACEBOOK POST

(OR SOME SUPER BUSINESSY STUFF)

THANKSGIVING SIDES (BEST TO WORST)

OR A MORE USEFUL (BUT STUPID) LIST

1
2
3
4
5
6
7
8
9
10
11
12

WORST TIMES TO SAY 'THANKS, YOU TOO'

OR A LIST OF LITERALLY ANYTHING ELSE

1
2
3
4
5
6
7
8
9
10
11
12

NOVEMBER

:YEAR

21

YOUR WEEK AT A GLANCE

MONDAY	TUESDAY	WEDNESDAY	THURSDAY	FRIDAY	SATURDAY ☐
TODAY ☐	TODAY ☐	TODAY ☐	TODAY ☐	TODAY ☐	☐ SUNDAY

IT'S NATIONAL STUFFING DAY

CONTROVERSIAL OPINION, BUT WE'LL PASS ON THE SOGGY BUTT BREAD.

BJORK WAS BORN IN 1965

MICHAEL STRAHAN WAS BORN IN 1971

9 AM

10 AM

11 AM

NOON

1 PM

2 PM

3 PM

4 PM

5 PM

6 PM

ON THIS DAY IN 1959: JACK BENNY & RICHARD NIXON PLAYED A MUSICAL DUET.

NOTES AND/OR DOODLES

22

YOUR WEEK AT A GLANCE

MONDAY	TUESDAY	WEDNESDAY	THURSDAY	FRIDAY	SATURDAY ☐
TODAY ☐	TODAY ☐	TODAY ☐	TODAY ☐	TODAY ☐	☐ SUNDAY

IT'S START YOUR OWN COUNTRY DAY

OVER 400 ACTIVE MICRONATIONS CURRENTLY EXIST.

HAILEY BIEBER WAS BORN IN 1996

MARK RUFFALO WAS BORN IN 1967

9 AM

10 AM

11 AM

NOON

1 PM

2 PM

3 PM

4 PM

5 PM

6 PM

ON THIS DAY IN 1954: THE HUMANE SOCIETY OF THE U.S. IS FORMED.

NOTES AND/OR DOODLES

YEAR: NOVEMBER

YOUR WEEK AT A GLANCE

MONDAY ☐ TODAY | TUESDAY ☐ TODAY | WEDNESDAY ☐ TODAY | THURSDAY ☐ TODAY | FRIDAY ☐ TODAY | SATURDAY ☐ | ☐ SUNDAY

23

NOTES AND/OR DOODLES

IT'S EAT A CRANBERRY DAY

THEY FLOAT, SO FLOODING AIDS HARVEST—THEY AREN'T GROWN IN WATER.

VINCENT CASSEL WAS BORN IN 1966

ROBIN ROBERTS WAS BORN IN 1960

9 AM

10 AM

11 AM

NOON

1 PM

2 PM

3 PM

4 PM

5 PM

6 PM

ON THIS DAY IN 1991: FREDDIE MERCURY CONFIRMED HIS AIDS DIAGNOSIS.

YOUR WEEK AT A GLANCE

MONDAY ☐ TODAY | TUESDAY ☐ TODAY | WEDNESDAY ☐ TODAY | THURSDAY ☐ TODAY | FRIDAY ☐ TODAY | SATURDAY ☐ | ☐ SUNDAY

24

NOTES AND/OR DOODLES

IT'S CELEBRATE YOUR UNIQUE TALENT DAY

1 PERCENT OF PEOPLE CAN TOUCH THEIR ELBOW WITH THEIR TONGUE.

SARAH HYLAND WAS BORN IN 1990

COLIN HANKS WAS BORN IN 1977

9 AM

10 AM

11 AM

NOON

1 PM

2 PM

3 PM

4 PM

5 PM

6 PM

ON THIS DAY 1971: D.B. COOPER ESCAPED VIA PARACHUTE W/ $200K IN RANSOM.

LISTS, NOTES & MEMOIRS

POTENTIAL TOUR RIDER DEMANDS

OR A LIST OF LITERALLY ANYTHING ELSE

1
2
3
4
5
6
7
8
9
10
11
12

FOODS THAT LOOK LIKE CELEBRITIES

OR A MORE USEFUL (BUT STUPID) LIST

1
2
3
4
5
6
7
8
9
10
11
12

A DRAWING OF A QUESTIONABLE THEME PARK RIDE

(OR SOME SUPER BUSINESSY STUFF)

PHRASES THAT SHOULD NEVER BE SAID

OR SOME BORING TO-DO LIST

1
2
3
4
5
6
7
8
9
10
11
12

USELESS THINGS I'VE MEMORIZED

OR A GROCERY LIST OR SOMETHING

1
2
3
4
5
6
7
8
9
10
11
12

YEAR: **NOVEMBER**

YOUR WEEK AT A GLANCE

MONDAY	TUESDAY	WEDNESDAY	THURSDAY	FRIDAY	SATURDAY ☐
☐ TODAY	☐ TODAY	☐ TODAY	☐ TODAY	☐ TODAY	☐ SUNDAY

25

NOTES AND/OR DOODLES

IT'S NATIONAL PARFAIT DAY

IN FRENCH, THE WORD LITERALLY MEANS 'SOMETHING PERFECT.'

BEN STEIN WAS BORN IN 1944 AMY GRANT WAS BORN IN 1960

9 AM

10 AM

11 AM

NOON

1 PM

2 PM

3 PM

4 PM

5 PM

6 PM

ON THIS DAY IN 1963: THE FUNERAL FOR PRESIDENT JOHN F. KENNEDY WAS HELD.

YOUR WEEK AT A GLANCE

MONDAY	TUESDAY	WEDNESDAY	THURSDAY	FRIDAY	SATURDAY ☐
☐ TODAY	☐ TODAY	☐ TODAY	☐ TODAY	☐ TODAY	☐ SUNDAY

26

NOTES AND/OR DOODLES

IT'S GOOD GRIEF DAY

DURING THE 1980s, SALLY WAS VOICED BY FERGIE.

TINA TURNER WAS BORN IN 1939 RITA ORA WAS BORN IN 1990

9 AM

10 AM

11 AM

NOON

1 PM

2 PM

3 PM

4 PM

5 PM

6 PM

ON THIS DAY IN 2003: THE CONCORDE COMPLETED ITS FINAL FLIGHT.

27

YOUR WEEK AT A GLANCE

MONDAY	TUESDAY	WEDNESDAY	THURSDAY	FRIDAY	SATURDAY ☐
TODAY ☐	TODAY ☐	TODAY ☐	TODAY ☐	TODAY ☐	☐ SUNDAY

IT'S NATIONAL ELECTRIC GUITAR DAY

IN 2001 CHRIS BLACK, A BRITISH MUSICIAN, MARRIED HIS STRATOCASTER.

(HER NAME IS FENDA, BTW)

BRUCE LEE WAS BORN IN 1940 JIMI HENDRIX WAS BORN IN 1942

9 AM

10 AM

11 AM

NOON

1 PM

2 PM

3 PM

4 PM

5 PM

6 PM

ON THIS DAY IN 2005: 50 CENT & AEROSMITH HEADLINED A BAT MITZVAH.

NOTES AND/OR DOODLES

28

YOUR WEEK AT A GLANCE

MONDAY	TUESDAY	WEDNESDAY	THURSDAY	FRIDAY	SATURDAY ☐
TODAY ☐	TODAY ☐	TODAY ☐	TODAY ☐	TODAY ☐	☐ SUNDAY

IT'S NATIONAL FRENCH TOAST DAY

ITALIANS LIKE TO PUT MOZZARELLA IN BETWEEN TWO SLICES OF IT.

BRYSHERE Y. GRAY WAS BORN IN 1993 ED HARRIS WAS BORN IN 1950

9 AM

10 AM

11 AM

NOON

1 PM

2 PM

3 PM

4 PM

5 PM

6 PM

ON THIS DAY IN 1994: SERIAL KILLER JEFFREY DAHMER WAS KILLED IN PRISON.

NOTES AND/OR DOODLES

YOUR WEEK AT A GLANCE

MONDAY	TUESDAY	WEDNESDAY	THURSDAY	FRIDAY	SATURDAY ☐
☐ TODAY	☐ TODAY	☐ TODAY	☐ TODAY	☐ TODAY	☐ SUNDAY

29

NOTES AND/OR DOODLES

IT'S NATIONAL LEMON CREME PIE DAY

DURING THE RENAISSANCE, WOMEN REDDENED THEIR LIPS W/ LEMON JUICE.

ANNA FARIS WAS BORN IN 1976

C.S.LEWIS WAS BORN IN 1898

9 AM

10 AM

11 AM

NOON

1 PM

2 PM

3 PM

4 PM

5 PM

6 PM

ON THIS DAY IN 1972: ATARI REVEALED THEIR ARCADE GAME 'PONG.'

YOUR WEEK AT A GLANCE

MONDAY	TUESDAY	WEDNESDAY	THURSDAY	FRIDAY	SATURDAY ☐
☐ TODAY	☐ TODAY	☐ TODAY	☐ TODAY	☐ TODAY	☐ SUNDAY

30

NOTES AND/OR DOODLES

IT'S NATIONAL MASON JAR DAY

SAFELY PRESERVES FOOD & REFRESHES HIPSTERS.

CHRISSY TEIGEN WAS BORN IN 1985

WINSTON CHURCHILL WAS BORN IN 1874

9 AM

10 AM

11 AM

NOON

1 PM

2 PM

3 PM

4 PM

5 PM

6 PM

ON THIS DAY IN 2004: KEN JENNINGS LOST ON 'JEOPARDY!' (AFTER 74 WINS).

NOVEMBER IN REVIEW

REASONS THAT NOVEMBER WAS GREAT

'IT ENDED' IS A VALID ANSWER

1
2
3
4
5
6
7
8
9
10
11
12

MY NOVEMBER ACCOMPLISHMENTS

- THREW AWAY A DECOMPOSING PUMPKIN ☐
- PLANNED TO GET SHOPPING DONE EARLY ☐
- DIDN'T BUY A SINGLE GIFT ☐
- GOT ICE CREAM WHEN IT WAS 50° OUT ☐
- BOUGHT HALF-PRICED CANDY CORN ☐
- REALIZED CANDY CORN IS GROSS ☐
- FINALLY STARTED RAKING THE YARD ☐
- CURSED AT NATURE ☐
- DECIDED TO HOST THANKSGIVING ☐
- IMMEDIATELY REGRETTED THAT DECISION ☐
- BOUGHT A TURKEY LIKE AN ADULT ☐
- FORGOT TO THAW THE FROZEN TURKEY ☐
- SERVED BURNT TURKEY AT 9PM ☐
- WAS THANKFUL THANKSGIVING WAS OVER ☐
- DIDN'T GET TRAMPLED ONCE ☐

IF NOVEMBER WAS A MOVIE, DRAW THE STARRING ROLES

CLICHÉS OVERHEARD THIS MONTH

- ☐ 'WE GET FRIDAY OFF, RIGHT?
- ☐ 'SCARY MASK, BUT HALLOWEEN'S OVER'
- ☐ 'DO WE HAVE TO GO OVER THERE?'
- ☐ 'I'M DONE WITH MY SHOPPING ALREADY'
- ☐ 'WHO HAS TO BLOW UP THE BALLOONS?'
- ☐ 'HASHTAG BLESSED'
- ☐ 'DO WE SERIOUSLY HAVE TO WATCH THIS?'
- ☐ 'I HATE HOW IT GETS DARK SO EARLY'
- ☐ 'HAPPY 'EXTRA HOUR OF SLEEP' DAY!'
- ☐ 'I ALREADY HAVE MY TREE UP'
- ☐ 'IT'S LIKE THESE LEAVES GROW ON TREES'
- ☐ 'I LOVE THANKSGIVING LEFTOVERS!'
- ☐ 'DID GRANDMA JUST FALL ASLEEP?'
- ☐ 'SHOULD I WEAR MY HEAVY COAT?'
- ☐ 'OH WOW, IT'S SNOWING!'
- ☐ 'THERE'S ALWAYS ROOM FOR PIE'
- ☐ 'TIME TO PUT ON MY EATING PANTS'

REASONS THAT I'M GLAD NOVEMBER IS OVER

USE ADDITIONAL PAPER IF NEEDED

1
2
3
4
5
6
7
8
9
10
11
12
13
14

NOVEMBER IN REVIEW

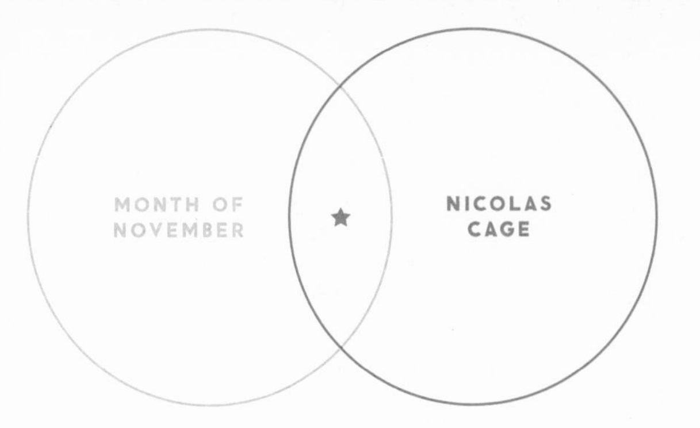

NOVEMBER VENN DIAGRAM

WHAT DID THEY HAVE IN COMMON?

KNOWN FOR MAKING TURKEYS 1

2

3

4

5

6

7

8

AWKWARD THINGS THAT HAPPENED

(AND WILL KEEP ME UP AT NIGHT)

1

2

3

4

5

6

7

8

9

10

11

12

13

14

15

16

17

ENJOYMENT OVER TIME

CHOOSE A COLOR KEY

LINE	ITEM
——	BEING WITH RELATIVES
— —	DRINKING HEAVILY
	HEARING CHRISTMAS MUSIC
	HEARING OTHER MUSIC
	SPENDING 12 HRS COOKING
	EATING LEFTOVERS
	CHINESE FOOD
	WATCHING A PARADE ON TV
	CROWDS OF PEOPLE
	DISCOUNT ELECTRONICS

NOVEMBER ENJOYMENT INDEX

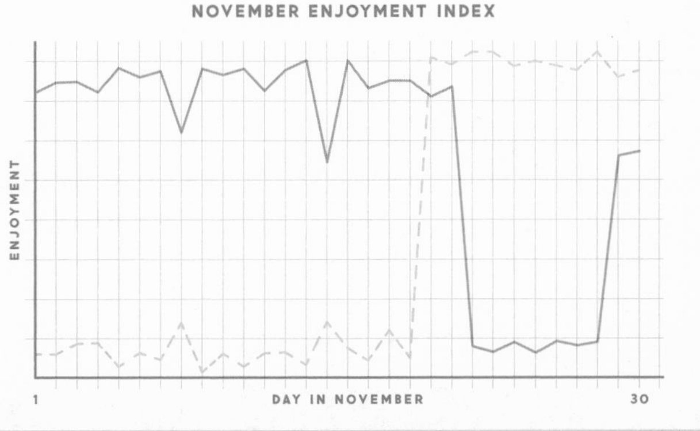

ORIGINALLY THE TENTH MONTH OF THE YEAR (IN THE ROMAN CALENDAR).

WELCOME TO

× DECEMBER ×

OF WHATEVER YEAR
YOU SAY IT IS.

LET'S GO WITH:

ITS NAME COMES FROM THE LATIN WORD 'DECEM' (MEANING TEN).

DECEMBER AT A GLANCE :YEAR

YOU MADE IT
TO DECEMBER

✖

CELEBRATE, IT'S:

UNIVERSAL HUMAN RIGHTS MONTH

NATIONAL PEAR MONTH

NATIONAL CAR DONATION MONTH

AIDS AWARENESS MONTH

SPIRITUAL LITERACY MONTH

✖

OFFICIAL SYMBOLS:

BIRTHSTONE: TURQUOISE

FLOWERS: NARCISSUS & HOLLY

TREES: HORNBEAM, FIG, & BEECH

SAGITTARIUS (NOV 22 / DEC 21)

CAPRICORN (DEC 22 / JAN 19)

DATES TO KNOW*
LIKE, IMPORTANT ONES

✖

WORLD AIDS DAY
DECEMBER 1ST

FEAST OF OUR LADY OF GUADALUPE
(MEXICAN)
DECEMBER 12TH

HANUKKAH
(JUDAISM)
STARTS ON THE 25TH DAY OF THE HEBREW MONTH OF KISLEV (USUALLY DECEMBER)

START OF WINTER
(WINTER SOLSTICE)
DECEMBER 21ST (OR 22ND)

CHRISTMAS DAY
DECEMBER 25TH

BOXING DAY
(UNITED KINGDOM)
DECEMBER 26TH

KWANZAA
STARTS ON DECEMBER 26TH

NEW YEAR'S EVE
DECEMBER 31ST

THINGS TO ACCOMPLISH THIS MONTH
FOR EXAMPLE: FILL OUT A TO-DO LIST

1
2
3
4
5
6
7
8
9
10
11
12
13
14
15

THINGS THAT ARE NEVER GOING TO HAPPEN
THERE'S ALWAYS NEXT YEAR

1
2
3
4
5
6
7
8
9
10
11
12
13
14
15

*A DISCLAIMER OF SORTS

HEY THERE. WE HERE AT BRASS MONKEY LIKE TO JOKE AROUND...BUT WE ALSO WANT TO TAKE A MINUTE TO RECOGNIZE JUST A FEW OF THE MANY HOLIDAYS & EVENTS THAT ARE IMPORTANT TO OUR FRIENDS AROUND THE GLOBE (AND AT HOME). YOU MAY BE DIFFERENT THAN US. WE MAY HAVE NEVER MET. BUT WE LOVE YOU ALL THE SAME.

SO IF YOU HAVEN'T HEARD OF A DAY, LOOK IT UP. LEARNING ABOUT & APPRECIATING CULTURES DIFFERENT THAN YOURS IS IMPORTANT...WAY MORE THAN POSTING A FEW 'STRAWBERRY JAM DAY' SELFIES.

DECEMBER AT A GLANCE

YEAR:

IT'S DECEMBER

START PLANNING

×

START OF WINTER*
DECEMBER 21ST (OR 22ND)

CHRISTMAS DAY
DECEMBER 25TH

NEW YEAR'S EVE
DECEMBER 31ST

×

BIRTHDAYS

TO REMEMBER

*PSST: SINCE THIS HOLIDAY MOVES AROUND EACH YEAR (AND WE DON'T KNOW WHEN IN THE FUTURE YOU'RE USING THIS), HELP US OUT AND ADD IT TO THE CALENDAR.

ALSO, ARE THERE JET PACKS YET? OUR FINGERS ARE CROSSED.

DAY OF WEEK S M T W T F S	DAY OF WEEK S M T W T F S	DAY OF WEEK S M T W T F S	DAY OF WEEK S M T W T F S	DAY OF WEEK S M T W T F S	DAY OF WEEK S M T W T F S	DAY OF WEEK S M T W T F S
01	02	03	04	05	06	07
08	09	10	11	12	13	14
15	16	17	18	19	20	21
22	23	24	CHRISTMAS DAY 25	26	27	28
29	30	NEW YEAR'S EVE 31	NOTES:			

DECEMBER, AS EXPRESSED IN A DRAWING

DECEMBER PREVIEW

DECEMBER VENN DIAGRAM

WHAT DO THEY HAVE IN COMMON?

1 BEARDED GUYS W/ OCCUPIED LAPS

2

3

4

5

6

7

8

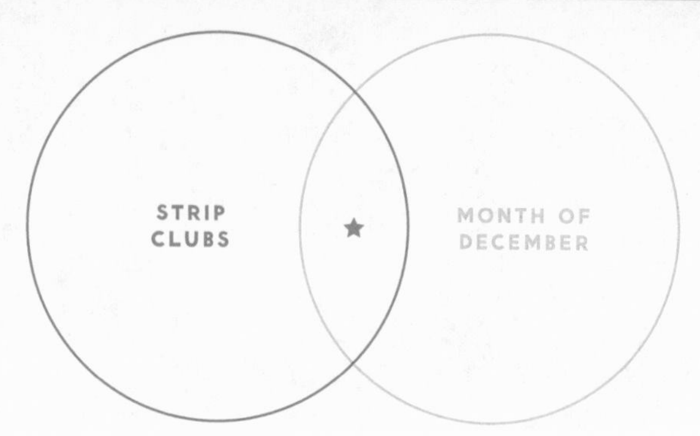

A DRAWING OF A LITERAL WAR ON CHRISTMAS

SUPPLIES NEEDED FOR THE MONTH

ALCOHOL, AND OTHER NECESSITIES

1

2

3

4

5

6

7

8

9

10

11

12

13

14

15

16

17

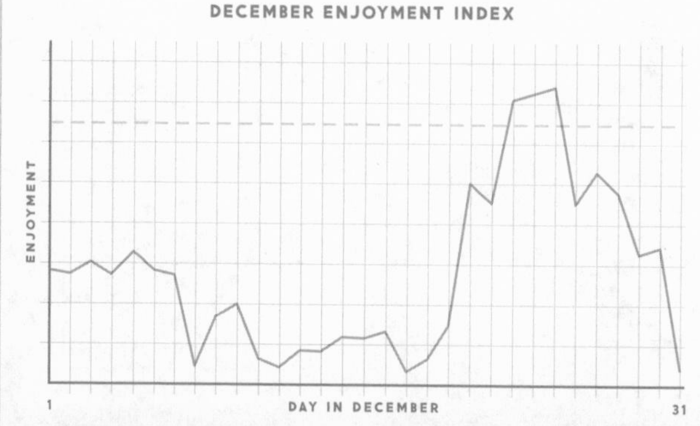

ENJOYMENT OVER TIME

CHOOSE A COLOR KEY

LINE	ITEM
——	SNOW BLIZZARDS
– –	DAIRY QUEEN BLIZZARDS
	WEARING UGLY THINGS
	TALKING ABOUT FRUITCAKE
	LOOKING AT LIGHT BULBS
	SITTING ON LAPS
	WEARING NUMBER GLASSES
	COUNTING WHILE YELLING
	DRINKING (EGGNOG)
	DRINKING (ANYTHING)

YEAR: **DECEMBER**

YOUR WEEK AT A GLANCE

MONDAY	TUESDAY	WEDNESDAY	THURSDAY	FRIDAY	SATURDAY ☐
☐ TODAY	☐ TODAY	☐ TODAY	☐ TODAY	☐ TODAY	☐ SUNDAY

01

NOTES AND/OR DOODLES

IT'S NATIONAL CHRISTMAS LIGHTS DAY

THOMAS EDISON SHOWCASED THE 1ST LIT CHRISTMAS TREE IN 1882.

RICHARD PRYOR WAS BORN IN 1940

BETTE MIDLER WAS BORN IN 1945

9 AM

10 AM

11 AM

NOON

1 PM

2 PM

3 PM

4 PM

5 PM

6 PM

ON THIS DAY IN 1955: ROSA PARKS WAS ARRESTED, IGNITING THE BUS BOYCOTT.

YOUR WEEK AT A GLANCE

MONDAY	TUESDAY	WEDNESDAY	THURSDAY	FRIDAY	SATURDAY ☐
☐ TODAY	☐ TODAY	☐ TODAY	☐ TODAY	☐ TODAY	☐ SUNDAY

02

NOTES AND/OR DOODLES

IT'S PLAY BASKETBALL DAY

THE AVERAGE NBA PLAYER HAS A VERTICAL LEAP OF 28 INCHES.

BRITNEY SPEARS WAS BORN IN 1981

LUCY LIU WAS BORN IN 1968

9 AM

10 AM

11 AM

NOON

1 PM

2 PM

3 PM

4 PM

5 PM

6 PM

ON THIS DAY IN 1997: 'GOOD WILL HUNTING' WAS RELEASED.

03

YOUR WEEK AT A GLANCE

MONDAY	TUESDAY	WEDNESDAY	THURSDAY	FRIDAY	SATURDAY ☐
TODAY ☐	TODAY ☐	TODAY ☐	TODAY ☐	TODAY ☐	☐ SUNDAY

IT'S NATIONAL GREEN BEAN CASSEROLE DAY

THE ORIGINAL RECIPE IS IN THE NATIONAL INVENTOR'S HALL OF FAME.

BRENDAN FRASER WAS BORN IN 1968

DASCHA POLANCO WAS BORN IN 1982

9 AM

10 AM

11 AM

NOON

1 PM

2 PM

3 PM

4 PM

5 PM

6 PM

ON THIS DAY IN 1976: AN ASSASSINATION ATTEMPT WAS MADE ON BOB MARLEY.

NOTES AND/OR DOODLES

04

YOUR WEEK AT A GLANCE

MONDAY	TUESDAY	WEDNESDAY	THURSDAY	FRIDAY	SATURDAY ☐
TODAY ☐	TODAY ☐	TODAY ☐	TODAY ☐	TODAY ☐	☐ SUNDAY

IT'S NATIONAL DICE DAY

THE DOTS ON TRADITIONAL DICE ARE KNOWN AS 'PIPS.'

JAY-Z WAS BORN IN 1969

FRED ARMISEN WAS BORN IN 1966

9 AM

10 AM

11 AM

NOON

1 PM

2 PM

3 PM

4 PM

5 PM

6 PM

ON THIS DAY IN 1980: LED ZEPPELIN OFFICIALLY DISBANDED.

NOTES AND/OR DOODLES

YEAR: **DECEMBER**

YOUR WEEK AT A GLANCE

MONDAY	TUESDAY	WEDNESDAY	THURSDAY	FRIDAY	SATURDAY ☐
☐ TODAY	☐ TODAY	☐ TODAY	☐ TODAY	☐ TODAY	☐ SUNDAY

05

NOTES AND/OR DOODLES

IT'S THE DAY OF THE NINJA

SOME USED A CODE TO PASS COVERT MESSAGES USING COLORED RICE.

(IT'S CALLED 'GOSHIKIMAI')

WALT DISNEY WAS BORN IN 1901

FRANKIE MUNIZ WAS BORN IN 1985

9 AM

10 AM

11 AM

NOON

1 PM

2 PM

3 PM

4 PM

5 PM

6 PM

ON THIS DAY IN 1933: PROHIBITION ENDED (THANKS TO THE 21ST AMENDMENT).

YOUR WEEK AT A GLANCE

MONDAY	TUESDAY	WEDNESDAY	THURSDAY	FRIDAY	SATURDAY ☐
☐ TODAY	☐ TODAY	☐ TODAY	☐ TODAY	☐ TODAY	☐ SUNDAY

06

NOTES AND/OR DOODLES

IT'S NATIONAL MICROWAVE DAY

IT WAS INVENTED BY ACCIDENT WHILE WORKING ON RADARS FOR WWII.

AGNES MOOREHEAD WAS BORN IN 1900

PRINCESS SOFIA WAS BORN IN 1984

9 AM

10 AM

11 AM

NOON

1 PM

2 PM

3 PM

4 PM

5 PM

6 PM

ON THIS DAY IN 1964: 'RUDOLPH THE RED-NOSED REINDEER' DEBUTED.

07

YOUR WEEK AT A GLANCE

MONDAY	TUESDAY	WEDNESDAY	THURSDAY	FRIDAY	SATURDAY ☐
TODAY ☐	TODAY ☐	TODAY ☐	TODAY ☐	TODAY ☐	☐ SUNDAY

IT'S LETTER WRITING DAY

LET'S BE PEN PALS. SERIOUSLY, WE'LL WRITE BACK.

(1107 HICKORY ST. KANSAS CITY, MO 64101)

LARRY BIRD WAS BORN IN 1956

TERRELL OWENS WAS BORN IN 1973

9 AM

10 AM

11 AM

NOON

1 PM

2 PM

3 PM

4 PM

5 PM

6 PM

ON THIS DAY IN 1941: PEARL HARBOR, HAWAII, WAS ATTACKED BY JAPAN.

NOTES AND/OR DOODLES

08

YOUR WEEK AT A GLANCE

MONDAY	TUESDAY	WEDNESDAY	THURSDAY	FRIDAY	SATURDAY ☐
TODAY ☐	TODAY ☐	TODAY ☐	TODAY ☐	TODAY ☐	☐ SUNDAY

IT'S NATIONAL BROWNIE DAY

ACCORDING TO OUR CORRECT OPINION, CENTER PIECES ARE THE BEST.

DIEGO RIVERA WAS BORN IN 1886

NICKI MINAJ WAS BORN IN 1982

9 AM

10 AM

11 AM

NOON

1 PM

2 PM

3 PM

4 PM

5 PM

6 PM

ON THIS DAY IN 1995: THE GRATEFUL DEAD ANNOUNCED THEIR BREAK UP.

NOTES AND/OR DOODLES

LISTS, NOTES & MEMOIRS

WORST PRESENTS I'VE EVER RECEIVED

OR SOME BORING TO-DO LIST

1
2
3
4
5
6
7
8
9
10
11
12

WORST PRESENTS I'VE EVER GIVEN

OR A GROCERY LIST OR SOMETHING

1
2
3
4
5
6
7
8
9
10
11
12

A DRAWING OF THE SKELETONS (AND/OR CLOTHES) IN MY CLOSET

(OR SOME SUPER BUSINESSY STUFF)

MOVIES I'M NOT READY TO WATCH

OR A MORE USEFUL (BUT STUPID) LIST

1
2
3
4
5
6
7
8
9
10
11
12

MORE ACCURATE INSPIRATIONAL PHRASES

OR A LIST OF LITERALLY ANYTHING ELSE

1
2
3
4
5
6
7
8
9
10
11
12

09

YOUR WEEK AT A GLANCE

MONDAY	TUESDAY	WEDNESDAY	THURSDAY	FRIDAY	SATURDAY ☐
TODAY ☐	TODAY ☐	TODAY ☐	TODAY ☐	TODAY ☐	☐ SUNDAY

IT'S NATIONAL LLAMA DAY

WHEN AGITATED, THEY CAN SPIT DISTANCES OF OVER 15 FEET.

JUDI DENCH WAS BORN IN 1934

JOHN MALKOVICH WAS BORN IN 1953

9 AM

10 AM

11 AM

NOON

1 PM

2 PM

3 PM

4 PM

5 PM

6 PM

ON THIS DAY IN 1965: 'A CHARLIE BROWN CHRISTMAS' PREMIERED.

NOTES AND/OR DOODLES

10

YOUR WEEK AT A GLANCE

MONDAY	TUESDAY	WEDNESDAY	THURSDAY	FRIDAY	SATURDAY ☐
TODAY ☐	TODAY ☐	TODAY ☐	TODAY ☐	TODAY ☐	☐ SUNDAY

IT'S NATIONAL LAGER DAY

THE PILGRIMS WERE LOW ON BEER, SO THEY STOPPED AT PLYMOUTH ROCK.

MICHAEL DUNCAN WAS BORN IN 1957

EMILY DICKINSON WAS BORN IN 1830

9 AM

10 AM

11 AM

NOON

1 PM

2 PM

3 PM

4 PM

5 PM

6 PM

ON THIS DAY IN 1967: OTIS REDDING WAS KILLED IN A PLANE CRASH.

NOTES AND/OR DOODLES

YEAR: **DECEMBER**

YOUR WEEK AT A GLANCE

MONDAY	TUESDAY	WEDNESDAY	THURSDAY	FRIDAY	SATURDAY ☐
☐ TODAY	☐ TODAY	☐ TODAY	☐ TODAY	☐ TODAY	☐ SUNDAY

11

NOTES AND/OR DOODLES

IT'S INTERNATIONAL MOUNTAIN DAY

ON AVERAGE, 6 PEOPLE DIE EVERY YEAR TRYING TO CLIMB MT. EVEREST.

REY MYSTERIO WAS BORN IN 1974

HAILEE STEINFELD WAS BORN IN 1996

9 AM

10 AM

11 AM

NOON

1 PM

2 PM

3 PM

4 PM

5 PM

6 PM

ON THIS DAY IN 1769: VENETIAN BLINDS WERE PATENTED BY EDWARD BEVAN.

YOUR WEEK AT A GLANCE

MONDAY	TUESDAY	WEDNESDAY	THURSDAY	FRIDAY	SATURDAY ☐
☐ TODAY	☐ TODAY	☐ TODAY	☐ TODAY	☐ TODAY	☐ SUNDAY

12

NOTES AND/OR DOODLES

IT'S NATIONAL POINSETTIA DAY

NAMED AFTER JOEL R. POINSETT, THE 1ST U.S. AMBASSADOR TO MEXICO.

FRANK SINATRA WAS BORN IN 1915

MAYIM BIALIK WAS BORN IN 1975

9 AM

10 AM

11 AM

NOON

1 PM

2 PM

3 PM

4 PM

5 PM

6 PM

ON THIS DAY IN 1987: 'FAITH' BY GEORGE MICHAEL HIT NUMBER 1.

LISTS, NOTES & MEMOIRS

FIRST SNOW ACTIVITIES

OR A LIST OF LITERALLY ANYTHING ELSE

1
2
3
4
5
6
7
8
9
10
11
12

SUBSEQUENT SNOW ACTIVITIES

OR A MORE USEFUL (BUT STUPID) LIST

1
2
3
4
5
6
7
8
9
10
11
12

A DRAWING OF A TREASURE MAP (OR A TREASURE TRAIL)

(OR SOME SUPER BUSINESSY STUFF)

MONTHS OF THE YEAR (BEST TO WORST)

OR SOME BORING TO-DO LIST

1
2
3
4
5
6
7
8
9
10
11
12

DUMB THINGS THAT MAKE ME CRY

OR A GROCERY LIST OR SOMETHING

1
2
3
4
5
6
7
8
9
10
11
12

YEAR: **DECEMBER**

YOUR WEEK AT A GLANCE

MONDAY	TUESDAY	WEDNESDAY	THURSDAY	FRIDAY	SATURDAY ☐
☐ TODAY	☐ TODAY	☐ TODAY	☐ TODAY	☐ TODAY	☐ SUNDAY

13

NOTES AND/OR DOODLES

IT'S NATIONAL VIOLIN DAY

THE ACT OF PLAYING BURNS APPROXIMATELY 170 CALORIES PER HOUR.

TAYLOR SWIFT WAS BORN IN 1989

NATASCHA MCELHONE WAS BORN IN 1969

9 AM

10 AM

11 AM

NOON

1 PM

2 PM

3 PM

4 PM

5 PM

6 PM

ON THIS DAY IN 1950: JAMES DEAN BEGAN HIS CAREER (IN A PEPSI COMMERCIAL).

YOUR WEEK AT A GLANCE

MONDAY	TUESDAY	WEDNESDAY	THURSDAY	FRIDAY	SATURDAY ☐
☐ TODAY	☐ TODAY	☐ TODAY	☐ TODAY	☐ TODAY	☐ SUNDAY

14

NOTES AND/OR DOODLES

IT'S ROAST CHESTNUTS DAY

ROASTING OVER AN OPEN FIRE? SCORE THE SKINS SO THEY DON'T EXPLODE.

VANESSA HUDGENS WAS BORN IN 1988

AWKWAFINA WAS BORN IN 1988

9 AM

10 AM

11 AM

NOON

1 PM

2 PM

3 PM

4 PM

5 PM

6 PM

ON THIS DAY IN 2008: AN IRAQI JOURNALIST THREW A SHOE AT GEORGE W. BUSH.

15

YOUR WEEK AT A GLANCE

MONDAY	TUESDAY	WEDNESDAY	THURSDAY	FRIDAY	SATURDAY ☐
TODAY ☐	TODAY ☐	TODAY ☐	TODAY ☐	TODAY ☐	☐ SUNDAY

IT'S NATIONAL WEAR YOUR PEARLS DAY

THEY ARE THE ONLY GEMSTONE TO COME FROM A LIVING CREATURE.

DON JOHNSON WAS BORN IN 1949

MAUDE APATOW WAS BORN IN 1997

9 AM

10 AM

11 AM

NOON

1 PM

2 PM

3 PM

4 PM

5 PM

6 PM

ON THIS DAY IN 2001: THE TOWER OF PISA REOPENED AFTER $27M IN REPAIRS.

NOTES AND/OR DOODLES

16

YOUR WEEK AT A GLANCE

MONDAY	TUESDAY	WEDNESDAY	THURSDAY	FRIDAY	SATURDAY ☐
TODAY ☐	TODAY ☐	TODAY ☐	TODAY ☐	TODAY ☐	☐ SUNDAY

IT'S STUPID TOY DAY

THE FIRST MR. POTATO HEAD REQUIRED AN ACTUAL POTATO.*

(*ROOT VEGETABLE NOT INCLUDED)

ANNA POPPLEWELL WAS BORN IN 1988

BENJAMIN BRATT WAS BORN IN 1963

9 AM

10 AM

11 AM

NOON

1 PM

2 PM

3 PM

4 PM

5 PM

6 PM

ON THIS DAY IN 1773: THE BOSTON TEA PARTY TOOK PLACE.

NOTES AND/OR DOODLES

YEAR: **DECEMBER**

YOUR WEEK AT A GLANCE

MONDAY	TUESDAY	WEDNESDAY	THURSDAY	FRIDAY	SATURDAY ☐
☐ TODAY	☐ TODAY	☐ TODAY	☐ TODAY	☐ TODAY	☐ SUNDAY

17

NOTES AND/OR DOODLES

IT'S NATIONAL MAPLE SYRUP DAY

IN 2012, THIEVES STOLE 6 MILLION LBS. OF IT (WORTH $18 MILLION).

MILLA JOVOVICH WAS BORN IN 1975

MANNY PACQUIAO WAS BORN IN 1978

9 AM

10 AM

11 AM

NOON

1 PM

2 PM

3 PM

4 PM

5 PM

6 PM

ON THIS DAY IN 1892: THE 1ST ISSUE OF 'VOGUE' MAGAZINE WAS PUBLISHED.

YOUR WEEK AT A GLANCE

MONDAY	TUESDAY	WEDNESDAY	THURSDAY	FRIDAY	SATURDAY ☐
☐ TODAY	☐ TODAY	☐ TODAY	☐ TODAY	☐ TODAY	☐ SUNDAY

18

NOTES AND/OR DOODLES

IT'S NATIONAL TWIN DAY

1 TO 2 PERCENT OF ALL FRATERNAL TWINS HAVE DIFFERENT DADS.

BRAD PITT WAS BORN IN 1963

SIA WAS BORN IN 1975

9 AM

10 AM

11 AM

NOON

1 PM

2 PM

3 PM

4 PM

5 PM

6 PM

ON THIS DAY IN 1997: COMEDIAN CHRIS FARLEY DIED FROM A DRUG OVERDOSE.

DECEMBER :YEAR

19

YOUR WEEK AT A GLANCE

MONDAY	TUESDAY	WEDNESDAY	THURSDAY	FRIDAY	SATURDAY ☐
TODAY ☐	TODAY ☐	TODAY ☐	TODAY ☐	TODAY ☐	☐ SUNDAY

IT'S HOLLY DAY

ROMANS BELIEVED THAT IT PROTECTED AGAINST LIGHTNING STRIKES.

(THERE'S EVIDENCE THAT THIS MAY BE PARTIALLY TRUE, BTW)

ALYSSA MILANO WAS BORN IN 1972 — TYSON BECKFORD WAS BORN IN 1970

9 AM

10 AM

11 AM

NOON

1 PM

2 PM

3 PM

4 PM

5 PM

6 PM

NOTES AND/OR DOODLES

ON THIS DAY IN 1986: 'LITTLE SHOP OF HORRORS' DEBUTED IN THEATERS.

20

YOUR WEEK AT A GLANCE

MONDAY	TUESDAY	WEDNESDAY	THURSDAY	FRIDAY	SATURDAY ☐
TODAY ☐	TODAY ☐	TODAY ☐	TODAY ☐	TODAY ☐	☐ SUNDAY

IT'S NATIONAL SANGRIA DAY

OR TRY MANGRIA: 3 PARTS RED WINE, 1 PART VODKA, & 1 PART O.J.

DICK WOLF WAS BORN IN 1946 — LARA STONE WAS BORN IN 1983

9 AM

10 AM

11 AM

NOON

1 PM

2 PM

3 PM

4 PM

5 PM

6 PM

NOTES AND/OR DOODLES

ON THIS DAY IN 1957: ELVIS PRESLEY WAS DRAFTED (HE WOULD SERVE 2 YRS).

HONEST DESCRIPTIONS OF U.S. STATES

OR SOME BORING TO-DO LIST

1
2
3
4
5
6
7
8
9
10
11
12

CHRISTMAS SONGS WORSE THAN TORTURE

OR A GROCERY LIST OR SOMETHING

1
2
3
4
5
6
7
8
9
10
11
12

A DRAWING OF A MALL SANTA

(OR SOME SUPER BUSINESSY STUFF)

WORST SONGS TO HAVE SEX TO

OR A MORE USEFUL (BUT STUPID) LIST

1
2
3
4
5
6
7
8
9
10
11
12

ALTERNATE MEANINGS FOR ACRONYMS

OR A LIST OF LITERALLY ANYTHING ELSE

1
2
3
4
5
6
7
8
9
10
11
12

21

YOUR WEEK AT A GLANCE

MONDAY	TUESDAY	WEDNESDAY	THURSDAY	FRIDAY	SATURDAY ☐
TODAY ☐	TODAY ☐	TODAY ☐	TODAY ☐	TODAY ☐	☐ SUNDAY

IT'S CROSSWORD PUZZLE DAY

IN 1926 A MAN IN BUDAPEST COMMITTED SUICIDE & LEFT ONE AS HIS NOTE.

(HAPPY HOLIDAYS)

SAMUEL L. JACKSON WAS BORN IN 1948

RAY ROMANO WAS BORN IN 1957

NOTES AND/OR DOODLES

9 AM

10 AM

11 AM

NOON

1 PM

2 PM

3 PM

4 PM

5 PM

6 PM

ON THIS DAY IN 2012: THE WORLD ENDED (ACCORDING TO THE MAYAN CALENDAR).

22

YOUR WEEK AT A GLANCE

MONDAY	TUESDAY	WEDNESDAY	THURSDAY	FRIDAY	SATURDAY ☐
TODAY ☐	TODAY ☐	TODAY ☐	TODAY ☐	TODAY ☐	☐ SUNDAY

IT'S NATIONAL COOKIE EXCHANGE DAY

IF YOU HAVE ANY LEFT OVER, YOU KNOW WHERE TO FIND US.

(WE'LL SEND YOU SOMETHING BACK)

JORDAN SPARKS WAS BORN IN 1989

MEGHAN TRAINOR WAS BORN IN 1993

NOTES AND/OR DOODLES

9 AM

10 AM

11 AM

NOON

1 PM

2 PM

3 PM

4 PM

5 PM

6 PM

ON THIS DAY IN 1808: LUDWIG VAN BEETHOVEN'S FIFTH SYMPHONY PREMIERED.

YEAR: **DECEMBER**

YOUR WEEK AT A GLANCE

MONDAY	TUESDAY	WEDNESDAY	THURSDAY	FRIDAY	SATURDAY ☐
☐ TODAY	☐ TODAY	☐ TODAY	☐ TODAY	☐ TODAY	☐ SUNDAY

23

NOTES AND/OR DOODLES

IT'S FESTIVUS

WRITER DAN O'KEEFE BASED IT ON HIS FATHER'S REAL TRADITION.

MADAM C.J. WALKER WAS BORN IN 1967 EDDIE VEDDER WAS BORN IN 1964

9 AM

10 AM

11 AM

NOON

1 PM

2 PM

3 PM

4 PM

5 PM

6 PM

ON THIS DAY IN 1888: VINCENT VAN GOGH CUT OFF PART OF HIS LEFT EAR.

YOUR WEEK AT A GLANCE

MONDAY	TUESDAY	WEDNESDAY	THURSDAY	FRIDAY	SATURDAY ☐
☐ TODAY	☐ TODAY	☐ TODAY	☐ TODAY	☐ TODAY	☐ SUNDAY

24

NOTES AND/OR DOODLES

IT'S CHRISTMAS EVE

OH, AND IT'S ALSO NATIONAL EGGNOG DAY.

LEE DANIELS WAS BORN IN 1959 RYAN SEACREST WAS BORN IN 1974

9 AM

10 AM

11 AM

NOON

1 PM

2 PM

3 PM

4 PM

5 PM

6 PM

ON THIS DAY IN 1955: NORAD TRACKS SANTA FOR THE FIRST TIME.

LISTS, NOTES & MEMOIRS

ANIMALS THAT LOOK LIKE MY IN-LAWS
OR A LIST OF LITERALLY ANYTHING ELSE

1
2
3
4
5
6
7
8
9
10
11
12

STORES THAT SHOULD NEVER CLOSE
OR A MORE USEFUL (BUT STUPID) LIST

1
2
3
4
5
6
7
8
9
10
11
12

A DRAWING OF THE FUTURE OF FASHION

(OR SOME SUPER BUSINESSY STUFF)

HOBBIES TO START & QUICKLY REGRET
OR SOME BORING TO-DO LIST

1
2
3
4
5
6
7
8
9
10
11
12

CRIMES I'D LIKELY BE GOOD AT
OR A GROCERY LIST OR SOMETHING

1
2
3
4
5
6
7
8
9
10
11
12

YEAR: **DECEMBER**

YOUR WEEK AT A GLANCE

MONDAY	TUESDAY	WEDNESDAY	THURSDAY	FRIDAY	SATURDAY ☐
☐ TODAY	☐ TODAY	☐ TODAY	☐ TODAY	☐ TODAY	☐ SUNDAY

25

NOTES AND/OR DOODLES

IT'S CHRISTMAS DAY

OH, AND IT'S ALSO NATIONAL PUMPKIN PIE DAY.

ADUT AKECH WAS BORN IN 1999 — DIDO WAS BORN IN 1971

9 AM

10 AM

11 AM

NOON

1 PM

2 PM

3 PM

4 PM

5 PM

6 PM

ON THIS DAY IN 1959: RINGO STARR GOT HIS FIRST DRUM SET.

YOUR WEEK AT A GLANCE

MONDAY	TUESDAY	WEDNESDAY	THURSDAY	FRIDAY	SATURDAY ☐
☐ TODAY	☐ TODAY	☐ TODAY	☐ TODAY	☐ TODAY	☐ SUNDAY

26

NOTES AND/OR DOODLES

IT'S NATIONAL CANDY CANE DAY

CELEBRATE BY BUYING THEM ON DISCOUNT I GUESS. CHRISTMAS IS OVER.

(SERIOUSLY, WHO DECIDED ON THIS DATE?)

KIT HARINGTON WAS BORN IN 1986 — ALEXANDER WANG WAS BORN IN 1983

9 AM

10 AM

11 AM

NOON

1 PM

2 PM

3 PM

4 PM

5 PM

6 PM

ON THIS DAY IN 1966: THE FIRST DAY OF THE FIRST KWANZAA IS CELEBRATED.

27

YOUR WEEK AT A GLANCE

MONDAY TODAY ☐ | TUESDAY TODAY ☐ | WEDNESDAY TODAY ☐ | THURSDAY TODAY ☐ | FRIDAY TODAY ☐ | SATURDAY ☐ | ☐ SUNDAY

IT'S MAKE CUT OUT SNOWFLAKES DAY

IN 1988, A SCIENTIST FOUND TWO IDENTICAL SNOW CRYSTALS.

JOHN AMOS WAS BORN IN 1939

MARLENE DIETRICH WAS BORN IN 1901

9 AM

10 AM

11 AM

NOON

1 PM

2 PM

3 PM

4 PM

5 PM

6 PM

ON THIS DAY IN 1932: RADIO CITY MUSIC HALL OPENED IN NEW YORK CITY.

NOTES AND/OR DOODLES

28

YOUR WEEK AT A GLANCE

MONDAY TODAY ☐ | TUESDAY TODAY ☐ | WEDNESDAY TODAY ☐ | THURSDAY TODAY ☐ | FRIDAY TODAY ☐ | SATURDAY ☐ | ☐ SUNDAY

IT'S NATIONAL CARD PLAYING DAY

A DECK CAN BE ARRANGED MORE WAYS THAN THERE ARE ATOMS ON EARTH.

JOHN LEGEND WAS BORN IN 1978

MAGGIE SMITH WAS BORN IN 1934

9 AM

10 AM

11 AM

NOON

1 PM

2 PM

3 PM

4 PM

5 PM

6 PM

ON THIS DAY IN 2007: MISCHA BARTON WAS ARRESTED IN WEST HOLLYWOOD.

NOTES AND/OR DOODLES

YEAR: **DECEMBER**

YOUR WEEK AT A GLANCE

MONDAY	TUESDAY	WEDNESDAY	THURSDAY	FRIDAY	SATURDAY ☐
☐ TODAY	☐ TODAY	☐ TODAY	☐ TODAY	☐ TODAY	☐ SUNDAY

29

NOTES AND/OR DOODLES

IT'S TICK TOCK DAY

THERE ARE ONLY 259,140 SECONDS LEFT IN THE YEAR.

(AS OF 12:01 A.M.)

TWINKLE KHANNA WAS BORN IN 1973

JUDE LAW WAS BORN IN 1972

9 AM

10 AM

11 AM

NOON

1 PM

2 PM

3 PM

4 PM

5 PM

6 PM

ON THIS DAY IN 1862: THE MODERN BOWLING BALL WAS INVENTED.

YOUR WEEK AT A GLANCE

MONDAY	TUESDAY	WEDNESDAY	THURSDAY	FRIDAY	SATURDAY ☐
☐ TODAY	☐ TODAY	☐ TODAY	☐ TODAY	☐ TODAY	☐ SUNDAY

30

NOTES AND/OR DOODLES

IT'S BICARBONATE OF SODA DAY

BAKING SODA & WATER CAN BE USED AS TOOTHPASTE IN A PINCH.

PATTI SMITH WAS BORN IN 1946

LEBRON JAMES WAS BORN IN 1984

9 AM

10 AM

11 AM

NOON

1 PM

2 PM

3 PM

4 PM

5 PM

6 PM

IN 2011: THIS DAY NEVER HAPPENED IN SAMOA (DUE TO A TIMEZONE CHANGE).

DECEMBER :YEAR

31

YOUR WEEK AT A GLANCE

MONDAY	TUESDAY	WEDNESDAY	THURSDAY	FRIDAY	SATURDAY ☐
TODAY ☐	TODAY ☐	TODAY ☐	TODAY ☐	TODAY ☐	☐ SUNDAY

IT'S NEW YEAR'S EVE

OH, AND IT'S ALSO NATIONAL CHAMPAGNE DAY.

GABBY DOUGLAS WAS BORN IN 1995

ANTHONY HOPKINS WAS BORN IN 1937

9 AM

10 AM

11 AM

NOON

1 PM

2 PM

3 PM

4 PM

5 PM

6 PM

ON THIS DAY IN 1907: THE 1ST ANNUAL BALL DROP WAS HELD IN TIMES SQUARE.

NOTES AND/OR DOODLES

A DRAWING OF BABY NEW YEAR

(OR BABY SPICE)

ILLNESSES BETTER THAN A CHAMPAGNE HANGOVER

OR A GROCERY LIST OR SOMETHING

1
2
3
4
5
6
7
8
9
10
11
12
13
14
15
16
17
18

DECEMBER IN REVIEW

MY DECEMBER ACCOMPLISHMENTS

- [ ] USED UP EVERY VACATION DAY
- [ ] AVOIDED HEARING 'CHRISTMAS SHOES'
- [ ] PRAYED FOR THE HOLIDAY MUSIC TO STOP
- [ ] BOUGHT A REAL TREE THIS YEAR
- [ ] SWEPT UP NEEDLES FOR TWENTY DAYS
- [ ] WENT TO THE OFFICE CHRISTMAS PARTY
- [ ] ENJOYED THE OPEN BAR
- [ ] DON'T REMEMBER THE OFFICE PARTY
- [ ] STARTED & FINISHED SHOPPING IN 1 DAY
- [ ] WAITED IN LINE FOR A MALL SANTA
- [ ] DISCOVERED THAT THERE'S AN AGE LIMIT
- [ ] COMPLIMENTED AN UGLY SWEATER
- [ ] WAS ACTUALLY JUST A NORMAL SWEATER
- [ ] SET UNREALISTIC NYE EXPECTATIONS
- [ ] ATE A BLOCK OF CHEESE & FELL ASLEEP

REASONS THAT DECEMBER WAS GREAT

'IT ENDED' IS A VALID ANSWER

1
2
3
4
5
6
7
8
9
10
11
12

IF DECEMBER WAS PERSONIFIED, DRAW ITS DRINK OF CHOICE

REASONS THAT I'M GLAD DECEMBER IS OVER

USE ADDITIONAL PAPER IF NEEDED

1
2
3
4
5
6
7
8
9
10
11
12
13
14

CLICHÉS OVERHEARD THIS MONTH

- [ ] 'SEE YA NEXT YEAR!'
- [ ] 'IT WAS THE THOUGHT THAT COUNTS'
- [ ] 'THANKS, I LOVE IT'
- [ ] 'JUST IN CASE, IS THERE A RECEIPT?'
- [ ] 'WOW THAT SURE IS SOMETHING'
- [ ] 'OH WOW, IT'S A BOX'
- [ ] 'WHAT DID SANTA BRING YOU THIS YEAR?'
- [ ] 'NICE BLINKER, ASSHOLE'
- [ ] 'NOW DON'T SPEND TOO MUCH ON ME'
- [ ] 'DIE HARD IS A CHRISTMAS MOVIE'
- [ ] 'IT'S GOING TO BE A WHITE CHRISTMAS'
- [ ] 'WERE YOU GOOD THIS YEAR?'
- [ ] 'WELL, 'TIS THE SEASON'
- [ ] 'ALRIGHT, TIME TO GO BACK TO BED'
- [ ] 'WELL DON'T YOU LOOK FESTIVE'
- [ ] 'NEXT YEAR WILL BE BETTER'
- [ ] 'OKAY, WINTER CAN BE OVER NOW'

ANCIENT EGYPTIANS CALLED THE APPENDIX THE 'WORM' OF THE BOWEL.

FINALLY, A USEFUL

× APPENDIX ×

GUARANTEED NOT TO EXPLODE
AND TRY TO KILL YOU.

THE YEAR IS:

HARRY HOUDINI DIED DUE TO A RUPTURED APPENDIX.

MEASUREMENT CONVERSION CHART

GIVE THEM 25.4 MM AND THEY'LL TAKE A MILE.

×

MM	DEC	FRACTION OF INCH	FRACTION OF INCH	DEC	MM
0.397	.016"	1/64	33/64	.516"	13.10
0.794	.031"	1/32	17/32	.531"	13.49
1.191	.047"	3/64	35/64	.547"	13.89
1.588	.063"	1/16	9/16	.563"	14.29
1.984	.078"	5/64	37/64	.578"	14.68
2.381	.094"	3/32	19/32	.594"	15.08
2.788	.109"	7/64	39/64	.609"	15.48
3.175	.125"	1/8	5/8	.625"	15.88
3.572	.141"	9/64	41/64	.641"	16.27
3.969	.156"	5/32	21/32	.656"	16.67
4.366	.172"	11/64	43/64	.672"	17.07
4.762	.188"	3/16	11/16	.688"	17.46
5.159	.203"	13/64	45/64	.703"	17.86
5.556	.219"	7/32	23/32	.719"	18.26
5.953	.234"	15/64	47/64	.734"	18.65
6.350	.250"	1/4	3/4	.750"	19.05
6.747	.266"	17/64	49/64	.766"	19.45
7.144	.281"	9/32	25/32	.781"	19.84
7.541	.297"	19/64	51/64	.797"	20.24
7.938	.313"	5/16	13/16	.812"	20.64
8.334	.328"	21/64	53/64	.828"	21.03
8.731	.344"	11/32	27/32	.844"	21.43
9.128	.359"	23/64	55/64	.859"	21.83
9.525	.375"	3/8	7/8	.875"	22.23
9.922	.391"	25/64	57/64	.891"	22.62
10.31	.406"	13/32	29/32	.906"	23.02
10.72	.422"	27/64	59/64	.922"	23.42
11.11	.439"	7/16	15/16	.938"	23.81
11.51	.453"	29/64	61/64	.953"	24.21
11.91	.469"	15/32	31/32	.969"	24.61
12.30	.484"	31/64	63/64	.984"	25.00
12.70	.500"	1/2	1	1.00"	25.40
MM	DEC	FRACTION OF INCH	FRACTION OF INCH	DEC	MM

COMMONLY MISPELLED WORDS

FOR EXAMPLE: MISSPELLED.

×

A

ABSENCE
ABUNDANCE
ACCUMULATE
ACQUIRE
ALLEGED
AMATEUR
APPARATUS
APPARENT
ASCEND
ATTENDANCE
AUXILIARY

B

BARBECUE
BEGGAR
BENEFICIAL

C

CALENDAR
CAMOUFLAGE
CANDIDATE
CIGARETTE
COLONEL
COMMITMENT
COMPETENT
CONCEIVABLE
CONDEMN
CONDESCEND
CONSCIENCE
CONSCIOUS
CONVENIENT
CORRELATE
CRITICISM

D

DECEIVE
DEFENDANT
DEFINITELY
DEFINITION
DEPENDENT
DESIRABLE
DESPAIR
DESPERATE
DIFFERENCE
DILEMMA
DRUNKENNESS

E

ECSTASY
EFFICIENCY
ENVIRONMENT
EQUIVALENT
EXPERIENCE
EXUBERANCE

F

FACSIMILE
FALLACIOUS
FEASIBLE
FEBRUARY
FICTITIOUS
FIERY
FINANCIALLY
FLUORESCENT
FORFEIT
FUELING

G

GRIEVOUS
GUARANTEE
GUERRILLA

H

HANDKERCHIEF
HEINOUS
HEMORRHAGE
HOARSE
HYGIENE

I

IDIOSYNCRASY
IGNORANCE
INDICTED
INEVITABLE
INFLUENTIAL
INOCULATE
INSURANCE
INTELLIGENCE

J

JUDICIAL

K

KNOWLEDGE

L

LEISURE
LICENSE
LIEUTENANT
LIKELIHOOD

M

MAINTENANCE
MANEUVER
MATHEMATICS
MILLENNIUM
MINIATURE
MINUSCULE
MISCHIEVOUS
MISSPELLED
MOSQUITO
MURMUR
MYSTERIOUS

N

NARRATIVE
NATURALLY
NECESSARY
NECESSITY
NUISANCE

O

OBEDIENCE
OCCURRENCE
OFFICIAL

P

PAVILION
PERMANENT
PERMISSIBLE
PIECE
PILGRIMAGE
POSSESS
POTATOES
PRAIRIE
PRECEDENCE
PREJUDICE
PRESCRIPTION
PRINCIPAL
PRINCIPLE
PROPAGANDA

Q

QUARANTINE

R

RECEIPT
RECEIVE
RELEVANT
REMINISCENCE
RESERVOIR
RESTAURANT
RIDICULOUS

S

SACRILEGIOUS
SACRIFICE
SECEDE
SEPARATE
SERGEANT
SIEGE
SIMILE
SIMULTANEOUS
SKIING
SOPHOMORE
SOUVENIR
SPECIMEN
SPONTANEOUS
STATISTICS
STUBBORNNESS
SUFFICIENT
SUPERSEDE
SUSCEPTIBLE
SYNONYMOUS

T

TECHNIQUE
TEMPERATURE
TOMORROW
TOURNAMENT
TRAGEDY
TWELFTH
TYRANNY

U

UNANIMOUS
UNDOUBTEDLY

V

VACUUM
VENGEANCE
VIGILANT
VILLAIN

W

WARRANT
WEDNESDAY
WEIRD
WHETHER
WHOLLY
WIELD
WINTRY
WITHDRAWAL

Y

YACHT
YIELD

MORSE AND NATO ALPHABETS

• • — •   — • — —   • •

LTR	NATO	MORSE CODE	MORSE CODE	NATO	LTR
A	ALPHA	• —	— •	NOVEMBER	N
B	BRAVO	— • • •	— — —	OSCAR	O
C	CHARLIE	— • — •	• — — •	PAPA	P
D	DELTA	— • •	— — • —	QUEBEC	Q
E	ECHO	•	• — •	ROMEO	R
F	FOXTROT	• • — •	• • •	SIERRA	S
G	GOLF	— — •	—	TANGO	T
H	HOTEL	• • • •	• • —	UNIFORM	U
I	INDIA	• •	• • • —	VICTOR	V
J	JULIET	• — — —	• — —	WHISKEY	W
K	KILO	— • —	— • • —	X-RAY	X
L	LIMA	• — • •	— • — —	YANKEE	Y
M	MIKE	— —	— — • •	ZULU	Z

CAPITALS OF THE UNITED STATES

BONUS: INCLUDES U.S. TERRITORIES.

STATE NAME	CAPITAL	SINCE	2019 POP.	LARGEST CITY
ALABAMA	MONTGOMERY	1846	198,525	BIRMINGHAM
ALASKA	JUNEAU	1906	32,113	ANCHORAGE
ARIZONA	PHOENIX	1912	1,680,992	PHOENIX
ARKANSAS	LITTLE ROCK	1821	197,312	LITTLE ROCK
CALIFORNIA	SACRAMENTO	1854	513,624	LOS ANGELES
COLORADO	DENVER	1867	727,211	DENVER
CONNECTICUT	HARTFORD	1875	122,105	BRIDGEPORT
DELAWARE	DOVER	1777	38,079	WILMINGTON
FLORIDA	TALLAHASSEE	1824	194,500	JACKSONVILLE
GEORGIA	ATLANTA	1868	506,811	ATLANTA
HAWAII	HONOLULU	1845	345,064	HONOLULU
IDAHO	BOISE	1865	228,959	BOISE
ILLINOIS	SPRINGFIELD	1837	114,230	CHICAGO
INDIANA	INDIANAPOLIS	1825	876,384	INDIANAPOLIS
IOWA	DES MOINES	1857	214,237	DES MOINES
KANSAS	TOPEKA	1856	125,310	WICHITA

CAPITALS OF THE UNITED STATES

BONUS: INCLUDES U.S. TERRITORIES.

×

STATE NAME	CAPITAL	SINCE	2019 POP.	LARGEST CITY
KENTUCKY	FRANKFORT	1792	27,679	LOUISVILLE
LOUISIANA	BATON ROUGE	1880	220,236	NEW ORLEANS
MAINE	AUGUSTA	1832	18,681	PORTLAND
MARYLAND	ANNAPOLIS	1694	39,174	BALTIMORE
MASS.	BOSTON	1630	692,600	BOSTON
MICHIGAN	LANSING	1847	118,210	DETROIT
MINNESOTA	SAINT PAUL	1849	308,096	MINNEAPOLIS
MISSISSIPPI	JACKSON	1821	160,628	JACKSON
MISSOURI	JEFFERSON C.	1826	42,838	KANSAS CITY
MONTANA	HELENA	1875	32,315	BILLINGS
NEBRASKA	LINCOLN	1867	289,102	OMAHA
NEVADA	CARSON CITY	1861	55,916	LAS VEGAS
N. HAMPSHIRE	CONCORD	1808	43,627	MANCHESTER
NEW JERSEY	TRENTON	1784	83,203	NEWARK
NEW MEXICO	SANTA FE	1610	84,683	ALBUQUERQUE
NEW YORK	ALBANY	1797	96,460	NEW YORK C.
N. CAROLINA	RALEIGH	1792	474,069	CHARLOTTE
N. DAKOTA	BISMARK	1883	73,529	FARGO
OHIO	COLUMBUS	1816	898,553	COLUMBUS
OKLAHOMA	OKLAHOMA C.	1910	655,057	OKLAHOMA C.
OREGON	SALEM	1855	174,365	PORTLAND
PENNSYLVANIA	HARRISBURG	1812	49,528	PHILADELPHIA
RHODE ISLAND	PROVIDENCE	1900	179,883	PROVIDENCE
S. CAROLINA	COLUMBIA	1786	131,674	COLUMBIA
S. DAKOTA	PIERRE	1889	13,646	SIOUX FALLS
TENNESSEE	NASHVILLE	1826	670,820	MEMPHIS
TEXAS	AUSTIN	1839	978,908	HOUSTON
UTAH	SALT LAKE C.	1858	200,567	SALT LAKE C.
VERMONT	MONTPELIER	1805	7,855	BURLINGTON
VIRGINIA	RICHMOND	1780	230,436	VIRGINIA BEACH
WASHINGTON	OLYMPIA	1853	46,478	SEATTLE
W. VIRGINIA	CHARLESTON	1885	46,536	CHARLESTON
WISCONSIN	MADISON	1838	259,680	MILWAUKEE
WYOMING	CHEYENNE	1869	64,235	CHEYENNE
AMER. SAMOA	PAGO PAGO	1899	3,656	PAGO PAGO
GUAM	HAGÅTÑA	1898	1,051	DEDEDO
N. MARIANA ISL	SAIPAN	1947	48,220	SAIPAN
PUERTO RICO	SAN JUAN	1898	395,326	SAN JUAN
U.S. VIRGIN ISL	CHAR. AMALIE	1917	18,481	SAINT CROIX

IMPORTANT CONTACT INFORMATION

IN CASE YOU DROP YOUR PHONE IN A TOILET.

FRIENDS

NAME

NUMBER

ADDRESS

NAME

NUMBER

ADDRESS

NAME

NUMBER

ADDRESS

NAME

NUMBER

ADDRESS

NAME

NUMBER

ADDRESS

NAME

NUMBER

ADDRESS

NAME

NUMBER

ADDRESS

DEPENDING ON THE DAY

FAMILY

NAME

NUMBER

ADDRESS

NAME

NUMBER

ADDRESS

NAME

NUMBER

ADDRESS

NAME

NUMBER

ADDRESS

NAME

NUMBER

ADDRESS

NAME

NUMBER

ADDRESS

NAME

NUMBER

ADDRESS

LIKE IT OR NOT

IMPORTANT CONTACT INFORMATION

IN CASE YOU DROP YOUR PHONE IN A TOILET.

ENEMIES

NAME
NUMBER
ADDRESS

NAME
NUMBER
ADDRESS

NAME
NUMBER
ADDRESS

NAME
NUMBER
ADDRESS

NAME
NUMBER
ADDRESS

NAME
NUMBER
ADDRESS

NAME
NUMBER
ADDRESS

KEEP THEM CLOSE

ACQUAINTANCES

NAME
NUMBER
ADDRESS

NAME
NUMBER
ADDRESS

NAME
NUMBER
ADDRESS

NAME
NUMBER
ADDRESS

NAME
NUMBER
ADDRESS

NAME
NUMBER
ADDRESS

NAME
NUMBER
ADDRESS

WHO AGAIN?

AN HONEST REVIEW OF WHAT I JUST ATE

WITHOUT SAYING 'MOUTHFEEL' ONCE.

×

THE AMBIANCE WAS UNDERWHELMING

FROZEN PIZZAS HAVE FLAVOR PROFILES TOO.

MY LAST WILL AND TESTAMENT

OR SOME EROTIC FAN FICTION.

×

TO WHOM IT MAY CONCERN

SO ANYWAY, SEE YA.

MY INSPIRATIONAL & HEARTFELT POETRY

FULL OF MEANINGFUL INSIGHTS ON LIFE.

×

THERE ONCE WAS A MAN FROM NANTUCKET

BRAVO.

AN OPEN LETTER TO 8 YEAR-OLD ME

A FEW THINGS TO KEEP IN MIND.

×

STOP WORRYING ABOUT QUICKSAND

SEX IS PRETTY COOL, BTW.